THE
NUMERIC
PERSONALITY

THE NUMERIC PERSONALITY

by

RICHARD ELLIOTT POOLE

DOUBLEDAY

NEW YORK   LONDON   TORONTO   SYDNEY   AUCKLAND

ACKNOWLEDGMENTS

I am grateful to my many good friends, who were so supportive of my writing and who shared my interests. I must thank first and foremost my friend, Adam Bourgeois, who inspired me. He gave me an insight into numbers that triggered an important rebirth in my approach to life — and because of him, this book was born. My very close friend, Dr. Brugh Joy, took a great deal of time out of his busy schedule to pore over my work. His remarkably objective comments and sage perspective allowed me to clarify and perfect my ideas and observations. Lorraine and Elliot Lubin were extremely generous and supportive of me and my work, and shared my joys as I explored the numbers. Suzanne de Passe and her husband Paul Le Mat not only read the manuscript with great sensitivity, but also encouraged me tremendously during the creation of this book. My mother Bernice Poole, who had never heard of the wisdom of numbers, supported my creative efforts with loving interest and understanding. I am grateful to Rita Aero, who right from the beginning, understood exactly what I was doing and, along with Esther Mitgang, edited my work and helped me make it into the book I had visualized. And especially I want to thank my wife, Eileen, who read and reread the manuscript with interest and enthusiasm. Her help was joyously given, and she was directly instrumental in bringing this book into existence.

Published by Doubleday, a division of
Bantam Doubleday Dell Publishing Group, Inc.
666 Fifth Avenue, New York, New York 10103

Doubleday and the portrayal of anchor with a
dolphin are trademarks of Doubleday, a division of
Bantam Doubleday Dell Publishing Group, Inc.

Library of Congress Cataloging-in-Publication Data

Poole, Richard Elliott.
    The numeric personality.

    1. Symbolism of numbers.   2. Personality—
Miscellanea.   3. Interpersonal relations—
Miscellanea.   4. Fortune-telling.   I. Title.
BF1623.P9P66   1989   133.3'35   89-1540
ISBN 0-385-24888-1

FIRST EDITION

To my wife Eileen
and my daughter Sharon
with all my love.

CONTENTS

INTRODUCTION

As amazing as it may seem, it is possible to harness the natural energy of numbers to help us understand and appreciate the uniqueness of our personalities. Certainly, this is not a revolutionary idea — numbers and their mathematics have been the basis of much philosophical investigation, both Eastern and Western. Using the month and day of birth as a reference point, we can discover remarkable and useful information about ourselves and those who share our world.

The day of your birth makes you one of forty-five distinct numeric personalities that share similar perceptions, aptitudes, and patterns of behavior. Each personality group represents between 0.8 and 4.3 percent of the total population. No particular group is stronger or more important than another, and each has a special place in the harmonic design of life. The ability to recognize and understand the similarities and differences among the numeric personalities can greatly enhance your ability to appreciate yourself and improve your relationships. Why does your boss hold back praise? Why does your partner need more time alone? Why is everyone except you athletic in your family? Why does your child want to become an actor instead of an architect? The numeric personality profiles can help you recognize and understand the unique characteristics of those around you, and they can enable you to understand the attraction you have toward some people and the conflict you may have with others.

This book begins with descriptions of the forty-five personality *sets*. As part of each description you will find a list of notable individuals who share that set and act as its archetypes, as well as each set's relevant dates and numbers and work space where you can keep track of your own research. Don't hesitate to write down your personal observations. By matching family, friends, and acquaintances to the different numeric personalities, you will make fascinating and insightful discoveries about them, and see important patterns in your relationships that might otherwise escape your attention.

In Parts II and III we will explore, in greater detail, the meanings of the numbers in your life. Here you can discover the potential for compatibility or conflict between yourself and individuals with different numeric backgrounds. You will also learn how to use numbers in your day-to-day life to bring clarity to confusing situations at home, on the job, and in your environment. Part IV contains an alphabetical listing of more than four thousand well-known men and women, along with their birth dates, occupations, and numeric personality set numbers.

At the back of the book, the numeric personality charts will help you keep track of the numbers and sets of people who are important in your life. Here, you will discover the numeric interactions that most frequently appear in your relationships, and have the opportunity to gain profound insight into the patterns in your connections to others. Several copies of the chart are included so you can, if you wish, group your relationships by family, friends, career acquaintances, and so forth.

To jump right in and learn about your own numeric personality, locate your month and day of birth on the Numeric Personality Set Calendar, pages 11 and 12. The year of birth is not important. When you have found your birth date, look at the slashed number, running down the left-hand column across from it. This is your set number.

Another way to find your set is to add together the digits in the month of your birth until you get a single numeral. April is four, for example, while December (twelve) is one plus two, or three. Then, add together the digits in the day of your birth. Finally, put the smaller of the two numbers first. For example: If you were born on May 9, your set is Five/Nine; if you were born on October 10, your set is One/One; if you were born on December 8, your set is Three/Eight.

NUMERIC PERSONALITY SET CALENDAR

JANUARY

SET	DAY OF THE MONTH			
1/1	1	10	19	28
1/2	2	11	20	29
1/3	3	12	21	30
1/4	4	13	22	31
1/5	5	14	23	
1/6	6	15	24	
1/7	7	16	25	
1/8	8	17	26	
1/9	9	18	27	

APRIL

SET	DAY OF THE MONTH			
1/4	1	10	19	28
2/4	2	11	20	29
3/4	3	12	21	30
4/4	4	13	22	
4/5	5	14	23	
4/6	6	15	24	
4/7	7	16	25	
4/8	8	17	26	
4/9	9	18	27	

FEBRUARY

SET	DAY OF THE MONTH			
1/2	1	10	19	28
2/2	2	11	20	29
2/3	3	12	21	
2/4	4	13	22	
2/5	5	14	23	
2/6	6	15	24	
2/7	7	16	25	
2/8	8	17	26	
2/9	9	18	27	

MAY

SET	DAY OF THE MONTH			
1/5	1	10	19	28
2/5	2	11	20	29
3/5	3	12	21	30
4/5	4	13	22	31
5/5	5	14	23	
5/6	6	15	24	
5/7	7	16	25	
5/8	8	17	26	
5/9	9	18	27	

MARCH

SET	DAY OF THE MONTH			
1/3	1	10	19	28
3/2	2	11	20	29
3/3	3	12	21	30
3/4	4	13	22	31
3/5	5	14	23	
3/6	6	15	24	
3/7	7	16	25	
3/8	8	17	26	
3/9	9	18	27	

JUNE

SET	DAY OF THE MONTH			
1/6	1	10	19	28
2/6	2	11	20	29
3/6	3	12	21	30
4/6	4	13	22	
5/6	5	14	23	
6/6	6	15	24	
6/7	7	16	25	
6/8	8	17	26	
6/9	9	18	27	

NUMERIC PERSONALITY SET CALENDAR

JULY

SET	DAY OF THE MONTH			
1/7	1	10	19	28
2/7	2	11	20	29
3/7	3	12	21	30
4/7	4	13	22	31
5/7	5	14	23	
6/7	6	15	24	
7/7	7	16	25	
7/8	8	17	26	
7/9	9	18	27	

OCTOBER

SET	DAY OF THE MONTH			
1/1	1	10	19	28
1/2	2	11	20	29
1/3	3	12	21	30
1/4	4	13	22	31
1/5	5	14	23	
1/6	6	15	24	
1/7	7	16	25	
1/8	8	17	26	
1/9	9	18	27	

AUGUST

SET	DAY OF THE MONTH			
1/8	1	10	19	28
2/8	2	11	20	29
3/8	3	12	21	30
4/8	4	13	22	31
5/8	5	14	23	
6/8	6	15	24	
7/8	7	16	25	
8/8	8	17	26	
8/9	9	18	27	

NOVEMBER

SET	DAY OF THE MONTH			
1/2	1	10	19	28
2/2	2	11	20	29
2/3	3	12	21	30
2/4	4	13	22	
2/5	5	14	23	
2/6	6	15	24	
2/7	7	16	25	
2/8	8	17	26	
2/9	9	18	27	

SEPTEMBER

SET	DAY OF THE MONTH			
1/9	1	10	19	28
2/9	2	11	20	29
3/9	3	12	21	30
4/9	4	13	22	
5/9	5	14	23	
6/9	6	15	24	
7/9	7	16	25	
8/9	8	17	26	
9/9	9	18	27	

DECEMBER

SET	DAY OF THE MONTH			
1/3	1	10	19	28
2/3	2	11	20	29
3/3	3	12	21	30
3/4	4	13	22	31
3/5	5	14	23	
3/6	6	15	24	
3/7	7	16	25	
3/8	8	17	26	
3/9	9	18	27	

PART I

THE FORTY-FIVE NUMERIC PERSONALITY PROFILES

How can I tell what I think
until I see what I say? — E. M. Forster

THE ONE/ONE SET AFFINITIES

THE ONE/ONE NUMBERS ARE: 1 1 2

ODD NUMBERS: 1 1   EVEN NUMBERS: 2

SET INTERVAL: 0 (Double 1)

FAMILY NUMBER: 2

THE ONE/ONES REPRESENT 2.2 PERCENT OF THE POPULATION.

PEOPLE I KNOW WHO ARE ONE/ONES:

_____   _____

_____   _____

_____   _____

_____   _____

_____   _____

MY ONE/ONE OBSERVATIONS:

_____

_____

_____

_____

_____

_____

_____

DISPOSITION

— LONERS — INDEPENDENT —

— OPINIONATED — INTENSE — TRUTHFUL — ZEALOTS —

— WILLFUL —

— NOT SWAYED BY MAJORITY VIEWS —

Intensity of conviction and a passion for living.

ONE/ONE

*The eight days of the year
that would make you a ONE/ONE are:*

January 1	*January 19*	*October 1*	*October 19*
January 10	*January 28*	*October 10*	*October 28*

One/Ones view the world as a set of absolutes. Although they may listen to the opinions of others, their mind holds no room for relative or multiple truths. One/Ones are rarely swayed by popular or majority beliefs — whatever they believe in is, to them, the absolute truth. This includes their belief that what is good for them is good for all. With such single-minded determination, unusual zeal, and independent spirit, One/Ones make excellent pioneers. Their depth of conviction makes them ready and willing to take chances in order to succeed. Adversity seldom stops them, and they seem to gain strength from their struggles.

One/Ones are extremely ambitious, and success is very important to them. Their view of life is serious and determined. They are eager and efficient, truthful and optimistic, and their sense of purpose usually takes priority over their sense of comfort.

With One/Ones, what you see is what you get. If they are boring, they are colossally boring; if they are interesting, they are dazzling. They tend to be either intensely connected to their family, or quite indifferent toward them. They prefer working alone but, when given a choice of independence or leadership, they opt to work with others. One/Ones are very generous to those in their favor and quite unforgiving of those who cross them. They become impatient with others easily, are often frustrated, and are not pleased with what they consider to be weaknesses or personal shortcomings. One/Ones have great difficulty laughing at themselves. Not prone to frivolous behavior, they are usually conservative, quite patriotic, and follow habitual daily routines.

One/Ones are excellent visionaries and conceptualists. They have their own unique ideas and can be quite eccentric. They have a strong sense of intuition, but many times they do not trust it, especially if it conflicts with their habits or beliefs. While they sometimes vacillate when making decisions, once they decide, One/Ones make a firm commitment and move straight ahead. They are quite willful and refuse to be held back. When they act, they do it with conviction and responsibility to their personal ideals.

Alan Alda
Jack Anderson
Julie Andrews
Eddie Arcaro
Francis Bacon
Mikhail Baryshnikov
Pat Benatar
Ray Bolger
Amy Carter
Paul Cézanne
Colette
Phil Everly
W. C. Fields
E. M. Forster
Hank Greenberg
Laurence Harvey
Helen Hayes
Edith Head
J. Edgar Hoover
Janis Joplin
John Le Carré
Robert E. Lee
Richard Lester
John Lithgow
Robert MacNeil
Guy Madison
Walter Matthau
Peter Max
Sal Mineo
Thelonious Monk
Terry Moore
Bonnie Parker
Dolly Parton
George Peppard
Edgar Allan Poe
Johnnie Ray
David Lee Roth
J. D. Salinger
Jonas Salk
Rod Stewart
Alfred Stieglitz
Jean-Antoine Watteau

No bird soars too high,
if he soars with his own wings. — William Blake

THE ONE/TWO SET AFFINITIES

THE ONE/TWO NUMBERS ARE: 1   1   2   3

ODD NUMBERS: 1   1   3   EVEN NUMBERS: 2

SET INTERVAL: 1

FAMILY NUMBER: 3

THE ONE/TWOS REPRESENT 4.3 PERCENT OF THE POPULATION.

PEOPLE I KNOW WHO ARE ONE/TWOS:

_____   _____
_____   _____
_____   _____
_____   _____
_____   _____

MY ONE/TWO OBSERVATIONS:

_____
_____
_____
_____
_____
_____
_____
_____

DISPOSITION

— QUICK — BRIGHT — EXECUTIVES — GENERALS —

— PHYSICAL — CONFIDENT — FRUSTRATED — BURNED OUT —

— ADVERSARIAL — FAST MOVERS — RUTHLESS —

— DECISIVE —

Confidence and determination, running from post to post.

ONE/TWO

*The sixteen days of the year
that would make you a ONE/TWO are:*

January 2	February 1	October 2	November 1
January 11	February 10	October 11	November 10
January 20	February 19	October 20	November 19
January 29	February 28	October 29	November 28

One/Twos have intense personal vision. They take themselves quite seriously and like to make their own rules. They are quick to act — so quick that sometimes they fail to get all the facts first. Consequently, they appear both decisive and indecisive; they have a tendency to charge forward and then suddenly, without explanation, pull back. Precocious as children, One/Twos are fast learners and extremely versatile, with fertile imaginations and quick bodily responses. They are a pleasant, admired, popular set that others find attractive because of their physical appearance, attitudes, or air of authority.

One/Twos have very strong egos. They need to control those around them and are convinced they know what is best for others. They want things done their way and do not like to explain their actions. They like to set goals, but tend to expect too much from themselves and others. One/Twos need to slow down, since their emotions directly affect their physical health and well-being.

Although One/Twos have a good sense of humor, they rarely tell jokes about themselves. They do not hesitate to take credit for their successes but have difficulty accepting blame for their mistakes. At times they are prone to martyrdom. One/Twos are frequently impatient and frustrated with the indecisiveness of others, and diplomacy is not one of their strong characteristics. When thwarted, they may sulk and not speak for days. When angered, they tend to avoid rather than confront, but when cornered they are ferocious and violent.

One/Twos are gamblers who are always willing to take a chance. They feel they have a specific mission in life. Born inventors, they can create tools or systems for practical needs, and are always willing to tackle manual tasks, no matter what their station in life. They approach projects, mental or physical, single-handedly and with confidence. Their superb ability to be decisive and their generally adversarial attitude, coupled with their quickness to grasp a situation and take action, make One/Twos splendid executives, warriors, and generals.

Bud Abbott
Stella Adler
Mario Andretti
Isaac Asimov
Justine Bateman
William Blake
Bertolt Brecht
Joyce Brothers
George Burns
Richard Burton
Roy Campanella
Nicolaus Copernicus
Stephen Crane
Jimmy Durante
Federico Fellini
Roberta Flack
Larry Flynt
John Forsythe
Jodie Foster
Clark Gable
Indira Gandhi
Berry Gordy, Jr.
Graham Greene
Daryl Hall
Margaux Hemingway
Calvin Klein
Lee Marvin
Groucho Marx
Carson McCullers
Vincente Minnelli
Judd Nelson
Merle Oberon
Linus Pauling
Leontyne Price
Arthur Rimbaud
Smokey Robinson
Eleanor Roosevelt
Tom Selleck
Muriel Spark
Sting
Tiffany
Robert Wagner

17

Do what thy manhood bids thee do, from none but self expect applause;
He noblest lives and noblest dies who
makes and keeps his self-made laws. — Sir Richard F. Burton

THE ONE/THREE SET AFFINITIES

THE ONE/THREE NUMBERS ARE: 1 2 3 4

ODD NUMBERS: 1 3   EVEN NUMBERS: 2 4

SET INTERVAL: 2

FAMILY NUMBER: 4

THE ONE/THREES REPRESENT 4.3 PERCENT OF THE POPULATION.

PEOPLE I KNOW WHO ARE ONE/THREES:

_____   _____
_____   _____
_____   _____
_____   _____
_____   _____
_____   _____

MY ONE/THREE OBSERVATIONS:

_____
_____
_____
_____
_____
_____
_____
_____

DISPOSITION

— EXPLORERS — TRENDSETTERS — ARTISTIC —

— STYLISH — QUICK TO LEARN —

— FRIENDLY — RITUALISTIC — GENEROUS —

— HARDWORKING —

Carrying the torch of new ideas.

ONE/THREE

*The sixteen days of the year
that would make you a ONE/THREE are:*

January 3	March 1	October 3	December 1
January 12	March 10	October 12	December 10
January 21	March 19	October 21	December 19
January 30	March 28	October 30	December 28

One/Threes are colorful, full-spectrum individuals in an orderly, self-contained package. They are sophisticated, creative, understanding, innovative, sensitive, and romantic, with open, straightforward feelings. They enjoy ritual and ceremony, but refuse to adhere to tradition for tradition's sake, preferring to set their own trends. Receptive to change and new ideas, they gain much from travel and particularly enjoy music. One/Threes have a good mechanical sense and approach life in a methodical, practical manner.

Money, physical appearance, and stylishness are very important to One/Threes. They enjoy hard work, and their mind requires intellectual stimulation. They like to know everything, tend to be well read and current on all topics, are careful listeners, and quickly decide where they stand on any issue. They are international in their thinking and attracted to groups and ideas that address social inequities. They are kindhearted, enjoy giving gifts, and can be generous to a fault. When their generosity is not reciprocated, however, One/Threes can feel betrayed. They need to feel needed and crave constant companionship and communication; they love the telephone. Yet, as they grow older, One/Threes may develop a strong desire for solitude and become hermitlike.

One/Threes are quite dominating and dislike sharing leadership; as employers, they accept no nonsense from employees. They are decisive, quick to act, and levelheaded in emergencies. They will go to impossible lengths to prove a point. They respond to aggression with an iron fist rather than a velvet glove. However, they usually follow such drastic actions with negotiation. If thwarted or frustrated, they may take refuge in martyrdom.

Always ready to explore the new, One/Threes are quick to recognize original ideas. They feel comfortable with technical innovations and are able to incorporate them easily into their lives. Although they are good speakers or performers, they can become withdrawn when they feel out of their element and should remember Thomas Wolfe's words, "The surest cure for vanity is loneliness." With their tremendous enthusiasm for new projects, One/Threes are often found in artistic pursuits and can be prolific artists or writers.

Woody Allen
Ursula Andress
Charles Atlas
Harry Belafonte
Pierre Bonnard
Sir Richard F. Burton
Kirk Cameron
Chubby Checker
Glenn Close
Samuel Taylor Coleridge
Aleister Crowley
Marion Davies
Roger Daltry
Emily Dickinson
Christian Dior
Wyatt Earp
Gene Hackman
Ron Howard
Wolfman Jack
Dorothy Lamour
Richard E. Leakey
Claude Lelouch
Jack London
Louis Malle
Mary Martin
Bette Midler
Jack Nicklaus
Luciano Pavarotti
Emily Post
Ezra Pound
Victoria Principal
Richard Pryor
Vanessa Redgrave
Paul Revere
Joan Rivers
Franklin D. Roosevelt
Grace Slick
J. R. R. Tolkien
Gore Vidal
Woodrow Wilson
Henry Winkler
Thomas Wolfe

Fear created gods; audacity created kings.
— Prosper Jolyat de Crebillon

THE ONE/FOUR SET AFFINITIES

THE ONE/FOUR NUMBERS ARE: 1 3 4 5

ODD NUMBERS: 1 3 5 EVEN NUMBERS: 4

SET INTERVAL: 3

FAMILY NUMBER: 5

THE ONE/FOURS REPRESENT 3.3 PERCENT OF THE POPULATION.

PEOPLE I KNOW WHO ARE ONE/FOURS:

_____   _____
_____   _____
_____   _____
_____   _____
_____   _____
_____   _____

MY ONE/FOUR OBSERVATIONS:

_____
_____
_____
_____
_____
_____
_____
_____

DISPOSITION

— MASKED — PRECISE — WORKAHOLICS —

— PERSISTENT — PROUD — DEMANDING OF SELF AND OTHERS —

— LOGICAL — HOMEBODIES — EXCELLENT DECORATORS —

— GENERALLY SUCCESSFUL —

"Wear a shield of diligence and a mask of propriety."

ONE/FOUR

The twelve days of the year
that would make you a ONE/FOUR are:

January 4	January 31	April 19	October 13
January 13	April 1	April 28	October 22
January 22	April 10	October 4	October 31

One/Fours are bold, daring, adventuresome beings. They fling themselves at life with incredible intensity and have strong personal magnetism. They have remarkable patience with both the very young and the old. They love their homes, enjoy working around them, and may be avid collectors of objects of personal interest or of art. They can be powerful leaders with an intense sense of duty and a compulsion for work. Ambitious, versatile, and bright, One/Fours adhere to strong principles and seldom do things that conflict with them.

One/Fours need order in their lives; they do not function well in chaos. There is a mathematical precision and determination about the things they do. No group has higher personal expectations than One/Fours. Perfectionists, they need to be the best in all aspects of their lives: best mate, best worker, best boss, best parent, best friend. They are workaholics who tend to overextend themselves, which creates conflicts in their personal relationships. If One/Fours feel dissatisfied with their achievements, no amount of adoration from others will suffice. They will often wear a mask of indifference or detachment to cover their sense of inadequacy or weakness.

In their work, One/Fours have great respect for tradition, but, convinced that everything can be improved upon, they embrace new ideas and practical concepts. They follow orders well, but they like to feel in charge and function best when left to their own devices. If they accept a challenge, it is to the bitter end — they will not stop until they achieve their goals. This persistence usually makes them successful in the material world. As employers, they expect their employees to be as dedicated as they are. Their ego and pride make it difficult for them to say no when their expertise or help is sought, making them susceptible to early burn-out.

One/Fours make great doctors, dentists, or detectives. They feel they should know all the answers, so they will doggedly pursue a mysterious ailment, element, clue, or criminal. They also make excellent artists, decorators, and inventors, relying on their keen sense of order, design, and style combined with their flair for creative organization.

Don Adams
Horatio Alger
Armand Assante
Tallulah Bankhead
Otto von Bismarck
Linda Blair
Louis Braille
Lord George Byron
John Candy
Chuck Connors
Catherine Deneuve
Eddy Duchin
Jeff Goldblum
Lee Grant
D. W. Griffith
Rutherford B. Hayes
Charlton Heston
Chiang Kai-shek
Buster Keaton
Patti LaBelle
Lily Langtry
Timothy Leary
Harper Lee
Doris Lessing
Norman Mailer
Ann-Margret
Toshiro Mifune
Dudley Moore
John O'Hara
Marie Osmond
Eden Pastora
Floyd Patterson
Paloma Picasso
Robert Rauschenberg
Debbie Reynolds
Damon Runyon
Susan Sarandon
Robert Stack
Art Tatum
Margaret Thatcher
Jan Vermeer
Jane Wyman

Humanity i love you because
when you're hard up you pawn your intelligence
to buy a drink. — e. e. cummings

THE ONE/FIVE SET AFFINITIES

THE ONE/FIVE NUMBERS ARE: 1 4 5 6

ODD NUMBERS: 1 5 EVEN NUMBERS: 4 6

SET INTERVAL: 4

FAMILY NUMBER: 6

THE ONE/FIVES REPRESENT 2.7 PERCENT OF THE POPULATION.

PEOPLE I KNOW WHO ARE ONE/FIVES:

_____   _____
_____   _____
_____   _____
_____   _____
_____   _____
_____   _____

MY ONE/FIVE OBSERVATIONS:

_____
_____
_____
_____
_____
_____
_____
_____

DISPOSITION

— YOUTHFUL — PLAYFUL — POWERFUL —

— CONTROLED — IMPATIENT — GRANDIOSE DREAMERS —

— DETERMINED — QUICK TONGUED —

— EXTROVERTED — DECISIVE —

ONE/FIVE

*The ten days of the year
that would make you a ONE/FIVE are:*

January 5	May 1	May 19	October 5
January 14	May 10	May 28	October 14
January 23			October 23

One/Fives are happy-go-lucky individuals with an aura of physical and mental youthfulness. Capable of being all things to all people, they thrive in social situations where they are in control or at the center of attention. They are ruled by an interesting mixture of logic, order, and impulse, which makes them risk-takers, gamblers, and idealists. One/Fives have an authoritative attitude and seldom doubt their self-styled genius. Their strong feelings and opinions compel them to speak their mind no matter what the consequences. They are attracted to grandiose projects — the bigger, the better. Details, however, are not their strong point — they like to delegate these to others. Because they are open to change and new ideas, it is not unusual for One/Fives to travel far from their birthplaces physically, mentally, or spiritually. Despite this, they resist changes in others, especially in their family or friends.

One/Fives are quite intuitive. They have tremendous discipline and tenacity when pursuing a specific goal. At the same time, they are given to comfort and self-indulgence, and can easily fall into addictions. They are rarely overeaters, however, since physical appearance is very important to them. Social interaction with others is of special significance to them, and their connections to family are very strong. They are seldom hermits, and some form of recreation or entertainment is a daily necessity.

One/Fives are compulsive workers, always in a rush to do something, meet someone, or be somewhere. They love to organize and direct, and will go to great lengths to do something for others. However, they are quite unforgiving and vengeful if they feel they have been treated badly. They have long memories and will seldom forget a real or imagined injustice. They generally mask their deep inner feelings and, when flustered, can appear brusque and abrasive.

One/Fives are attracted to the social, dramatic, artistic, and political arenas of life. Keen judges of character, they can easily spot weaknesses and strengths in others and use this skill to great advantage. As a result, they make great talk-show hosts, salespeople, entertainers, raconteurs, and politicians.

Alvin Ailey
Benedict Arnold
Chester A. Arthur
Fred Astaire
Léon Bakst
Jason Bateman
Cecil Beaton
Humphrey Bogart
Julian Bond
John Wilkes Booth
Johnny Carson
Judy Collins
Rita Coolidge
e. e. cummings
Donovan
John Dos Passos
Faye Dunaway
Robert Duval
Dwight D. Eisenhower
Ian Fleming
Glenn Ford
Bob Geldof
Lillian Gish
Lorraine Hansberry
Joseph Heller
Ho Chi Minh
Grace Jones
Diane Keaton
Ernie Kovacs
Ralph Lauren
Malcolm X
Édouard Manet
Katherine Mansfield
Yukio Mishima
Roger Moore
Jeanne Moreau
Jack Parr
Pelé
Albert Schweitzer
David O. Selznick
Jim Thorpe
Pete Townshend

Whoever fights monsters should see to it that in the process he does not become a monster.
And when you look long into an abyss,
the abyss also looks into you. — Friedrich Nietzsche

THE ONE/SIX SET AFFINITIES

THE ONE/SIX NUMBERS ARE: 1 5 6 7

ODD NUMBERS: 1 5 7   EVEN NUMBERS: 6

SET INTERVAL: 5

FAMILY NUMBER: 7

THE ONE/SIXES REPRESENT 2.7 PERCENT OF THE POPULATION.

PEOPLE I KNOW WHO ARE ONE/SIXES:

_____   _____
_____   _____
_____   _____
_____   _____
_____   _____

MY ONE/SIX OBSERVATIONS:

_____
_____
_____
_____
_____
_____
_____

DISPOSITION

— FOLLOWERS — CULTISTS — LEADERS —

— SEARCHERS — GOAL-ORIENTED — DRAWN TO FAME —

— ACHIEVERS — SAVIORS — MAGNETIC —

— ACTIVE/VACILLATING —

"Follow the leader or lead the followers; attract fame, and serve glory."

ONE/SIX

*The ten days of the year
that would make you a ONE/SIX are:*

January 6	June 1	June 19	October 6
January 15	June 10	June 28	October 15
January 24			October 24

One/Sixes, with their magnetism and mystique, can be both peace-loving problem-solvers and wild-eyed zealots. They combine practical idealism with an intuitive perception of symmetry, rhythm, and beauty. Because they sense a definite, but difficult-to-define mission in life, they sometimes feel as though their feet are moving simultaneously in two different directions. They enjoy the processes of discovery and invention, yet some One/Sixes can become superstitious and may even hear voices and commands. They can quickly move from reason to impulse and from friendship to enmity. They are particularly sensitive to real or imagined wrongs.

Prone to extremes, One/Sixes need to belong to or be a part of something greater than themselves. Security is important to them, yet so are liberty and independence — a dilemma that often creates conflict in their actions and relationships. A strong desire to please others prompts them to promise things that are beyond their control. Yet their sensitivity to their personal shortcomings makes their inability to fulfill these promises weigh heavily on their conscience.

To tell One/Sixes that something is impossible is like waving a red cape at a bull. Still, they are cool-headed fighters with good judgment and tenacious vision. They are hard workers who function best in situations where they are pursuing important personal goals. Although they usually seek expert advice before undertaking projects, if the advice does not suit them they may put it aside and act impulsively. They should try to avoid work that requires the intervention of others for completion.

One/Sixes are attracted to the areas of social achievement, fame, and mystic search. They make excellent pioneers — many One/Sixes become the first to achieve something significant. At times they can assume an attitude of suffering coupled with a need for atonement, and they can degenerate into tragic figures when they take themselves too seriously. Because they possess a quality that makes them attractive to the public, they can be moving orators, rallying others against injustice or toward some spiritual or political belief. As a result, they are strong religious leaders, dramatic and persuasive attorneys, or hypnotic performers.

Shana Alexander
Joan of Arc
Clyde Beatty
John Belushi
Pat Boone
Lloyd Bridges
Mel Brooks
Charo
Alan Cranston
André Derain
Neil Diamond
Gustave Doré
Judy Garland
Janet Gaynor
Andy Griffith
Moss Hart
Thor Heyerdahl
Lee Iacocca
Reverend Ike
Martin Luther King, Jr.
Natassja Kinski
Gene Krupa
Le Corbusier
Jenny Lind
Carole Lombard
Tom Mix
Molière
Marilyn Monroe
Friedrich Nietzsche
Aristotle Onassis
Gilda Radner
Oral Roberts
Gena Rowlands
Carl Sandburg
Arthur Schlesinger
Wallis Simpson
Sharon Tate
Danny Thomas
Edith Wharton
P. G. Wodehouse
Loretta Young
Bill Wyman

Discouragement seizes us only when
we can no longer count on chance. — George Sand

THE ONE/SEVEN SET AFFINITIES

THE ONE/SEVEN NUMBERS ARE: 1 6 7 8

ODD NUMBERS: 1 7 EVEN NUMBERS: 6 8

SET INTERVAL: 6

FAMILY NUMBER: 8

THE ONE/SEVENS REPRESENT 2.7 PERCENT OF THE POPULATION.

PEOPLE I KNOW WHO ARE ONE/SEVENS:

_____   _____
_____   _____
_____   _____
_____   _____
_____   _____

MY ONE/SEVEN OBSERVATIONS:

_____
_____
_____
_____
_____
_____
_____

DISPOSITION

— BIG THINKERS — GOAL ORIENTED — EXECUTIVES —

— CUNNING — MATERIALISTIC — BENEFACTORS —

— DEMANDING — IMMERSED IN WORK — INTUITIVE —

— TRENDSETTING — LOGICAL —

Charging onward to the top of the mountain.

ONE/SEVEN

*The ten days of the year
that would make you a ONE/SEVEN are:*

January 7	July 1	July 19	October 7
January 16	July 10	July 28	October 16
January 25			October 25

One/Sevens want to lead and direct. They are ambitious, they think big, and their motto is "Go for it!" Their executive abilities include the foresight to clearly and systematically define and pursue a set of goals, which puts them on a path of steady advancement. Drawn to strong people who may help them attain their goals, One/Sevens start at the top, yet always question situations. Even as children, "Why?" is the most frequently used word when One/Sevens want to get to the root of a situation.

Power is very important to One/Sevens. If they feel they do not have it, they will seek out and attach themselves to someone or something that does. Personal recognition and material success are also very important to their happiness and well-being. They tend to be big spenders and may have trouble actually saving money. One/Sevens love to enjoy life and always want more out of it. Despite this, they are fairly rigid in their habits and have definite likes and dislikes.

One/Sevens are basically loners in their work, yet they would be driven to despair if they felt they were nothing more than an anonymous entity. They need to surround themselves with a supportive, familylike atmosphere. They always operate from a set of high standards and expectations, and are exacting employers, expecting a great deal from those who work for them. Although generous to a fault with their money and possessions, they are reluctant to share the limelight with others. Their strong sense of pride makes it difficult for them to be in subservient positions or accept personal shortcomings or failure. In fact, it is so difficult for One/Sevens to acknowledge an error that they are more likely to try to save a sinking ship than to say, "I goofed."

Seldom without a goal, One/Sevens enjoy mental challenges, and their methodical, logical minds are tenacious when pursuing something important. They usually have a very accurate feel for the pulse of their time and always manage to be where the action is. Their excellent sense of timing makes it important for them to listen to their own inner voice rather than follow the counsel of those whose timeliness is not so acute.

Nick Adams
June Allyson
Corazon Aquino
Arthur Ashe
Dan Aykroyd
Albert Bierstadt
Karen Black
David Brinkley
Joe E. Brown
Genevieve Bujold
Robert Burns
Leslie Caron
John Carpenter
Edgar Degas
Olivia De Havilland
Andy Devine
Princess Diana
Günter Grass
Arlo Guthrie
Deborah Harry
R. D. Laing
Angela Lansbury
Estée Lauder
Charles Laughton
Kenny Loggins
Ethel Merman
Ilie Nastase
Eugene O'Neill
Jackie Kennedy Onassis
Pablo Picasso
Sydney Pollack
Marcel Proust
Jean-Pierre Rampal
George Sand
Sally Struthers
Twyla Tharp
Bishop Desmond Tutu
Rudy Vallee
James McNeill Whistler
Oscar Wilde
Virginia Woolf
William Wyler

The cat in gloves
catches no mice. — *Benjamin Franklin*

THE ONE/EIGHT SET AFFINITIES

THE ONE/EIGHT NUMBERS ARE: 1 7 8 9

ODD NUMBERS: 1 7 9   EVEN NUMBERS: 8

SET INTERVAL: 7

FAMILY NUMBER: 9

THE ONE/EIGHTS REPRESENT 2.7 PERCENT OF THE POPULATION.

PEOPLE I KNOW WHO ARE ONE/EIGHTS:

_____   _____
_____   _____
_____   _____
_____   _____
_____   _____
_____   _____

MY ONE/EIGHT OBSERVATIONS:

_____
_____
_____
_____
_____
_____
_____
_____

DISPOSITION

— CHARISMATIC — CORNER CUTTERS — DAREDEVILS —

— UNFORGIVING — ADDICTIVE PERSONALITIES —

— POWER SEEKERS — FORCEFUL —

— ATTRACTED TO THE UNUSUAL —

*"A powerful thought can manifest
a world of change."*

ONE/EIGHT

*The ten days of the year
that would make you a ONE/EIGHT are:*

January 8	August 1	August 19	October 8
January 17	August 10	August 28	October 17
January 26			October 26

One/Eights have ambitious natures, a strong sense of personal destiny, and definite daredevil tendencies. They are very competitive and will rarely turn down a challenge or dare. They are sensitive to their health and tend to keep themselves physically fit, a trait they also admire in others. With multifaceted talents and interests, their major problem is finding the right occupation. Pageantry and the unusual, exotic, or mystical can appeal to them. They have great intuition, can be very creative, are quite opinionated, and can be ruthless. They would rather to do things their way and be wrong than follow someone else's path and be right.

Power, success, and personal recognition are important to One/Eights. They need to control situations, crave possessions such as fast cars and fine horses, and prefer notoriety to a lack of acknowledgment. Bright and naturally stubborn, they will not hesitate to tailor circumstances to suit themselves. They are impatient and like to take shortcuts and cut corners, which can cost them dearly in the long run. They are particularly susceptible to substance abuse, a weakness that can be devastating to them and cause them to mistreat others. Moderation does not come easily to them, and they can vacillate between excess and zealous abstinence.

One/Eights have a fine sense of organization, are capable of great accomplishments, and work hard to achieve fame. They are individualists who work better alone or with subordinates. They would rather give orders than take them, and they have high expectations of their employees and family. Generally slow to anger, they can be explosive when they reach the limits of their tolerance, and very unforgiving when deeply hurt or let down. They can save themselves much needless sorrow and anxiety if they can learn to laugh at themselves.

One/Eights are natural leaders. With their strong egos, nothing challenges them more than to be told that they cannot or should not do something. They enjoy pushing themselves to extremes and are often drawn to danger. They prefer action to dreams, and their independent spirits love the exciting. One/Eights are often found in politics, competitive sports, or show business, where they are dramatic hands-on players.

Rosanna Arquette
Jean Arthur
Rona Barrett
David Bowie
Charles Boyer
Edward Burne-Jones
Al Capone
Coco Chanel
Chevy Chase
Anton Chekhov
Montgomery Clift
Jackie Coogan
Angela Davis
Dom De Luise
Jules Feiffer
Eddie Fisher
Benjamin Franklin
Jerry Garcia
Bill Graham
Wayne Gretzky
Rita Hayworth
Herbert Hoover
Jesse Jackson
James Earl Jones
Margot Kidder
Eartha Kitt
Evel Knievel
Herman Melville
Arthur Miller
Paul Newman
Lou Piniella
Elvis Presley
Yves Saint Laurent
Vidal Sassoon
Mack Sennett
Norma Shearer
Willie Shoemaker
Jaclyn Smith
Sigourney Weaver
Betty White
Orville Wright
Jane Wyatt

Will you, won't you,
will you, won't you,
will you join the dance? — Lewis Carroll

THE ONE/NINE SET AFFINITIES

THE ONE/NINE NUMBERS ARE: 1 1 8 9

ODD NUMBERS: 1 1 9 EVEN NUMBERS: 8

SET INTERVAL: 8

FAMILY NUMBER: 1

THE ONE/NINES REPRESENT 2.7 PERCENT OF THE POPULATION.

PEOPLE I KNOW WHO ARE ONE/NINES:

_____   _____
_____   _____
_____   _____
_____   _____
_____   _____

MY ONE/NINE OBSERVATIONS:

_____
_____
_____
_____
_____
_____
_____
_____

DISPOSITION

— TRAILBLAZERS — TEACHERS — EXECUTIVES —

— SUCCESSFUL — ORGANIZERS — ETHICAL —

— TRAVELERS — ANALYTICAL —

— CREATIVE — PERFECTIONISTS —

"Nurture the dream and give it attention,
then watch the show."

ONE/NINE

The ten days of the year
that would make you a ONE/NINE are:

January 9	September 1	September 19	October 9
January 18	September 10	September 28	October 18
January 27			October 27

Life for One/Nines is an experience in variety. With their wide range of interests, capacity for intense concentration, and tenacity when pursuing a goal, they tend to be successful in almost any field they enter. Innovators rather than imitators, they are attracted to the dramatic and the powerful. Along with their clear, analytical minds, they frequently have an exceptional talent or ear for music. They enjoy travel, are interested in global issues, and can be very eclectic in their tastes. They view life in broad terms and are more open to the unconventional than most.

One/Nines believe in action and are not afraid of unpopular issues; the need for approval, however, remains important to them. They thrive on appreciation and attention, and are drawn to whatever will allow them to shine in brilliance and glory. Needing to be the best "anything" in the world, they are unable to accept personal weakness and cannot tolerate feelings of inferiority. They have a strong ethical viewpoint, but their mistake lies in believing that others operate from the same standards. One/Nines' ethical sense is so powerful that they will face a roaring crowd to defend a friend falsely accused of impropriety, yet they may flounder if their personal integrity is challenged.

Although quite serious, One/Nines have a good sense of humor and can laugh at themselves. They are tireless workers who function best when allowed to express their independent spirit. They do not enjoy taking orders or being told what to do. They have a fine sense of organization, quickly grasp the essence of new things, and easily spot any flaws in a system or idea. Their exceptional ability to focus on a single issue can make them appear aloof to others. This, coupled with their perfectionist tendencies, can present problems for them in relationships.

One/Nines usually are a "class act." Their presence is always memorable. Their powerful sense of responsibility and their genuine concern for others bring intense social consciousness into whatever they do. Yet they possess a streak of elitism and, although they may champion the causes of the common people, they seldom think of themselves as common. They make great spiritual leaders, teachers, and executives.

Muhammad Ali
Joan Baez
George Balanchine
Chuck Berry
Jackson Browne
Edgar Rice Burroughs
Al Capp
Lewis Carroll
Yvonne De Carlo
Frances Farmer
José Feliciano
Crystal Gayle
William Golding
Cary Grant
Oliver Hardy
Jeremy Irons
Amy Irving
Danny Kaye
John Lennon
Roy Lichtenstein
Roger Maris
Wynton Marsalis
Marcello Mastroianni
Melina Mercouri
Wolfgang A. Mozart
Martina Navratilova
Lee Harvey Oswald
Sylvia Plath
Arthur Rackham
Donna Reed
Theodore Roosevelt
George C. Scott
Ed Sullivan
Dylan Thomas
Lily Tomlin
Margaret Trudeau
Pierre Trudeau
Twiggy
Lee Van Cleef
Fay Wray
Susannah York
Moon Unit Zappa

THE TWO/TWO SET AFFINITIES

THE TWO/TWO NUMBERS ARE: 2 2 4

ODD NUMBERS: None   EVEN NUMBERS: 2 2 4

SET INTERVAL: 0 (Double 2)

FAMILY NUMBER: 4

THE TWO/TWOS REPRESENT 2.2 PERCENT OF THE POPULATION.

PEOPLE I KNOW WHO ARE TWO/TWOS:

_____   _____
_____   _____
_____   _____
_____   _____
_____   _____
_____

MY TWO/TWO OBSERVATIONS:

_____
_____
_____
_____
_____
_____
_____
_____

DISPOSITION

— EMPATHETIC — CREATURES OF HABIT — ON THE EDGE —

— VENGEFUL — STUBBORN —

— DETAIL ORIENTED — SELF-IMPORTANT —

— REGIMENTED — IMPULSIVE —

Life as a battle with the Dragon of Balance.

TWO/TWO

*The eight days of the year
that would make you a TWO/TWO are:*

February 2	February 20	November 2	November 20
February 11	February 29	November 11	November 29

Two/Twos face the dilemma of balancing their impulsive, sensitive natures with their desire to have everything under control. They intuitively see the overall pattern and essence of situations, but they need to find a way to integrate this sensitivity into mainstream consciousness. Some Two/Twos respond like ambulance drivers who, faced with daily tragedy, desensitize themselves. Others create emotional buffer zones by bringing strong structure and organization into their lives. An interesting mixture of extravagance and frugality, they can throw away dollars and pinch pennies. They are attracted to the spiritual or occult, and relate best to others on a one-to-one basis. They want to be personally involved, and often champion some social cause as an outlet for their emotional natures.

Two/Twos tend to cling to habitual patterns of behavior. Disharmony causes them great anxiety, making them overly sensitive or pessimistic. They are always open to new ideas and will listen to both sides of any issue. They have a stubborn streak, however, and will not accept ideas that threaten their scheme of order. They must follow a plan, and the plan must be their plan. There are no shortcuts for them, and often the hard way is the best way. Their flair for detail lets nothing material escape their attention, but their emotions and their need for self-importance can blind them.

Two/Twos are hard workers who are not comfortable being idle. If their work feels harmonious, they thrive; if not, they either leave it or get sick by staying. Given half a chance, they will organize everyone around them. They sometimes take things far too personally, which can trigger a destructive self-pity syndrome. When deeply hurt, they turn suddenly vengeful; if their anger can not find another target, they focus it on themselves.

Naturally empathetic, Two/Twos make excellent therapists and friends. They often find that the arts let them express their dramatic, impulsive nature within a protective framework. Music, with its emotional impact and organizational precision, and painting, with its expressionistic potential and compositional structure, are ideal. Writing and acting, which allow for the expression of intense emotion within a safe, detached setting, are also excellent occupations for Two/Twos.

Ansel Adams
Louisa May Alcott
Balthus
Judy Canova
Yakima Canutt
Alistair Cooke
Bo Derek
James Dickey
Barry Diller
Jimmy Dorsey
Fyodor Dostoevsky
Sandy Duncan
Thomas A. Edison
Farrah Fawcett
Enzo Ferrari
Eva Gabor
Bonita Granville
Patty Hearst
Alger Hiss
James Joyce
Robert F. Kennedy
Burt Lancaster
C. S. Lewis
Chuck Mangione
Demi Moore
Ozzie Nelson
Pat O'Brien
Jennifer O'Neill
George Patton
Sidney Poitier
Stephanie Powers
Mary Quant
Ayn Rand
Burt Reynolds
Robert Ryan
Buffy Saint-Marie
Dick Smothers
Tom Smothers
Gloria Vanderbilt
Kurt Vonnegut
Édouard Vuillard
Jonathan Winters

A community is like a ship;
everyone ought to be prepared to take the helm. — Henrik Ibsen

THE TWO/THREE SET AFFINITIES

THE TWO/THREE NUMBERS ARE: 1 2 3 5

ODD NUMBERS: 1 3 5 EVEN NUMBERS: 2

SET INTERVAL: 1

FAMILY NUMBER: 5

THE TWO/THREES REPRESENT 4.1 PERCENT OF THE POPULATION.

PEOPLE I KNOW WHO ARE TWO/THREES:

_____   _____
_____   _____
_____   _____
_____   _____
_____   _____
_____   _____

MY TWO/THREE OBSERVATIONS:

_____
_____
_____
_____
_____
_____
_____
_____

DISPOSITION

— SAINTS AND SINNERS — DRIVEN — AMBITIOUS —

— DUTIFUL — CHANGEABLE — SICKLY — ACCIDENT PRONE —

— CHANCE-TAKERS — DRAMATIC —

— SAVIORS —

> *"A good crisis puts color in the cheeks and*
> *fire in the loins."*

TWO/THREE

The fifteen days of the year
that would make you a TWO/THREE are:

February 3	March 11	November 12	December 11
February 12	March 20	November 21	December 20
February 21	March 29	November 30	December 29
March 2	November 3	December 2	

Two/Threes, filled with dreams of service to others and visions of heroic glory, strive to be leaders. Part introvert, part extrovert, they are a complex mix of saint and sinner, humanitarian and con artist. They hold strong opinions and never fear taking a controversial position. They are quite intuitive but, under normal circumstances, they do not trust their inner voice. Designed for action in times of crisis, they are flames looking for a reason to burn. When no crisis exists, they are on the prowl for the emergency that will hurl them into decisive acts and concentrate their energy. Confronted by crisis, they become completely focused, ready to lead, direct, and experience life. Lacking such an emergency, they can be indecisive and doubting. The great lesson for Two/Threes is to learn to enjoy the present without the stimulation of crisis.

Two/Threes are extremely ambitious, and success is very important to them. They have a great need for attention and affection from others, and are anchored in the arena of drama. If they cannot find the dramatic in their own lives, they will find it in the lives of friends or on the pages of their morning newspaper. Their need for the dramatic even finds expression in their illnesses: fallen arches are not their style; sleeping sickness or some other exotic affliction is more in keeping with their personal dynamics.

Two/Threes are gifted, bright, intense, and hardworking. They will not hesitate to roll up their sleeves and get their hands dirty, and they have very high expectations of performance from others. Their forceful opinions, however, often evoke strong responses and polarized reactions. Although they are demanding, they are generous, loyal friends. Sometimes Two/Threes can be torn between their need for personal success and the need to serve others, but they can always be depended on to aid the frail or the needy.

Two/Threes are chance-takers — but not necessarily gamblers — and are most often attracted to the arenas of politics, show business, and the arts. They are involved in the process of change and are always trying to modify themselves, someone else, or some situation. New art forms, alternate techniques, a different lifestyle, or a return to the good old days, anything that represents change, either forward or backward, is attractive to them.

Joseph Alioto
Adam Ant
Desi Arnaz
W. H. Auden
Pearl Bailey
Shelley Berman
Charles Bronson
Karen Carpenter
Winston Churchill
Dick Clark
Charles Darwin
Otto Dix
Morgan Fairchild
Hubert de Givenchy
Charles Goodyear
Mikhail Gorbachev
Lorne Greene
Goldie Hawn
William Hurt
Billy Idol
John Irving
Jennifer Jones
Grace Kelly
G. Gordon Liddy
Abraham Lincoln
René Magritte
Charles Manson
Mary Tyler Moore
Anais Nin
Bobby Orr
Laffit Pincay, Jr.
Carl Reiner
Norman Rockwell
Georges Seurat
Nina Simone
Aleksandr Solzhenitsyn
Gertrude Stein
Jonathan Swift
Fran Tarkenton
Mark Twain
Voltaire
Neil Young

Discipline is the soul of an army.
It makes small numbers formidable, procures success to the weak,
and esteem to all. — George Washington

THE TWO/FOUR SET AFFINITIES

THE TWO/FOUR NUMBERS ARE: 2 2 4 6

ODD NUMBERS: None   EVEN NUMBERS: 2 2 4 6

SET INTERVAL: 2

FAMILY NUMBER: 6

THE TWO/FOURS REPRESENT 2.7 PERCENT OF THE POPULATION.

PEOPLE I KNOW WHO ARE TWO/FOURS:

_____   _____
_____   _____
_____   _____
_____   _____
_____   _____
_____   _____

MY TWO/FOUR OBSERVATIONS:

_____
_____
_____
_____
_____
_____
_____

DISPOSITION

— DICTATORIAL — COMPARTMENTALIZED —

— ORGANIZED — DECISIVE — OPEN-MINDED —

— INTUITIVE — HISTRIONIC — VIGILANT —

— LONG-TERM FRIENDS —

Something to do and shape. Someone to direct.
Love, drama, order, and flowers.

TWO/FOUR

The ten days of the year
that would make you a TWO/FOUR are:

February 4	April 2	April 20	November 4
February 13	April 11	April 29	November 13
February 22			November 22

Two/Fours are difficult to categorize. They are masters of organization and communication, yet their air of authority and conviction separates them from the crowd. They are romantic, nostalgic, and sentimental, and often have dramatic emotional natures. They can be as hard as nails and amazingly detached if it suits them, yet tears and tantrums come easily to them. They have an exceptional ability to mentally compartmentalize, which allows them to switch from complete absorption in work to equally intense play: a quick change of costume, and they are off and running. They are particularly attracted to fashion and trendy styles, which their innately social personalities easily adopt as their own.

Two/Fours have a great desire for harmony and order in their lives. They have a very strong need to remain connected to friends and family, but they want to sit in the driver's seat. They will not remain powerless in a relationship or a job for long. If they find themselves in such a situation, they head for the door. If they are unable to move on, it can be devastating to their mental and physical health. Although they have extraordinary intuitive abilities, their determination to have things their own way can override their intuition. They do not want to hear anything they are not ready to accept and tend to seek validation from those who agree with them. They also resist changes that upset their personal timetable of priorities.

Two/Fours are very ambitious, accept and assume responsibility, and enjoy directing others. They are good at sorting through situations and communicating their ideas. Particularly fond of having the last word, they can be unforgiving when thwarted. They collect a broad assortment of friends, keep them forever, and tend to categorize them neatly. It is not unusual for Two/Fours to have tennis-playing friends, business friends, childhood friends, and concertgoing friends — whatever the occasion, they have the friends to match.

Two/Fours are exceptional organizers and decision makers. They also have quite a flair for art and design. With their great skill in communication, intense convictions, and innate sense of authority, they frequently land in positions of power. Whether running a country, a company, or a family, they are always the strongest personality in the room.

Hans Christian Andersen
Samuel Beckett
Luis Buñuel
Art Carney
Giovanni Casanova
Oleg Cassini
Stockard Channing
Charlemagne
Frédéric Chopin
Alice Cooper
Walter Cronkite
Jamie Lee Curtis
Rodney Dangerfield
Charles de Gaulle
Duke Ellington
Max Ernst
Tennessee Ernie Ford
Betty Friedan
André Gide
Whoopi Goldberg
Alec Guinness
William Randolph Hearst
Hirohito
Adolf Hitler
Edward Kennedy
Billie Jean King
Charles Lindbergh
Harold Lloyd
Ida Lupino
Chico Marx
Rod McKuen
Zubin Mehta
Edna St. Vincent Millay
Joan Miró
Ryan O'Neal
Geraldine Page
Eva Perón
Oliver Reed
Will Rogers
Robert Louis Stevenson
Grant Wood
Émile Zola

It is impossible to enjoy idling thoroughly
unless one has plenty of work to do. — Jerome K. Jerome

THE TWO/FIVE SET AFFINITIES

THE TWO/FIVE NUMBERS ARE: 2 3 5 7

ODD NUMBERS: 3 5 7   EVEN NUMBERS: 2

SET INTERVAL: 3

FAMILY NUMBER: 7

THE TWO/FIVES REPRESENT 2.7 PERCENT OF THE POPULATION.

PEOPLE I KNOW WHO ARE TWO/FIVES:

_____   _____
_____   _____
_____   _____
_____   _____
_____   _____
_____   _____

MY TWO/FIVE OBSERVATIONS:

_____
_____
_____
_____
_____
_____
_____
_____

DISPOSITION

— AMBITIOUS — FAMILY ORIENTED — DASHING —

— DISCIPLINED — CURIOUS —

— EXHIBITIONISTS — INSECURE — DUTIFUL —

— PRIVATE —

"A stage, an audience, something new to perform
— let the drama begin."

TWO/FIVE

The ten days of the year
that would make you a TWO/FIVE are:

February 5	May 2	May 20	November 5
February 14	May 11	May 29	November 14
February 23			November 23

Hank Aaron
Honoré de Balzac
Jack Benny
Irving Berlin
William S. Burroughs
Red Buttons
Vernon Castle
Catherine the Great
Prince Charles
Cher
Joe Cocker
Aaron Copland
Bing Crosby
Salvador Dalí
Moshe Dayan
Mamie Eisenhower
Peter Fonda
Martha Graham
Johannes Gutenberg
George Frederick Handel
Patrick Henry
Gregory Hines
John W. Hinkley, Jr.
James Hoffa
Bob Hope
Boris Karloff
George S. Kaufman
Billy the Kid
Veronica Lake
Vivien Leigh
Bob Marley
Harpo Marx
Claude Monet
Samuel Pepys
Dick Powell
Charlotte Rampling
Roy Rogers
Margaret Rutherford
Sam Shepard
Belle Starr
James Stewart
Ike Turner

"I move, therefore I exist" is the motto of the Two/Five set. Not happy being idle, they are generally on the move. They have an emotional nature that requires an occasional binge, and a natural curiosity that compels them to try almost anything once. Many of their frequent internal dialogues concern religion, the occult, and the mysteries of life. Strongly influenced by their early years, they use their past as a reference point and a springboard to the present or the future. They are generally showy, stylish individuals, in love with the idea of love. Yet they can be quite romantically naive and are very influenced by the social acceptability of their mates.

Two/Fives love attention and always want to get their own way, but they will frequently set aside their personal needs for the needs of others. They have an ongoing internal conflict between their strong sense of duty and personal propriety and their desire for quick results, change, and experimentation. Nevertheless, they seldom appear indecisive. They need to prove both to themselves and to others that they do achieve their goals, which they pursue with fanatic zeal. Physical appearance is important to them, and they usually take great pride in their health, grooming, and dress. They are attracted to affluence and achievement, and are motivated by success and social recognition.

Two/Fives work with high expectations and do not hesitate to take on responsibility. They enjoy directing others and can become quite dictatorial. They are capable of tremendous self-discipline, but their tendency to push themselves to the limit can adversely affect their health and mental well-being. Fortunately, they seldom get too carried away. Although strongly attached to their families and very social by nature, they relate best to others on a one-to-one basis and maintain a private and complex inner self.

Two/Fives have a keen business sense that makes them skillful and careful gamblers. They have a strong personal magnetism and project a sense of authority, which can make them powerful public speakers. They are often attracted to the glitter of show business. Excellent at social repartee, they love to entertain others. Nevertheless, they are quite discreet, and make solid and loyal friends.

Our swords shall play
the orators for us. — *Christopher Marlowe*

The Two/Six Set Affinities

THE TWO/SIX NUMBERS ARE: 2 4 6 8

ODD NUMBERS: None   EVEN NUMBERS: 2 4 6 8

SET INTERVAL: 4

FAMILY NUMBER: 8

THE TWO/SIXES REPRESENT 2.7 PERCENT OF THE POPULATION.

People I Know Who Are Two/Sixes:

_____   _____
_____   _____
_____   _____
_____   _____
_____   _____
_____   _____

My Two/Six Observations:

_____
_____
_____
_____
_____
_____
_____

Disposition

— POPULAR — TENDERHEARTED — POLITICAL —

— RESPONSIBLE — POLARIZED — OPINIONATED —

— STRUTTING — STUBBORN —

— LOYAL FRIENDS — GREGARIOUS —

Romance, drama — a reason to be.

TWO/SIX

*The ten days of the year
that would make you a TWO/SIX are:*

February 6	June 2	June 20	November 6
February 15	June 11	June 29	November 15
February 24			November 24

For Two/Sixes, life is a great spectacle, an adventure — the definitive drama. It is to be lived, not contemplated. They view the world as a conflict between good and evil, and tend to be either very liberal or very conservative, often switching views during the course of their life. They particularly enjoy conversations and debate. Their strongly expressed views invite argument, and yet somehow seem reassuring even to those who violently disagree with them. Popular, lively, and full of spirit, Two/Sixes stand out in a crowd and are very difficult to ignore. They may inspire love, hate, awe, or shock, but never indifference.

Two/Sixes want fame, love, creative success, adoration, power, glory, and any other bonuses that life can bestow. They are ruled more by their emotions than reason, and the romantic, social, and dramatic areas of life capture their attention. Because of their deep emotional makeup, they can be susceptible to addictions and obsessions. They may be quite nervous but seldom show it to others, usually masking it by being busy or involved in some cause or endeavor. They are very intuitive but may not be comfortable with this gift. They carry a strong sense of personal responsibility for the well-being of humanity, which they sometimes carry to extremes.

Two/Sixes are seldom bored, lead busy lives, and tend to be workaholics. They do not like being bothered by details and responsibilities — these they would gladly delegate to others. Their thinking is romantic, dramatic, and diverse, but it is always in terms of absolutes, never subtleties. While quite social, their polarized views and disdain for details can put others off, yet their powerful personal charisma is entrancing. It is on the personal level that Two/Sixes shine. They make incredibly loyal friends and mates.

Two/Sixes are very versatile and clever, and are usually attracted to the arts, social service, or politics. They are heroic rescuers of the downtrodden, defenders of the past, or initiators of the new. They make extraordinary storytellers and great show people. Never ones to fail to add sensational overtones or emphasis to any story, they bring a dramatic quality to even the mundane areas of life.

Susan B. Anthony
John Barrymore
Marisa Berenson
William F. Buckley
Gary Busey
Stokely Carmichael
Dale Carnegie
Natalie Cole
Jacques Cousteau
Joan Davis
Eric Dolphy
Nelson Eddy
Fabian
Sally Field
Errol Flynn
Zsa Zsa Gabor
Marvin Hamlisch
Thomas Hardy
Lillian Hellman
Winslow Homer
Hedda Hopper
James Jones
Scott Joplin
Cyndi Lauper
Mike Nichols
Georgia O'Keeffe
Lionel Richie
Peter Paul Rubens
Babe Ruth
Marquis de Sade
Maria Shriver
John Philip Sousa
Jeb Stuart
William Styron
Wayne Thiebaud
Henri de Toulouse-Lautrec
Rip Torn
François Truffaut
Mamie Van Doren
George Washington
Charlie Watts
Johnny Weissmuller

Each man's life represents
a road toward himself. — Hermann Hesse

THE TWO/SEVEN SET AFFINITIES

THE TWO/SEVEN NUMBERS ARE: 2 5 7 9

ODD NUMBERS: 5 7 9   EVEN NUMBERS: 2

SET INTERVAL: 5

FAMILY NUMBER: 9

THE TWO/SEVENS REPRESENT 2.7 PERCENT OF THE POPULATION.

PEOPLE I KNOW WHO ARE TWO/SEVENS:

_____   _____
_____   _____
_____   _____
_____   _____
_____   _____
_____   _____

MY TWO/SEVEN OBSERVATIONS:

_____
_____
_____
_____
_____
_____
_____

DISPOSITION

— ADMINISTRATORS — AMICABLE —

— PILGRIMS — SENSITIVE — UNCONVENTIONAL —

— ADDICTIVE PERSONALITIES — IMPETUOUS —

— IN THE SOCIAL WHIRL —

"Someone to serve. Something to do.
Approval and love is happiness through and through."

TWO/SEVEN

The ten days of the year
that would make you a TWO/SEVEN are:

February 7	July 2	July 20	November 7
February 16	July 11	July 29	November 16
February 25			November 25

Two/Sevens are on a journey of self-discovery. They seek to understand their relationships with their family, friends, associates, the world, and, finally, themselves. They are excitable, passionate individuals who are caring, sensitive, and giving. They are not comfortable with reality when it interferes with their idea of responsibility. They tend to distrust their considerable psychic abilities, and may disguise their unease about it with quiet skepticism. Their secret self is so sensitive that it is seldom allowed to come through. They can mask their insecurity with an endless variety of tasks to perform or with a constant stream of conversation.

Two/Sevens seek material success, social interaction, and a happy home life. They are ambitious organizers and planners, but tend to live for the moment and are not usually thrifty. They possess a strong sense of duty and social action that can cause them to be overly responsible for others. They do not put themselves first — it is usually late in their lives before they assign the worth to themselves that they so easily give to others. They tend to have addictive personalities and find escape through food, drugs, or social obligations. The great lesson for them is that they do not have to do or say anything — all they have to do is be.

Two/Sevens are always quick to take action, and impatient with the inefficiency and indecision of others. They make very poor hermits and are quite social within their circle of friends. They often try to find their identity through others, but this neither works for them nor is appreciated by others. Their desire to do things for others can trap them into a pattern of servitude. Not always judicious in deciding whom to help, they can accumulate a circle of selfish people with a "What have you done for me lately?" attitude. When they are able to free themselves from their self-inflicted burdens of responsibility, however, they are beacons of power and strength.

Two/Sevens are open to new ideas and fresh circumstances, speak with great eloquence and conviction, and usually find themselves at the forefront of contemporary thought. They can be equally at home in business or the arts. Skillful in sensing the connections between ideas, they make excellent researchers, administrators, arbitrators, agents, and promoters.

John Quincy Adams
Lola Albright
Jim Backus
Theda Bara
Lisa Bonet
Sonny Bono
Anthony Burgess
Albert Camus
Andrew Carnegie
Enrico Caruso
Professor Irwin Corey
Buster Crabbe
Marie Curie
Charles Dickens
Joe DiMaggio
Elizabeth Dole
John Foster Dulles
Galileo
Billy Graham
Dag Hammarskjöld
George Harrison
Hermann Hesse
Tab Hunter
John Kennedy, Jr.
Sinclair Lewis
John McEnroe, Jr.
Burgess Meredith
Joni Mitchell
László Moholy-Nagy
Benito Mussolini
Carry Nation
Petrarch
Pierre-Auguste Renoir
Carlos Santana
Leon Spinks
Joan Sutherland
Booth Tarkington
Virgil Thomson
Alexis de Tocqueville
Walter Wanger
E. B. White
Natalie Wood

Oh, to be seventy again!
— Oliver Wendell Holmes

THE TWO/EIGHT SET AFFINITIES

THE TWO/EIGHT NUMBERS ARE: 1   2   6   8

ODD NUMBERS: 1   EVEN NUMBERS: 2   6   8

SET INTERVAL: 6

FAMILY NUMBER: 1

THE TWO/EIGHTS REPRESENT 2.7 PERCENT OF THE POPULATION.

PEOPLE I KNOW WHO ARE TWO/EIGHTS:

_____   _____
_____   _____
_____   _____
_____   _____
_____   _____
_____   _____

MY TWO/EIGHT OBSERVATIONS:

_____
_____
_____
_____
_____
_____
_____
_____

DISPOSITION

— CONTRARY — SENTIMENTAL —

— NAIVE — INTROVERTS — ECCENTRIC —

— RAPACIOUS — SUSCEPTIBLE — UNREALISTIC —

— COGNITIVE —

"The old, the new, and the strange make the heart bright and brave."

TWO/EIGHT

The ten days of the year
that would make you a TWO/ EIGHT are:

February 8	August 2	August 20	November 8
February 17	August 11	August 29	November 17
February 26			November 26

Marian Anderson
Richard Attenborough
James Baldwin
Martin Buber
Madeleine Carroll
Johnny Cash
Buffalo Bill Cody
Honoré Daumier
James Dean
Alain Delon
Fats Domino
Jackie Gleason
Alex Haley
Christie A. Hefner
Katharine Hepburn
Oliver Wendell Holmes
Rock Hudson
Lauren Hutton
Eugène Ionesco
Michael Jackson
Jack Lemmon
Gordon Lightfoot
Myrna Loy
Margaret Mitchell
Nick Nolte
Peter O'Toole
Patti Page
Charlie Parker
Robert Plant
Chaim Potok
Tony Randall
John Ruskin
Charles Schulz
Martin Scorsese
General Wm. T. Sherman
Lee Strasberg
Jacqueline Susann
Lana Turner
Tina Turner
Jules Verne
King Vidor
Jack Warner

The words "my" and "more" must have been invented for Two/Eights. They are natural accumulators who collect and treasure both the exotic and the mundane: records, books, beer bottles, seashells, manhole covers, and so forth. They love art, music, and antiques, and have difficulty discarding the old and well worn. This is not due to possessiveness, but to a compulsion to be the world's last great storehouse and museum: they have visions of bequeathing their tattered Hawaiian shirt to a thankful citizen of another galaxy. They are intuitive observers who seldom miss anything, but they are easily distracted by new ideas or actions, and their innate curiosity can lead them on a winding path. They often operate in orderly confusion, yet somehow manage to fuse everything together.

Two/Eights are supersensitive to emotional discord and very selective of their friends and environment. They are not easy to know. Basically introverts, nonconformists, and loners, they have a strong need for privacy, and are more comfortable in intimate surroundings than public gatherings. They often romanticize or idealize situations and are not always practical. They can be extremely stubborn when they feel coerced, but, since they need more than normal devotion and approval from others, they are easily moved by praise. They require a good philosophical base to function well, and have unique personal ethics that can be difficult for others to understand.

Two/Eights are human think tanks, always moving from one busy thought to another. Filled with great ideas, they prefer leaving the detailed realization of these ideas to others. They have a long, slow-burning fuse and a sense of humor that, fortunately, tempers their intemperance. Their interactions with others are best on a one-to-one basis and, while they may quickly sever past ties, their basic instinct is to hold on to intimate associations.

Two/Eights are quick to analyze most situations accurately, yet they are not quick to act and can be procrastinators, dreamers, and visionaries. Once in action, however, they are very decisive and tireless. Although they may probe things deeply, they are seldom happy as specialists, and operate better with wide-ranging interests. Idealistic searchers for universal hidden truths, they are interested in history and foreign cultures, and often use the arts and humanities as vehicles of expression.

Look not mournfull into the past.
It comes not back again. Wisely improve the Present.
It is thine! — Henry Wadsworth Longfellow

THE TWO/NINE SET AFFINITIES

THE TWO/NINE NUMBERS ARE: 2 2 7 9

ODD NUMBERS: 7 9 EVEN NUMBERS: 2 2

SET INTERVAL: 7

FAMILY NUMBER: 2

THE TWO/NINES REPRESENT 2.7 PERCENT OF THE POPULATION.

PEOPLE I KNOW WHO ARE TWO/NINES:

_____   _____
_____   _____
_____   _____
_____   _____
_____   _____

MY TWO/NINE OBSERVATIONS:

_____
_____
_____
_____
_____
_____
_____

DISPOSITION

— RESILIENT — TENACIOUS — WANDERERS —

— CHAMELEONS — FICKLE —

— SELF-DEPRECATING — MULTIFACETED —

— SENTIENT —

Quick to learn, quick to turn — the rationale is resiliency.

TWO/NINE

The ten days of the year
that would make you a TWO/NINE are:

February 9	September 2	September 20	November 9
February 18	September 11	September 29	November 18
February 27			November 27

Two/Nines are like cats — when they fall, they land on their feet. They are very resilient, and have an incredible knack for working their way out of whatever problems strike them. There is no room for conflict or crisis in their schedule, and they are seldom penitents. Quick to move on, they believe that life needs to be lived now, and will not linger on their tragedies or follies. Two/Nines are generally open to new ideas and liberal in their thinking. Travel or life in foreign countries can have particular attraction for them. Very global in their outlook, they often wander far, physically or philosophically, from their roots.

Two/Nines know what they want and expect it to appear. They are ambitious, but never interested in either money or power for its own sake — it is the symbolic meaning of things that is important to them. Although interested in the occult or the unusual, they nevertheless remain logical and realistic. They need variety and diversion, and have trouble when they fixate on a single idea. They can be quite impulsive, although their concern and need for the approval of others often moderates their whimsy. They require harmony, believe life is to be really enjoyed and, although they can escape into drugs or alcohol, their sense of propriety usually acts as a safety net for them.

Two/Nines often have many admirers and are very popular. They need the appreciation of their family and associates, love to be wined and dined, and would never object to having their statue in the park. Yet, although they appear to be very outgoing, they are basically shy. There is always an emotional buffer zone around them, and even loved ones are seldom allowed inside this ring of defense. They will never show it, but they are very sensitive to what others may think or say about them. They are not comfortable in situations where they feel out of control, and, although they can be social, they need structure when dealing with large groups of people.

Two/Nines are very bright and intuitive, and have the ability to go right to the heart of matters. They have a very convincing, honest appearance, and others automatically find them both caring and credible. They enjoy helping others, but will seldom burden themselves unnecessarily. They are often found in the arts and other areas that allow for personal expression and interaction with others within a controlled setting.

Cleveland Amory
Gene Autry
Brigitte Bardot
François Boucher
Helen Gurley Brown
Imogene Coca
Ronald Colman
Jimmy Connors
Brian De Palma
Matt Dillon
Lawrence Durrell
Anita Ekberg
Linda Evans
Mia Farrow
Enrico Fermi
Greer Garson
Dexter Gordon
Madeline Kahn
Caroline Kennedy
Carole King
Stanley Kramer
Hedy Lamarr
D. H. Lawrence
Bruce Lee
Henry W. Longfellow
Sophia Loren
Carmen Miranda
Martha Mitchell
Toni Morrison
Jelly Roll Morton
Ralph Nader
Kim Novak
Yoko Ono
Eugene Ormandy
Carl Sagan
Upton Sinclair
John Steinbeck
Elizabeth Taylor
Louis Comfort Tiffany
John Travolta
Stanford White
Joanne Woodward

The cat. He walked by himself,
and all places were alike to him. — Rudyard Kipling

THE THREE/THREE SET AFFINITIES

THE THREE/THREE NUMBERS ARE: 3   3   6

ODD NUMBERS: 3   3   EVEN NUMBERS: 6

SET INTERVAL: 0 (Double 3)

FAMILY NUMBER: 6

THE THREE/THREES REPRESENT 2.2 PERCENT OF THE POPULATION.

PEOPLE I KNOW WHO ARE THREE/THREES:

_____   _____
_____   _____
_____   _____
_____   _____
_____   _____
_____   _____

MY THREE/THREE OBSERVATIONS:

_____
_____
_____
_____
_____
_____
_____

DISPOSITION

— DECISIVE — FIERY —

— RUTHLESS — DETERMINED — SURE-FOOTED —

— OPINIONATED — POTENT — OUTRIDERS —

— TEACHERS —

"Trust the moment, gauge the time, then go for it."

THREE/THREE

*The eight days of the year
that would make you a THREE/THREE are:*

March 3	March 21	December 3	December 21
March 12	March 30	December 12	December 30

Three/Threes would like their torch of truth to burn brightly in the hearts of their fellow beings. Their dynamic is one of decisive intensity, and they are not individuals to dismiss lightly. They are determined, self-contained, and strong-minded individuals who will not change to fit someone else's decor. "Fiery" is the word that describes their nature — and even in their most tranquil moments, they have a restless, combustible undercurrent. Although they walk by themselves and all places are the same to them, their concerns center around their family and their perceptions of the greater family of humanity. They can profit greatly from diverse life experiences and the thoughts and products of others.

Power and control are key factors in life for Three/Threes. They need to wield power or associate themselves with someone who has power. They carry a never-say-die energy, refuse to be rebuffed, and can, even in their softest voice, be firm and decisive. They are not easily swayed by argument, and, once their minds are made up, they have difficulty seeing other sides of issues. Yet they will experiment with new concepts, and are hopeful and adventurous. Their need to communicate their ideas to others is deeply ingrained in their being, and their strong intuitive powers serve them well. They have a keen sense of balance and harmony, and, when their conscious and subconscious wills are at odds with each other, they suffer from restlessness and a vague sense of dissatisfaction.

Three/Threes are fearless, righteous, and expect reparations to be made when they feel harmed. They love to direct others, and they use their keen understanding of people to advantage in their dealings with them. Their powerful personal magnetism makes them seem very persuasive, and others tend to accept even their offhand statements and assurances without question. They can, however, change direction like fire in a shifting wind, which sometimes results in conflict.

Three/Threes can be intense performers and artists — music and the arts give them great opportunities for the expression of their dynamic emotional presence. They are very high-pressure people who are always on the move. Drawn to politics and social service, they make strong leaders and teachers. They are often found in situations that satisfy their desires to both be of service and be in control, and excel in defending the rights of animals, the downtrodden, the aged, or the infirm.

Edward Albee
Broncho Billy Anderson
Johann Sebastian Bach
Warren Beatty
Alexander Graham Bell
Maria Callas
Eric Clapton
James Coco
Bo Diddley
Phil Donahue
Perry Ellis
Gustave Flaubert
Jane Fonda
Connie Francis
Astrud Gilberto
Jean-Luc Godard
Francisco de Goya
Jean Harlow
Al Jarreau
Jack Kerouac
Rudyard Kipling
Sandy Koufax
Chris Evert Lloyd
Liza Minnelli
Edvard Munch
Sean O'Casey
Ozzy Osbourne
Burt Parks
Donald T. Regan
Edward G. Robinson
Wally Schirra
Frank Sinatra
Joseph Stalin
Darryl Strawberry
James Taylor
Vincent Van Gogh
Paul Verlaine
Dionne Warwick
Grover Washington, Jr.
Andrew Young
Frank Zappa
Florenz Ziegfeld

I think, therefore I am.
— René Descartes

THE THREE/FOUR SET AFFINITIES

THE THREE/FOUR NUMBERS ARE: 1 3 4 7

ODD NUMBERS: 1 3 7   EVEN NUMBERS: 4

SET INTERVAL: 1

FAMILY NUMBER: 7

THE THREE/FOURS REPRESENT 3.3 PERCENT OF THE POPULATION.

PEOPLE I KNOW WHO ARE THREE/FOURS:

Patti   3/31/73

Cheryl G 3/13/60

MY THREE/FOUR OBSERVATIONS:

DISPOSITION

— EARTHY — VOLCANIC — ORGANIZERS —

— BOSSES — SHARP — SELF-CENTERED —

— JEALOUS — MOTHER HENS/BIG DADDIES — RELENTLESS —

— HOT AND COLD —

"Be in charge. But in charge of what? is the question."

THREE/FOUR

*The twelve days of the year
that would make you a THREE/FOUR are:*

March 4	March 31	April 21	December 13
March 13	April 3	April 30	December 22
March 22	April 12	December 4	December 31

The proof of existence for Three/Fours is "I think it, therefore it is." They want to create their own reality, and they do. Whether or not it works for them is a moot point — it is simply their way. Their natures are fiery and volcanic, yet they have an aura of self-assurance and dignity. They play to win, never hang around if they lose, and have the great ability to rebuild from defeat. They have a strong sense of self-importance that comes from their social position or from the divine authority of their religious beliefs. Still, they have sensitive egos — they can move mountains when they feel confident, and be devastated when their egos are hurt.

Three/ Fours are masters of shaping and directing. Their earthy intensity is centered on their domain, which can be their family, their job, or their country. Which domain they choose to focus on is determined by how much control they actually have. If they are powerless outside their home, they will focus on their mate or children; if they are powerless within their family, they will focus on work, pets, gardens, decor, or some other element of life that they can manage and direct. Tact and diplomacy are not their strong points, and they need to develop patience, adaptability, and more subtle outlets for their uniqueness.

Authority and a compulsion for hard work are the hallmarks of Three/ Fours. They often attempt to do too much, which can cause them frustration and anger. Operating from their deep convictions, they feel they really know what is best for those around them. They are very persuasive and often expend an enormous amount of energy on the affairs of others. Three/Fours are not easy to please, have very high expectations of themselves, and expect others to share their desire for perfection. They function best with a contented, subservient partner, although they have the ability to subordinate their need for power to a loved one. They can be quite jealous. Their anger, when expressed, is explosive; when suppressed, it can have debilitating effects upon their health and mental well-being.

Three/Fours tend to improve upon, rather than originate ideas. They are good observers and excellent organizers, and follow through on any course of action. This, combined with their serious, sincere characters, lets them function as strong and dynamic social figures. Sports, politics, the dramatic arts, and great humanitarian causes are excellent outlets for their talents.

Herb Alpert
Elizabeth Arden
Eve Arden
George Benson
Marlon Brando
Jeff Bridges
Charlotte Brontë
Thomas Carlyle
Richard Chamberlain
Cesar Chavez
Doris Day
John Denver
René Descartes
Queen Elizabeth II
John Garfield
Lionel Hampton
Herbie Hancock
Franz Joseph Haydn
Washington Irving
Wassily Kandinsky
Perry King
David Letterman
Patti Lupone
Marcel Marceau
Henri Matisse
Elaine May
Eddie Murphy
Pola Negri
Willie Nelson
Nero
Wayne Newton
Odetta
Paula Prentiss
Anthony Quinn
Knute Rockne
Stephen Sondheim
Donna Summer
Tiny Tim
Dick Van Dyke
Diane Von Furstenburg
Christopher Walken
Dennis Wilson

To err is human,
to forgive divine. — Alexander Pope

THE THREE/FIVE SET AFFINITIES

THE THREE/FIVE NUMBERS ARE: 2 3 5 8

ODD NUMBERS: 3 5   EVEN NUMBERS: 2 8

SET INTERVAL: 2

FAMILY NUMBER: 8

THE THREE/FIVES REPRESENT 2.7 PERCENT OF THE POPULATION.

PEOPLE I KNOW WHO ARE THREE/FIVES:

_____   _____
_____   _____
_____   _____
_____   _____
_____   _____
_____   _____

MY THREE/FIVE OBSERVATIONS:

_____
_____
_____
_____
_____
_____
_____

DISPOSITION

— AMBITIOUS — CREATIVE —

— SYMPATICO — SELF-CONSCIOUS — ENTHUSIASTIC —

— WHEELER-DEALERS — OUTSPOKEN — UNUSUAL —

— NOT EASY TO KNOW —

Travelers on a journey of change to a station of power.

THREE/FIVE

*The ten days of the year
that would make you a THREE/FIVE are:*

March 5	May 3	May 21	December 5
March 14	May 12	May 30	December 14
March 23			December 23

Three/Fives are members of one of the most elusive sets. "Change" must be their middle name — by the time others understand who they really are, Three/Fives have moved on to something else. They can arrive at their destination before their journey begins, and leave their own party before the guests arrive. They usually lead a nontraditional, varied life, have unconventional attitudes, and can be very frank. They are attracted to the arts and often have an aptitude for healing. Explorers of other lands, times, and ideas, they are interested in travel, antiques, history, and sports. They tend to learn through experience, not books.

Three/Fives are individuals who crave and enjoy the spotlight. They are not to be found in the back of the room unless they are waiting to make their grand entrance. Attracted to the lure of personal power, they thrive on crisis, have a great flair for the dramatic, and do not hesitate to make waves. They have restless, questioning, changeable minds, and are extraordinary in making quick contacts with people. The role of playing savior is not foreign to them, and they often try to please too many people.

Three/Fives have a gambler's instincts and they drive a hard bargain. It is not easy for family, friends, and loved ones to understand them because of the incredibly quick changes they manifest. Their outward social image masks the loner that resides within them, and they can be jealous and brooding. They may experience an incredible variety of physical symptoms when they are out of balance with their situation. Restless and sensual, they are easily bored, yet their enthusiasm and infectious energy can inspire more conventional individuals. Three/Fives love to urge others into motion. Those who embark on joint ventures with them, however, are often unsatisfied — although very conscious of detail, Three/Fives tend to move ahead and leave the dirty work for their helpers.

Three/Fives have strong executive abilities and can make charismatic leaders. They have great endurance and are able to inspire confidence in others. Their powerful psychic sense, honorable temperament, and magnetic personalities make them persuasive and effective talkers or writers. They are very creative, with intense powers of visualization that serve them well in music and on stage or screen.

Mary Astor
Burt Bacharach
Yogi Berra
James Brown
George Carlin
Joan Crawford
Billy Crystal
General George Custer
Joan Didion
Walt Disney
Albrecht Dürer
Samantha Eggar
Albert Einstein
Peter Carl Fabergé
Horton Foote
José Greco
Armand Hammer
Rex Harrison
Engelbert Humperdinck
Akira Kurosawa
Abbe Lane
Fritz Lang
Edward Lear
Golda Meir
Nostradamus
Alexander Pope
Otto Preminger
Lee Remick
Little Richard
Harold Robbins
Christina Rossetti
Dante Gabriel Rossetti
Henri Rousseau
Gayle Sayers
Pete Seeger
Johann Strauss
Mr. T
Irving Thalberg
Giovanni Tiepolo
Martin Van Buren
Fats Waller
Earl Wilson

If you want a golden rule that will fit everybody, this is it:
Have nothing in your houses that you do not know to be useful,
or believe to be beautiful. — William Morris

THE THREE/SIX SET AFFINITIES

THE THREE/SIX NUMBERS ARE: 3 3 6 9

ODD NUMBERS: 3 3 9   EVEN NUMBERS: 6

SET INTERVAL: 3

FAMILY NUMBER: 9

THE THREE/SIXES REPRESENT 2.7 PERCENT OF THE POPULATION.

PEOPLE I KNOW WHO ARE THREE/SIXES:

_____   _____
_____   _____
_____   _____
_____   _____
_____   _____
_____   _____

MY THREE/SIX OBSERVATIONS:

_____
_____
_____
_____
_____
_____
_____
_____

DISPOSITION

— PRECISE — AVARICIOUS — POWERFUL —

— SECRETIVE — ANALYTICAL — CONSERVATIVE —

— VENGEFUL — LOYAL —

— MONEY MANAGERS —

"Gamble on the surest game in town."

THREE/SIX

*The ten days of the year
that would make you a THREE/SIX are:*

March 6	June 3	June 21	December 6
March 15	June 12	June 30	December 15
March 24			December 24

Three/Sixes are breakers of tradition, yet they feel things should have a proper routine, ritual, and order. They are most often concerned with the relationships between money and commerce, self and humanity. Conservative, bright, and determined individuals, they like to see a definite pattern or progression in their lives. Although they believe that there is a time and place for everything, they may sometimes respond with a strong streak of impulsiveness.

Money always seems to play a significant role in the lives and decisions of Three/Sixes. No one seems to grasp the connection between money and society's stamp of approval more completely than they do. They invest most of their time in earning money in order to gain the power and privilege they need. Appearances dominate their thoughts, and they are very concerned with maintaining their chosen image. Presiding over their family is of prime importance to them, and they require harmony and balance in their life. Three/Sixes have addictive personalities. With an almost fetishlike attraction to something, someone, or someplace, their addiction can be to money, fame, drugs, routine, health, certain foods, or anything else their inventive minds envision.

Three/Sixes can be as foolish in personal relationships as they are astute in business matters. Unable to understand that money can buy companionship but not love, they are not always skillful when it comes to handling their emotional involvement with family and intimates. They tend to be very loyal to friends and coworkers, and very revengeful when they feel deeply wronged. Offended Three/Sixes are not to be taken lightly — the expression "Don't get mad, get even" describes their sense of retribution.

Three/Sixes are intuitive and brilliant in their ability to grasp group dynamics. They are social and charismatic individuals who know how to meet and interact with people. Still, there is a reclusive and secret self within them, and they frequently carry an air of mystery and intrigue. Able to quickly size up and take advantage of situations, they have the accountant's mind for detail and opportunity. This, combined with their sense of proprietorship, makes them excellent managers of money.

Maxwell Anderson
Fatty Arbuckle
Josephine Baker
Djuna Barnes
Clyde Barrow
Dave Brubeck
Kit Carson
Jeff Chandler
Lou Costello
Tony Curtis
Vic Damone
Jefferson Davis
Colleen Dewhurst
Anne Frank
Ava Gardner
Ira Gershwin
J. Paul Getty
Kahlil Gibran
Allen Ginsberg
Paulette Goddard
Leo Gorcey
William S. Hart
Judy Holliday
Lena Horne
Howard Hughes
Andrew Jackson
Don Johnson
Rockwell Kent
Ring Lardner
Mike Love
Gabriel García Márquez
Curtis Mayfield
Mary McCarthy
Ed McMahon
Michelangelo
Wes Montgomery
Rob Reiner
Jane Russell
Jean-Paul Sartre
I. F. Stone
Sly Stone
Edward Weston

*If a man does not keep pace with his companions, perhaps it is because he hears
a different drummer. Let him step to the music which he hears, however
measured or far away.— Henry David Thoreau*

THE THREE/SEVEN SET AFFINITIES

THE THREE/SEVEN NUMBERS ARE: 1 3 4 7

ODD NUMBERS: 1 3 7 EVEN NUMBERS: 4

SET INTERVAL: 4

FAMILY NUMBER: 1

THE THREE/SEVENS REPRESENT 2.7 PERCENT OF THE POPULATION.

PEOPLE I KNOW WHO ARE THREE/SEVENS:

_____   _____
_____   _____
_____   _____
_____   _____
_____   _____
_____   _____

MY THREE/SEVEN OBSERVATIONS:

_____
_____
_____
_____
_____
_____
_____

DISPOSITION

— PHILANTHROPIC — HARMONIOUS —

— DYNAMIC — DARING — INDEPENDENT — TRIED AND TRUE —

— OUTGOING — ARTISTIC —

— IMPETUOUS —

"Living life feeds the spirit."

THREE/SEVEN

*The ten days of the year
that would make you a THREE/SEVEN are:*

March 7	July 3	July 21	December 7
March 16	July 12	July 30	December 16
March 25			December 25

Three/Sevens are very popular, earthy individuals with outgoing personalities and sharp wits. They possess great ingenuity and active imaginations, and fate often seems to affect them significantly. Their strong, independent personality comes through early in life and, once they make up their mind, they act quickly. Their keen intuitive sense, when trusted, lets them pierce right to the heart of any issue. Very good at repartee, they are dramatic storytellers and do not hesitate to speak their minds — there is never any difficulty knowing where things stand with them. They have quick, fiery tempers and are quite impulsive. Usually endowed with special gifts, they tend to be quite stylish and often create their own fashions.

Three/Sevens make excellent hosts: they tend to have outgoing personalities that can light up a dark room. They are quite ready to believe anything but, for them, the proof of the pudding is in the eating. With a strong sense of loyalty and duty, and an eagerness to please others, they have an almost addictive need to prove themselves worthy of the praise of strangers and friends. They see themselves as troupers whose show must go on; the world is their stage, and even the rising of the sun and moon need their attention. Although they can be either extremely connected to or fairly detached from their families, it is particularly important for them to interact on a personal level with the people they encounter in their daily lives.

Three/Sevens are compulsively busy and often need little sleep. They can be very determined and can ultimately master any adversity. They are ambitious, but do not take direction from others very well. They work best when they can be emotionally detached from what they are doing, since their quick, impulsive nature can cause them to overlook important details.

Three/Sevens are charismatic, with an adventurous spirit and a particularly strong connection to nature, music, and the arts. They love to play Santa Claus and give gifts to others. They lean toward public service and will particularly champion the underdog. Experimenters and pioneers, they speak most eloquently through their work and make good leaders or teachers.

Gregg Allman
Paul Anka
Jane Austen
Clara Barton
Ludwig van Beethoven
Johnny Bench
Milton Berle
Emily Brontë
Anita Bryant
Ellen Burstyn
Cab Calloway
Geo. Washington Carver
George M. Cohan
Bill Cosby
Noel Coward
Hart Crane
Henry Ford
Aretha Franklin
Buckminster Fuller
Ernest Hemingway
Elton John
Franz Kafka
Dorothy Kilgallen
Jerry Lewis
James Madison
Barbara Mandrell
Marshall McLuhan
Piet Mondrian
Henry Moore
Kate Nelligan
Pablo Neruda
Isaac Newton
Arnold Schwarzenegger
Rod Serling
Sissy Spacek
Gloria Steinem
Isaac Stern
Cat Stevens
Henry David Thoreau
Rebecca West
Robin Williams
Andrew Wyeth

Seize the day, put no trust in the morrow!
—Horace

THE THREE/EIGHT SET AFFINITIES

THE THREE/EIGHT NUMBERS ARE: 2 3 5 8

ODD NUMBERS: 3 5   EVEN NUMBERS: 2 8

SET INTERVAL: 5

FAMILY NUMBER: 2

THE THREE/EIGHTS REPRESENT 2.7 PERCENT OF THE POPULATION.

PEOPLE I KNOW WHO ARE THREE/EIGHTS:

_____   _____
_____   _____
_____   _____
_____   _____
_____   _____
_____   _____

MY THREE/EIGHT OBSERVATIONS:

_____
_____
_____
_____
_____
_____
_____

DISPOSITION

— PRECOCIOUS — SENSUAL —

— UNCONVENTIONAL — INSECURE — STAR-CROSSED LOVERS —

— KEEN EYED — BRIGHT — INNOVATORS —

— AMBITIOUS —

"Who wants hearts and flowers?
An audience and a good script are hard to find."

THREE/EIGHT

The ten days of the year
that would make you a THREE/EIGHT are:

March 8	August 3	August 21	December 8
March 17	August 12	August 30	December 17
March 26			December 26

Steve Allen
Alan Arkin
Count Basie
Kim Basinger
Timothy Bottoms
James Caan
Cantinflas
David Carradine
Wilt Chamberlain
Nat King Cole
Sammy Davis, Jr.
Dolores Del Rio
Cecil B. De Mille
Lesley-Anne Down
Robert Frost
Kate Greenaway
Robert Guccione
Edith Hamilton
George Hamilton
Oliver Wendell Holmes
P. D. James
Erica Jong
Alan King
Huey Long
Fred MacMurray
Mao Tse-tung
Henry Miller
Jim Morrison
Leonard Nimoy
Rudolph Nureyev
Lynn Redgrave
Kenny Rogers
Diana Ross
Kurt Russell
Carole Bayer Sager
Martin Sheen
Mary Shelley
James Thurber
Leon Uris
Richard Widmark
Ted Williams
Tennessee Williams

Three/Eights try to establish definitive relationships with everyone and everything. They have a strong concern for others, but they also have a very strong sense of self. Early physical and emotional bloomers, they tend to be ahead of their time in their thoughts and actions. They love novelty and are attracted to the unusual. They have a wide variety of interests, and are unorthodox in their thinking. Extroverted introverts who always have a public and a secret side, they can be librarians by day and swingers by night, or police officers when on duty and revolutionaries on their own time. Their quick, bright minds make them very decisive, and they believe in action rather than abstract thought. They have good intuition and combine it successfully with their strong sense of style, design, and order.

Three/Eights are interested in their own emotional, physical, and material well-being. They are involved in a constant tug-of-war trying to define their purpose in life. Either withdrawn and hurt, or filled with spontaneity and impulse, their lives revolve around their relationships — to the opposite sex, their parents, their friends, their fellow workers, their children, their health, their career, their church, their government. Control over others is very important to them. They need to receive attention, and they thrive on public adoration. Even though they are very social, they are usually more comfortable with smaller groups.

Three/Eights are ambitious and enjoy material abundance. They can be amazingly pragmatic and are better suited emotionally to being leaders than followers. They can be far too direct, however. This directness, combined with their innate sensitivity, cause them to experience more than the average share of problems with the opposite sex. Still, despite their pragmatism and directness, deep within they are idealists and romantics looking for their Prince Charming or Cinderella, and hoping to live happily ever after.

Three/Eights are very effective in communicating with others, and their skill with words and music is great. They make excellent designers, artists, writers, and musicians. They can be charismatic leaders, and, despite their many self-doubts, they have the ability to successfully combine several fields simultaneously. Drawn to championing the causes of the needy or downtrodden, they are often found in politics or the social services.

Moral indignation is jealousy
with a halo. — H. G. Wells

THE THREE/NINE SET AFFINITIES

THE THREE/NINE NUMBERS ARE: 3 3 6 9

ODD NUMBERS: 3 3 9 EVEN NUMBERS: 6

SET INTERVAL: 6

FAMILY NUMBER: 3

THE THREE/NINES REPRESENT 2.7 PERCENT OF THE POPULATION.

PEOPLE I KNOW WHO ARE THREE/NINES:

_____   _____
_____   _____
_____   _____
_____   _____
_____   _____

MY THREE/NINE OBSERVATIONS:

_____
_____
_____
_____
_____
_____
_____
_____

DISPOSITION

— DESIGNERS — METICULOUS —

— WILLFUL — CAUTIOUS — SEEKERS OF RECOGNITION —

— STYLISH — SHY — VIGILANT —

— TENACIOUS —

"Oh, to be able to redesign people!"

THREE/NINE

The ten days of the year
that would make you a THREE/NINE are:

March 9	September 3	September 21	December 9
March 18	September 12	September 30	December 18
March 27			December 27

The word "design" has special meaning in the lives of Three/Nines. They are bright and breezy, with a strong sense of personal style. Designers and designing, their focus is on order, appearance, and success. They can become quite habitual in their daily lives, but express a quickness in their routine that reveals their strong sense of purpose. Although at times shy, they are generally quite social and always want to make some kind of statement about themselves and their position in the world. What they wish to convey is particularly well expressed through their choice of apparel. Although this may range from the avant-garde to the homespun, Three/Nines tend to be meticulous dressers, oriented to a well-tailored, fashionable look.

Being "in" is of primary importance for Three/Nines. They are especially concerned about how their actions look to others or how they can be brought to the notice of others: Three/Nines like to give, but they would never do so anonymously. They want to be in control of their lives, yet the conflict they sometimes feel between their desire for the unique and their need for conformity is one they have difficulty resolving. Although their style tends to run to the exotic, their need for acceptance is always a moderating influence, and the prevailing tastes of close friends and associates strongly influence them.

Three/Nines are hardworking, consistent, and always strive for success and achievement. Purpose and ambition mark their world. They can be the most insistent of individuals when refused anything, and nothing provokes them more than being told they cannot have something they have set their mind on. Their relationships to their family and their work, which they also consider a "family" relationship, underlie the dynamics in their life. They are seldom ambivalent about these, and are either strongly connected to or strongly alienated from them.

Three/Nines are clever and artistic, and actively shape their environment and life. They are gifted designers, and their mixture of common and exotic tastes allow them to excel in the fields of commercial art, fashion, and interior or industrial design. Their stylish nature also makes them popular entertainers.

Beau Bridges
Dick Butkus
Truman Capote
Irene Cara
Kitty Carlisle
Edgar Cayce
Maurice Chevalier
Ty Cobb
André Courrèges
Gerard Depardieu
Angie Dickinson
Marlene Dietrich
Kirk Douglas
Douglas Fairbanks, Jr.
Redd Foxx
Yuri Gagarin
Sydney Greenstreet
Emmett Kelly
Paul Klee
Alfred A. Knopf
Alan Ladd
Oscar Levant
Alison Lurie
Stephane Mallarmé
Johnny Mathis
H. L. Mencken
John Milton
Bill Murray
Donny Osmond
Jesse Owens
Louis Pasteur
Wilson Pickett
Keith Richards
Vita Sackville-West
Saki
Steven Spielberg
Mickey Spillane
Edward Steichen
Mies van der Rohe
Sarah Vaughan
Amerigo Vespucci
H. G. Wells

Do you believe in the life to come?
Mine was always that. — Samuel Beckett

THE FOUR/FOUR SET AFFINITIES

THE FOUR/FOUR NUMBERS ARE: 4 4 8

ODD NUMBERS: None   EVEN NUMBERS: 4 4 8

SET INTERVAL: 0 (Double 4)

FAMILY NUMBER: 8

THE FOUR/FOURS REPRESENT 0.8 PERCENT OF THE POPULATION.

PEOPLE I KNOW WHO ARE FOUR/FOURS:

_____   _____
_____   _____
_____   _____
_____   _____
_____   _____
_____   _____

MY FOUR/FOUR OBSERVATIONS:

_____
_____
_____
_____
_____
_____
_____
_____

DISPOSITION

— DOMESTIC — RIGID — PRECISE —

— ACQUISITIVE — SAGACIOUS — GIFTED —

— STRATEGISTS — HUMOROUS —

— SLIGHTLY CRAZY —

Makers of tomorrow . . . yours and theirs.

FOUR/FOUR

The three days of the year
that would make you a FOUR/FOUR are:

April 4
April 13
April 22

Four/Fours are the world's great logicians. Their time is often spent making maps of their tomorrows. They are keen observers of life, and seldom miss anything that goes on around them. This, coupled with their intuitive sense of order, makes them natural choreographers in the dance of life — give them anything to orchestrate or direct and they will do a superb job. Their precision is always saved from monotony by their good sense of humor and slight craziness. They are philanthropic, although sometimes very unconventionally so. They could, for example, become advocates of a shorter work week for ants. Their sense of propriety is more flexible than most lovers of order, but they will not storm the barricades of tradition unless their concepts of fairness are gravely insulted.

Despite their restless energy, Four/Fours are often in a state of slight disappointment, because nothing ever turns out exactly as planned. This, however, spurs them on to greater conscientiousness in their next endeavor. Four/Fours receive great pleasure and reassurance from their material achievements. They are quite social and love to interact with others, but they focus on their home life for inspiration.

Four/Fours are industrious, single-minded workers willing to undergo great sacrifices to attain their goals. Their strong organizational skills make their work compositionally excellent and structurally sound. They usually appear traditional to others and generally exert a great stabilizing effect on those around them, happily giving directions and advice. Sometimes Four/Fours hold uncompromising views and are rigid in the demands they make upon themselves and others. Whether stubborn and opinionated or principled and determined, they lack compassion for those who disagree with them.

Four/Fours are multitalented. They shine as commercial representatives, import/exporters, travel agents, lawyers, and military officers. The arts, music, drama, and writing provide them with an orderly but dramatic outlet for their emotions. Noted for fairness, keen judgment, and humor, they make excellent political leaders, inspiring teachers, and superb diplomatic officials.

Eddie Albert
Maya Angelou
Samuel Beckett
Elmer Bernstein
Joseph Bottoms
Glen Campbell
Richard Diebenkorn
Dorothea Dix
Stanley Donen
Marguerite Duras
James Ensor
Henry Fielding
Peter Frampton
Al Green
Gil Hodges
Thomas Jefferson
Immanuel Kant
Gary Kasparov
Howard Keel
Rosemary Lane
Thomas Lawrence
Cloris Leachman
Nikolai Lenin
Hal March
Yehudi Menuhin
Charles Mingus
Arthur Murray
Jack Nicholson
Robert J. Oppenheimer
Anthony Perkins
Margaret Price
Odilon Redon
Hans Richter
Ricky Schroder
Robert Sherwood
Aaron Spelling
Harold Stassen
John Cameron Swayze
Maurice de Vlaminck
Muddy Waters
Eudora Welty
F. W. Woolworth

I am as bad as the worst, but,
Thank God, I am as good as the best. — *Walt Whitman*

THE FOUR/FIVE SET AFFINITIES

THE FOUR/FIVE NUMBERS ARE: 1 4 5 9

ODD NUMBERS: 1 5 9   EVEN NUMBERS: 4

SET INTERVAL: 1

FAMILY NUMBER: 9

THE FOUR/FIVES REPRESENT 1.9 PERCENT OF THE POPULATION.

PEOPLE I KNOW WHO ARE FOUR/FIVES:

_____   _____
_____   _____
_____   _____
_____   _____
_____   _____
_____   _____

MY FOUR/FIVE OBSERVATIONS:

_____
_____
_____
_____
_____
_____
_____
_____

DISPOSITION

— FLAMBOYANT — DEMONSTRATIVE —

— OSTENTATIOUS — ACTORS — BOASTFUL —

— LAWYERS — DUALISTIC — AMBIVALENT —

— GREGARIOUS —

"Come help me lead — you be my guide."

FOUR/FIVE

*The seven days of the year
that would make you a FOUR/FIVE are:*

April 5	April 23	May 22
April 14	May 4	May 31
	May 13	

Duality in personality is a hallmark of Four/Fives. They shift between crushing self-deprecation and colossal self-importance. They are defenders of tradition and conspirators for change. Their minds are filled with visions of order and delusions of grandeur. They can be quite self-indulgent, and may have a problem holding onto their money. Life for them takes on great dramatic intensity. It is what might have been or what will be that concerns them. They are mentally alert and, despite their duality, refuse to be derailed once they have focused on their objective. Obstacles in their way simply spur them on to greater effort.

Four/Fives thrive on social interaction with others. They want to join the party, alleviate humanity's problems, and rediscover the mysteries of the past — they would never do well in solitary confinement. Their strong need to control often causes them difficulty in maintaining peaceful family relationships. While they can be very self-sufficient and great self-promoters, they have an underlying insecurity. They need an inordinate amount of attention and are very attracted to people who show them approval or provide them with distractions or variety.

Four/Fives are very hardworking, and their motto is "What is good for me is good for all." They play only to win and will fight only when winning is assured. Persistent, steady, quick-thinking, they are capable of moving mountains and achieving the impossible. They think of themselves as romantics, and they rarely see the people they love realistically. Although Four/Fives tend to be very dramatic, they are not easily moved to deep emotion. They are authoritative, strong-minded individuals, rigid in the demands they make on themselves and others.

Four/Fives attract the unconventional, are universal in their vision of things, and have a need to help others. They are filled with a restless energy and are often attracted to some form of public service. They need an audience for their work and are strongly drawn to the performing arts — some of our greatest actors are Four/Fives. They also make excellent trial lawyers, using the courtroom as a stage for their performances.

Luther Adler
Fred Allen
Don Ameche
Beatrice Arthur
Charles Aznavour
Richard Benjamin
Valerie Bertinelli
Georges Braque
Mary Cassatt
Julie Christie
Judith Crist
Bette Davis
Sandra Dee
Melvyn Douglas
Arthur Conan Doyle
Daphne du Maurier
Clint Eastwood
Denholm Elliott
Rainer Werner Fassbinder
Maynard Ferguson
Jean Honoré Fragonard
Sir John Gielgud
Keith Haring
Audrey Hepburn
Herbert von Karajan
Joe Louis
Loretta Lynn
Lee Majors
Marisol
Vladimir Nabokov
Joe Namath
Laurence Olivier
Gregory Peck
Pete Rose
William Shakespeare
Brooke Shields
Gale Storm
Shirley Temple Black
Spencer Tracy
J. M. W. Turner
Walt Whitman
Stevie Wonder

Things said or done long years ago / Or things I did not do or say /
But thought that I might say or do / Weigh me down, and not a day / But something is recalled /
My conscience or my vanity appalled. — William Butler Yeats

THE FOUR/SIX SET AFFINITIES

THE FOUR/SIX NUMBERS ARE: 1 2 4 6

ODD NUMBERS: 1 EVEN NUMBERS: 2 4 6

SET INTERVAL: 2

FAMILY NUMBER: 1

THE FOUR/SIXES REPRESENT 1.6 PERCENT OF THE POPULATION.

PEOPLE I KNOW WHO ARE FOUR/SIXES:

_____   _____
_____   _____
_____   _____
_____   _____
_____   _____
_____   _____

MY FOUR/SIX OBSERVATIONS:

_____
_____
_____
_____
_____
_____
_____

DISPOSITION

— INTELLECTUAL — LOYAL —

— FAMILY ORIENTED — DREAMERS — IMPATIENT —

— ACCURATE — QUICK STUDIES — FRIENDLY —

— FOCUSED — ANXIOUS —

Painting the world with a quick brushstroke.

FOUR/SIX

*The six days of the year
that would make you a FOUR/SIX are:*

April 6	April 24	June 4	June 13
April 15			June 22

Four/Sixes have minds that are like colorful kaleidoscopes of what might have been, or what will be. They tend to be dreamers, yet they are bright, opinionated, and intellectual in their approach to things. They have the ability to find interest in the mundane, and enjoy details and precision. They have a very pleasant, friendly appearance and personality. Their engaging manner and disarming approach to things make them popular with others.

Four/Sixes are quite social and enjoy the dramatic — they would love to put their life on instant replay and redirect each episode. They are drawn to routine and extreme accuracy, but they are open to new ideas and enjoy their traveling experiences. They like to be in control in their relationships with others, and often have special friends for special purposes. They are loyal friends themselves, and usually have a very strong connection to home and family. The phrases "gone, but not forgotten" and "till death do us part" always have special meaning to Four/Sixes. It is not easy for them to leave relationships, and they truly try to hold on to their friends forever.

Four/Sixes are hardworking and ambitious. They love success and tend to acquire many possessions. They are prone to more emotional tension and worry than is normal, and can be quite vengeful if deeply hurt. They have an uncanny ability to see the overall pattern of things very quickly, almost too quickly. At times they grasp things so speedily and with such ease that they miss the deeper meanings. When their deeper emotions are involved, however, their logical mind will often override their quick, intuitive insights, making them slow to act.

Four/Sixes are able to clearly separate work from play, which sometimes makes them seem like two different people. They are quick, logical thinkers who derive great satisfaction from directing others. They are gifted individuals, suited to a broad variety of occupations. They gravitate to areas that involve them with service organizations, and can often be found in situations that involve teaching others.

Luís W. Alvarez
Gene Barry
Bill Blass
Alfred Bloomingdale
Claudia Cardinale
Butch Cassidy
Gower Champion
Charlemagne
Christo
Leonardo Da Vinci
Willem De Kooning
Bruce Dern
John Dillinger
Freddy Fender
Merle Haggard
Leslie Howard
Walter Huston
Henry James
Kris Kristofferson
Anne Morrow Lindbergh
Shirley MacLaine
Neville Marriner
Elizabeth Montgomery
Gerry Mulligan
Joseph Papp
Michelle Phillips
André Previn
Raphael
Basil Rathbone
Rosalind Russell
Bessie Smith
Lincoln Steffens
Meryl Streep
Barbra Streisand
Lowell Thomas
Anthony Trollope
Robert Walker, Jr.
Robert Penn Warren
Harold Washington
Billy Wilder
Billy Dee Williams
William Butler Yeats

Man is so made that he can only find relaxation from one kind of labor
by taking up another. — Anatole France

THE FOUR/SEVEN SET AFFINITIES

THE FOUR/SEVEN NUMBERS ARE: 2 3 4 7

ODD NUMBERS: 3 7   EVEN NUMBERS: 2 4

SET INTERVAL: 3

FAMILY NUMBER: 2

THE FOUR/SEVENS REPRESENT 1.9 PERCENT OF THE POPULATION.

PEOPLE I KNOW WHO ARE FOUR/SEVENS:

_____   _____
_____   _____
_____   _____
_____   _____
_____   _____
                            _____

MY FOUR/SEVEN OBSERVATIONS:

_____
_____
_____
_____
_____
_____
_____
_____

DISPOSITION

— COMPULSIVE — MOTIVATED BY SUCCESS —

— DIRECTORS — LOVERS OF ORDER — ASPIRING —

— PERFECTIONISTS — INTUITIVE —

— REGIMENTED —

FOUR/SEVEN

The seven days of the year
that would make you a FOUR/SEVEN are:

April 7	April 25	July 22
April 16	July 4	July 31
	July 13	

Four/Sevens think they know what is best for others and, generally speaking, they give good, logical advice. Life, however, is not always logical, and decisions that are sound intellectually can be disastrous emotionally. Four/Sevens face the problem of how to fit their good advice to others into the context of their own lives and personal relationships, areas where they can be either overbearing or too naive. They frequently have unresolved issues with a parental figure. As a result, they tend to attach themselves to someone they can depend on, or they become someone who can be depended on — a champion of the forgotten and abandoned.

Four/Sevens are perfectionists who need to control their environment: If there is a change of plans, they must be the ones to make it; if spontaneity is expressed, they must be the ones to initiate it. They tend to have autocratic and elitist attitudes. They are motivated by success, which they define as the social acknowledgment of their expertise. Lovers of order, they need to conduct their lives in a methodical, logical manner, and are extremely fond of set routines. They have very bright, retentive minds, and enjoy displaying their memory skills publicly.

Four/Sevens are ambitious, compulsive workers. They are natural directors, and, given half a chance, they will quickly assume responsibility and command. However, the decisive qualities that make them so successful in their careers can create problems for them in their personal lives. They relate best on a one-to-one basis with other individuals and, though drawn to partnerships in business, they function better on their own. When their strong sense of propriety is threatened, their calm natures can erupt into volcanic anger. They mistrust their powerful intuition, and yet this intuitive gift is actually their great strength — combined with their zeal for work and organization, it makes whatever endeavor they pursue a success.

Four/Sevens are frequently involved in the world of commerce. Their keen sense of order also serves them well in sports or the arts, especially music. They are particularly sensitive to popular tastes and moods, and gravitate toward politics, but they function best in the more unrestricted areas of private enterprise. They love to train others and can make very successful careers out of telling others what to do.

Kareem Abdul-Jabbar
Edie Adams
Louis Armstrong
Hank Bauer
Stephen Vincent Benèt
Polly Bergen
Albert Brooks
Alexander Calder
Irene Castle
Charlie Chaplin
Geraldine Chaplin
Calvin Coolidge
Francis Ford Coppola
Oscar De La Renta
Ella Fitzgerald
Harrison Ford
Stephen Foster
David Frost
Giuseppe Garibaldi
James Garner
Nathaniel Hawthorne
Billie Holiday
Edward Hopper
Rose Kennedy
Ann Landers
Gina Lollobrigida
Henry Mancini
Cheech Marin
Paul Mazursky
Gregor Mendel
Edward R. Murrow
Al Pacino
Wayne Rogers
Ravi Shankar
Neil Simon
Dusty Springfield
Terence Stamp
Casey Stengel
Tokyo Rose
Peter Ustinov
Bobby Vinton
Walter Winchell

Not the fruit of experience,
but experience itself, is the end. — Walter Pater

THE FOUR/EIGHT SET AFFINITIES

THE FOUR/EIGHT NUMBERS ARE: 3 4 4 8

ODD NUMBERS: 3 EVEN NUMBERS: 4 4 8

SET INTERVAL: 4

FAMILY NUMBER: 3

THE FOUR/EIGHTS REPRESENT 1.9 PERCENT OF THE POPULATION.

PEOPLE I KNOW WHO ARE FOUR/EIGHTS:

_____   _____
_____   _____
_____   _____
_____   _____
_____   _____
_____   _____

MY FOUR/EIGHT OBSERVATIONS:

_____
_____
_____
_____
_____
_____
_____
_____

DISPOSITION

— HORSE TRADERS — DEAL MAKERS —

— ADMIRABLE — INTUITIVE — HARDWORKING —

— SOAPBOX PREACHERS — OPINIONATED —

— NOSTALGIC —

Champions of the lost cause, nostalgic for lost times.

FOUR/EIGHT

*The seven days of the year
that would make you a FOUR/EIGHT are:*

April 8	April 26	August 22
April 17	August 4	August 31
	August 13	

Four/Eights are a very outspoken group. They may appear soft-spoken, but they cannot be silenced when they have something important to say. They are not interested in vague promises or distant horizons, and will put their money where their mouth is. They can always be counted on for advice and direction, and, if they do not have the answers, they know who does. Four/Eights are natural horse traders who prefer the two-for-one deal. Getting something for free is even better, since they like achieving their goals at minimum expense. This talent serves them well, although their reluctance to make an even trade can work to their detriment and cost them dearly.

Four/Eights are attracted to power and the powerful. They have a strong need to control and shape events, and do so by making themselves indispensable to others. When it comes to family, they are usually in charge. All they desire is a secure, intimate relationship with the entire universe: animal, mineral, extraterrestrial, everything. Their attitudes can undergo many changes, but they seldom have doubts about their current beliefs. They like fixed routines and are very habitual. They are extremely connected to the past, and are often nostalgic for lost moments. Although they enjoy drama, they prefer to experience it vicariously. Still, they are prone to imagine a sinister element lurking to destroy the order and serenity they try to create in their lives.

Four/Eights have a strong social orientation, enjoy organizing and directing others, and leave a larger-than-life impression behind. They feel responsible for fighting injustice and improving the quality of life. Animals and children play an important part in the world they wish to create. They are very impatient for things to happen or change, and often take short cuts that can work against them. When they have been hurt or wronged, their memory is long and forgiveness distant.

Four/Eights have a fine sense of coming trends, and can be gamblers and risk takers. They can, however, be blinded by their beliefs or their love of nostalgia, which can cause them to ignore the future and make silly choices. They have wide-ranging interests but are drawn to social causes or ideas that capture their imagination. They make good organizers, missionaries, and entrepreneurs.

John J. Audubon
Richard Basehart
Carol Burnett
Fidel Castro
Ilka Chase
Eldridge Cleaver
James Coburn
Claude Debussy
Daniel Defoe
Ferdinand Delacroix
Isak Dinesen
Betty Ford
Richard Gere
Debbie Gibson
Buddy Hackett
Knut Hamsun
Valerie Harper
Sonja Henie
Alfred Hitchcock
William Holden
Olivia Hussey
Nikita Khrushchev
Dorothea Lange
Alan Jay Lerner
Bernard Malamud
Fredric March
Carmen McCrae
J. Pierpont Morgan
Van Morrison
Annie Oakley
Frederick Olmsted
Dorothy Parker
I. M. Pei
Itzhak Perlman
Mary Pickford
Ma Rainey
Harry Reasoner
Bobby Rydell
William Saroyan
Percy Bysshe Shelley
Thornton Wilder
Carl Yastrzemski

There, there is nothing else but grace and measure.
Richness, quietness and pleasure. — Charles Baudelaire

THE FOUR/NINE SET AFFINITIES

THE FOUR/NINE NUMBERS ARE: 4 4 5 9

ODD NUMBERS: 5 9   EVEN NUMBERS: 4 4

SET INTERVAL: 5

FAMILY NUMBER: 4

THE FOUR/NINES REPRESENT 1.6 PERCENT OF THE POPULATION.

PEOPLE I KNOW WHO ARE FOUR/NINES:

_____   _____
_____   _____
_____   _____
_____   _____
_____   _____
_____   _____

MY FOUR/NINE OBSERVATIONS:

_____
_____
_____
_____
_____
_____
_____

DISPOSITION

— FULL OF DESIRE — RESPONSIBLE —

— YOUTHFUL — LOYAL — WRY —

— DISCIPLINED — STUBBORN —

— PLANNERS —

FOUR/NINE

The six days of the year
that would make you a FOUR/NINE are:

| April 9 | April 27 | September 4 | September 13 |
| April 18 | | | September 22 |

Four/Nines are bundles of desire. They want everything: stability, revolution, sensuality, order, luxury, freedom, purpose, greatness. Without a definite direction, Four/Nines spin their wheels in a mire of indecision. With purpose and conviction, however, they are invincible. Responsible and persistent individuals, they are disciplined and thorough, and very loyal to their friends. They tend to be superstitious and can have more than the usual share of accidents and unusual experiences in their lives.

Four/Nines want a life of certainty and sureness. This is always an elusive dream for them. Habitually attracted to the unusual — or to their idea of the unusual — they often have a difficult time getting established or focused in their career or in life. They can be impulsive, eccentric, and changeable — they may like the old and worn, or may want a new change of apparel every day. Once their minds are made up, however, they can be quite stubborn.

Four/Nines are bright, hardworking, and youthful. They will assume great personal responsibility for the actions of those around them. This overconcern for others can diffuse their energy. Until they can find a point of personal focus they can stick with, Four/Nines may lead lives filled with scrambled details and nervous indecision. Once focused, however, they move fast and are able to perform the impossible. They have great expectations and can be extremely critical of themselves and others. Their attraction to detail can be annoying to partners and fellow workers, but it is very useful to them when pursuing their goals.

Four/Nines may seem cranky and crotchety, but they have a great, wry sense of humor. They take direction well and are exact followers of orders. With their innate ability to grasp technical details, they make good experimenters and researchers. Discovery is the reward that opens up new vistas for them. They are shrewd, excellent planners who perform very well in high-stress situations that call for action. Although they can be ruthless, they are often found in careers that make them champions of the underdog.

Anouk Aimee
Sherwood Anderson
Earl Anthony
Scott Baio
Charles Baudelaire
Jean-Paul Belmondo
Jacqueline Bisset
Ward Bond
Debby Boone
Scott Brady
Judy Carne
Claudette Colbert
Clarence Darrow
Sandy Dennis
Michael Faraday
J. William Fulbright
Ulysses S. Grant
Barbara Hale
Huntington Hartford
Hugh Hefner
John Houseman
Sol Hurok
Robert Indiana
Ivan the Terrible
Joan Jett
Coretta Scott King
Jack Klugman
Michael Learned
Hayley Mills
Paul Muni
Eadweard Muybridge
Blackjack Pershing
Dennis Quaid
Walter Reed
Mary Renault
Paul Robeson
Leopold Stokowski
Mel Torme
Victor Vasarely
Erich Von Stroheim
Richard Wright
Efrem Zimbalist

Life can only be understood backwards;
but it must be lived forwards. — Søren Kierkegaard

THE FIVE/FIVE SET AFFINITIES

THE FIVE/FIVE NUMBERS ARE: 1 5 5

ODD NUMBERS: 1 5 5 EVEN NUMBERS: None

SET INTERVAL: 0 (Double 5)

FAMILY NUMBER: 1

THE FIVE/FIVES REPRESENT 0.8 PERCENT OF THE POPULATION.

PEOPLE I KNOW WHO ARE FIVE/FIVES:

_____   _____
_____   _____
_____   _____
_____   _____
_____   _____
_____   _____

MY FIVE/FIVE OBSERVATIONS:

_____
_____
_____
_____
_____
_____
_____
_____

DISPOSITION

— PHYSICAL — UNCONVENTIONAL —

— ENERGETIC — EARTHY — SELF-CRITICAL —

— PROUD — MATERIALISTIC — POPULAR —

— COMBATIVE —

Churning with energy, catalysts for change.

FIVE/FIVE

*The three days of the year
that would make you a FIVE/FIVE are:*

*May 5
May 14
May 23*

Five/Fives believe that "now" is the time for action. They are in a constant state of flux, are generally impatient, and are always trying to change something or someone. They are not always practical, but they can be quite decisive in their actions — for better or worse. They are very earthy, intuitive, and opinionated, and have a tendency to be overly self-critical in small things. Often unconventional in their actions and beliefs, they feel less bound by traditions — social, family, or marital — than most people.

Five/Fives are particularly impressed by power and its material symbols, but consider personal freedom a priority. They have a constantly churning energy, and their minds are extremely busy. Their lives are always going up and down, running hot and cold. When focused, they are deep and profound thinkers, able to work very hard for a single principle. They can be very intellectual and brilliantly perceptive, but at the same time they will leap before looking. They believe that a rough landing is preferable to not taking off, and they have a childlike resiliency that lets them quickly pick themselves up after a fall.

Five/Fives are sociable and popular, but they often present a mask to the external world. They do this to cover their frequent failure to understand what they really want. They are very proud, but their feelings are hurt easily by things that may seem very minor or insignificant to someone else. To Five/Fives, however, nothing is ever insignificant, and everything can take on great importance. They can be unforgiving when their pride is deeply injured, and react to hurt with either an attitude of martyrdom or a call to battle. They never hide from a fight, but for them it is a duel to the death — they do not surrender or admit defeat.

Five/Fives have a strong sense for popular trends. They are catalysts for change and can capture public acclaim. They enjoy showing off. They like to do the expedient thing and can be successful in many trades. The material world attracts their attention, rather than the spiritual, and they tend to want their rewards now, not later.

*Barbara Barrie
James Beard
Sydney Bechet
David Byrne
Pat Carroll
Rosemary Clooney
Joan Collins
Oliver Cromwell
Scatman Crothers
Bobby Darin
Giorgio Di Sant'Angelo
Billie Dove
Douglas Fairbanks, Sr.
Gabriel Farhenheit
Alice Faye
Margaret Fuller
Betty Garrett
Thomas Gainsborough
James Gleason
Freeman Gosden
Libby Holman
Søren Kierkegaard
Otto Klemperer
Franz Kline
Carolus Linnaeus
George Lucas
Herbert Marshall
Karl Marx
Franz Anton Mesmer
Robert A. Moog
Patrice Munsel
Helen O'Connell
John Payne
Alan Garcia Peréz
Tyrone Power
Artie Shaw
Zutty Singleton
Bob Woodward
Tammy Wynette*

I do not know which makes a man more conservative
— to know nothing but the present,
or nothing but the past. — John Maynard Keynes

THE FIVE/SIX SET AFFINITIES

THE FIVE/SIX NUMBERS ARE: 1 2 5 6

ODD NUMBERS: 1 5 EVEN NUMBERS: 2 6

SET INTERVAL: 1

FAMILY NUMBER: 2

THE FIVE/SIXES REPRESENT 1.6 PERCENT OF THE POPULATION.

PEOPLE I KNOW WHO ARE FIVE/SIXES:

_____   _____
_____   _____
_____   _____
_____   _____
_____   _____
_____   _____

MY FIVE/SIX OBSERVATIONS:

_____
_____
_____
_____
_____
_____
_____

DISPOSITION

— ROMANTICS — MANIPULATORS —

— VERSATILE — COMPETITIVE — DETERMINED —

— PHILANTHROPISTS — PSYCHIC —

— PRIVATE —

Alone in the crowd — but controlling the scene.

FIVE/SIX

*The six days of the year
that would make you a FIVE/SIX are:*

May 6	May 24	June 5	June 14
May 15			June 23

Five/Sixes are marked by their dual natures and extreme versatility. Drawn to the traditional, but fascinated by the new and different, they can be quite nostalgic and conservative, yet they have open, adventurous spirits. They believe that change is the name of the game, but not too much change. And, while they are not prone to dance on the table at parties, it is difficult to ignore their quiet, strong presence. They have strong psychic abilities and are frequently attracted to the occult.

Five/Sixes want applause, but are not quite daring enough to hold center stage. They prefer to act as a master puppeteer, hiding behind a curtain yet controlling the action. They are ruled by emotions and affected by traditions. Their dual natures create confusion for them until they finally realize that it is all right to drive a Porsche, then come home to sit around a pot-bellied stove. They are interested in helping others and have very strong family ties. However, when their ideas are in conflict with those of their family, Five/Sixes can become quite frustrated and react in ways that are completely against their family's wishes. This can cause them serious problems until they learn that love and disagreement can coexist.

Five/Sixes are marked by their determination. They have a very competitive instinct that is not apparent at first glance. Their inner sensitivity and outer sense of privacy make them difficult to get to know. They take everything personally. Their attachment to a charitable cause is never on an intellectual level — they personally identify with the suffering of the afflicted. They are extremely loyal, long-lasting friends, but if they feel they have been wronged they can be vengeful. They are happiest in a love relationship, and they are usually very committed to their mate. Their problem is finding the right person and learning to trust them. As a result, they often marry late.

Five/Sixes are romantics at heart and usually enjoy books, music, and the arts. They tend to underestimate their great abilities and quiet strength. Their philanthropic nature makes them favor causes that will benefit the helpless; they can be excellent nurses and servants of the sick. Given carte blanche, Five/Sixes would love to be in charge of a close-knit organization that brings love, culture, prosperity, and freedom to the world.

Anna Maria Alberghetti
Laurie Anderson
Jean Anouilh
L. Frank Baum
Josephine Bonaparte
Margaret Bourke-White
June Carter
Thomas Chippendale
Joseph Cotten
Duke of Windsor
Bob Dylan
Clifton Fadiman
Bob Fosse
Sigmund Freud
Boy George
Stewart Granger
Che Guevara
Ross Hunter
Burl Ives
Jasper Johns
Ernst Ludwig Kirchner
Jerzy Kosinski
Trini Lopez
Federico García Lorca
James Mason
Elsa Maxwell
Willie Mays
Dorothy McGuire
Bill Moyers
Max Ophüls
Katherine Anne Porter
Priscilla Presley
Jerry Quarry
Tony Richardson
Maximilien Robespierre
Bob Seger
Toots Shor
Harriet Beecher Stowe
Rudolph Valentino
Queen Victoria
Pancho Villa
Orson Welles

Tact consists of knowing
how far is too far to go. — Jean Cocteau

THE FIVE/SEVEN SET AFFINITIES

THE FIVE/SEVEN NUMBERS ARE: 2 3 5 7

ODD NUMBERS: 3 5 7 EVEN NUMBERS: 2

SET INTERVAL: 2

FAMILY NUMBER: 3

THE FIVE/SEVENS REPRESENT 1.6 PERCENT OF THE POPULATION.

PEOPLE I KNOW WHO ARE FIVE/SEVENS:

_____   _____
_____   _____
_____   _____
_____   _____
_____   _____
_____   _____

MY FIVE/SEVEN OBSERVATIONS:

_____
_____
_____
_____
_____
_____
_____
_____

DISPOSITION

— SUREFOOTED — OUTSPOKEN —

— DRIVEN — FEARLESS — PRAGMATIC —

— DECISIVE — THRIFTY —

— ARTISTIC — SURVIVORS —

"The truth sometimes hurts — no matter, it feels right to me."

FIVE/SEVEN

*The six days of the year
that would make you a FIVE/SEVEN are:*

| May 7 | May 25 | July 5 | July 14 |
| May 16 | | | July 23 |

Five/Sevens are always on the move and looking ahead. They are planning their arrival at the top of the mountain before they take the first step. Their plans are pragmatic, however, and they are not idle dreamers: if the road to the top begins in a coal mine, they grab their pick and shovel and start moving the earth. They are very outspoken. The instant they formulate a thought, it passes from their lips in a quick, instinctive reflex. Hopeless in areas requiring subtlety or tact, they are seldom found in the diplomatic corps. They are very psychic but are uncomfortable with this talent. They often unnecessarily anticipate trouble, and they may express a foreboding of doom as a talisman to protect them from surprise if things go wrong.

Five/Sevens have a superhuman desire and drive to succeed. They are motivated by an underlying fear of failure. They feel that whatever they need to do to succeed is permissible, and they can be totally devastated and flustered when they feel out of control. This, however, is never a lasting state with them. They thrive on attention and approval. Prone to developing fast attachments, they are quick to come to the aid of friends and loved ones. They have a thrifty astuteness that makes them willing to clip coupons and save their money, and they will seldom pass up anything free. Yet they want, need, and strive for the best available.

Five/Sevens can be earthy showstoppers with volcanic tempers. They are survivors who can live by wit and hustle. They have high expectations, resist interference, and work best with others on a one-to-one basis. Intense and aggressive, they have the tenacity of bulldogs and usually accomplish whatever they attempt to do. With their prideful demeanor and their arrogant scorn, they often seem uppity, but this is simply their way to mask an inner nervousness and preoccupation with what they are doing.

Five/Sevens shine in fields that call for quick, decisive responses. They do well working for crisis-oriented organizations such as the Red Cross. They make great, sensitive writers, as putting words on paper helps to modulate their instinctive responses. Any endeavor that requires pragmatic decisiveness is an excellent outlet for the dynamic uniqueness of Five/Sevens.

Annabella
P. T. Barnum
Anne Baxter
Ingmar Bergman
Johannes Brahms
Robert Browning
Bennett Cerf
Raymond Chandler
Jean Cocteau
Gary Cooper
Jeanne Crain
Miles Davis
Gloria DeHaven
Ralph Waldo Emerson
Totie Fields
Henry Fonda
Gerald Ford
Woody Guthrie
Gabby Hayes
Woody Herman
Janis Ian
Gustav Klimt
Liberace
Archibald MacLeish
Billy Martin
Warren Oates
Pee Wee Reese
Dale Robertson
Bojangles Robinson
Beverly Sills
Isaac Bashevis Singer
Irving Stone
Margaret Sullivan
Pyotr Ilyich Tchaikovsky
Studs Terkel
Terry-Thomas
Josip Tito
Leslie Uggams
Johnny Unitas
Karen Valentine
Michael Wilding
Debra Winger

There's only one thing worse than the man who will argue over anything,
and that's the man who will argue over nothing. — Edward Gibbon

THE FIVE/EIGHT SET AFFINITIES

THE FIVE/EIGHT NUMBERS ARE: 3 4 5 8

ODD NUMBERS: 3 5   EVEN NUMBERS: 4 8

SET INTERVAL: 3

FAMILY NUMBER: 4

THE FIVE/EIGHTS REPRESENT 1.6 PERCENT OF THE POPULATION.

PEOPLE I KNOW WHO ARE FIVE/EIGHTS:

_____   _____
_____   _____
_____   _____
_____   _____
_____   _____

MY FIVE/EIGHT OBSERVATIONS:

_____
_____
_____
_____
_____
_____
_____
_____

DISPOSITION

— RESPONSIBLE — CANDID —

— SCRUPULOUS — PRINCIPLED — DETERMINED —

— VERSATILE — DEMONSTRATIVE —

— BRAVE —

"Wave the red, white, and blue — flash the tattoo, 'Death Before Dishonor.'"

FIVE/EIGHT

*The six days of the year
that would make you a FIVE/EIGHT are:*

May 8	*May 26*	*August 5*	*August 14*
May 17			*August 23*

For Five/Eights, everything comes down to principle — their principle. It is the mark of their being, the stamp of their individuality, their sacred line that must not be crossed or defiled. Although they can be impulsive, they will consider others' viewpoints; but once they have made a decision, they rarely change their mind. Five/Eights may well understand the folly of their position but, call it stubbornness or pride, adhering to it is a matter of principle to them, and they are willing to risk all for it. They tackle life with their sleeves rolled up, ready to act and take a stand. When they have doubts, they settle them through action rather than contemplation. They are extremely candid, quick, and bright, and tend to be very methodical.

Five/Eights approach life as something they must change and improve, rather than enjoy. In relationships and family matters, they will hold onto a situation because of the principle behind it — even when they know something is very wrong. They believe that they can overcome all opposition and achieve whatever goals they set through superhuman effort. They give their all, and are too busy plunging ahead to be daunted or dismayed by the odds against them. It can be devastating for them, however, to remain in circumstances where their principles are being trampled.

Five/Eights focus their attention on independence, power, and domains of power such as family, work, or politics. They are dogged, determined, and tireless workers who have high expectations, are very demanding, and like to take control. It is not easy for them to delegate authority and, when they do delegate tasks to others, they expect their instructions to be followed exactly. They feel overly responsible for the actions of others, and take it personally if anyone they are responsible for has shortcomings or problems. At the same time, they are protective of others and will quickly rally to their defense.

Five/Eights function best in situations where their actions speak for them. The contemplative areas of life hold little attraction for them, and they are never happy sitting behind a desk with nothing to do. They can do or be almost anything, and can be found in every field: drama, writing, music, law, religion, politics, business, and sports, to name a few. They are good communicators who are very persuasive, with a quality of deep conviction that instills confidence in others.

Conrad Aiken
James Arness
Lex Barker
Tony Bill
Peter Benchley
Angel Cordero
Barbara Eden
Jean Gabin
John Galsworthy
Oscar Hammerstein
Dennis Hopper
John Huston
Keith Jarrett
Al Jolson
Gene Kelly
Ayatola Khomeini
Peggy Lee
Sugar Ray Leonard
Shelley Long
Guy de Maupassant
Robert Morley
Rick Nelson
Stevie Nicks
Maureen O'Sullivan
Nehemiah Persoff
River Phoenix
Thomas Pynchon
Don Rickles
Sally K. Ride
Laurance S. Rockefeller
Roberto Rossellini
Mark Russell
Erik Satie
John Saxon
Rick Springfield
Susan St. James
Teresa Stratas
Robert Taylor
George Tooker
Harry S. Truman
John Wayne
Hank Williams, Jr.

I am myself and what is around me, and if I do not save it,
it shall not save me. — José Ortega y Gasset

THE FIVE/NINE SET AFFINITIES

THE FIVE/NINE NUMBERS ARE: 4 5 5 9

ODD NUMBERS: 5 5 9   EVEN NUMBERS: 4

SET INTERVAL: 4

FAMILY NUMBER: 5

THE FIVE/NINES REPRESENT 1.6 PERCENT OF THE POPULATION.

PEOPLE I KNOW WHO ARE FIVE/NINES:

_____   _____
_____   _____
_____   _____
_____   _____
_____   _____
_____   _____

MY FIVE/NINE OBSERVATIONS:

_____
_____
_____
_____
_____
_____
_____
_____

DISPOSITION

— HARD TO PLEASE —

— DISCIPLINED — INNOVATORS — ANALYTICAL — INTERNATIONAL —

— VIGILANT — AMBITIOUS — ELEGANT —

— PROMOTERS —

Life as the quest for the possible dream.

FIVE/NINE

*The six days of the year
that would make you a FIVE/NINE are:*

May 9	May 27	September 5	September 14
May 18			September 23

Five/Nines have large personalities, too expansive to fit into a single costume or occupation. Any attempt to put them into a neat little box misses one of their chief dynamics — that of strong, frequently diverse interests. A single focus does not suit their inquiring minds, and they usually pursue a variety of experiences simultaneously. Five/Nines are born with the feeling that they have an important role to play, and their sense of purpose usually makes them stand out at an early age. Others quickly come to view them as authorities or trend-setters. They have a strong "Don't fence me in" attitude, are quite vocal, and do not hesitate to speak their mind.

Five/Nines are happy warriors in search of a cause. They are always trying to change something, someone, or themselves. They have a built-in compulsion to be on the move, and are always heading toward some goal. They have a hard time being alone or doing nothing and, although their body may be still, their mind never is. They have high expectations and seem able to accomplish the impossible. Confronted by an obstacle that would stop most people, they plunge through it, go around it, dig under it, or turn it to their advantage in some mysterious way.

Five/Nines are dedicated workers with great ambition and desire. They have a very organized, analytical mind that lets them quickly develop their plans for accomplishing their goals. They are difficult to please, and often feel let down by others, as they tend to be perfectionists who can become irritated over tiny details. They are very disciplined, and their self-control often allows them to make a complete turnaround in their life, such as going from overweight to skinny.

Five/Nines are thought-provokers and masters of power and compromise. They are often found in diverse roles. Accountant and rock star, stripper and housewife, actor and art expert, corporate executive and martial arts expert — these are typical of the range of their talents and interests. They are respected, gutsy, and elegant, with a quality that captures public attention and admiration. They have an international outlook, see the world as their stage, and are often involved in championing the causes of others. The issues that draw their enthusiasm and imagination are global issues, such as the cultural plight of minorities or revolutionary changes in social behavior.

Johann Christian Bach
Candice Bergen
Daniel Berrigan
John Brown
John Cage
Frank Capra
Ray Charles
John Cheever
John Coltrane
Perry Como
William Devane
Isadora Duncan
Werner Erhard
Albert Finney
Margot Fonteyn
Pancho Gonzales
Walter Gropius
Dashiell Hammett
Wild Bill Hickok
Julio Iglesias
Glenda Jackson
Reggie Jackson
Jesse James
Billy Joel
Pope John Paul II
Henry Kissinger
Christopher Lee
Louis XIV
Bob Newhart
Walter Pidgeon
Vincent Price
Mickey Rooney
Georges Rouault
Bertrand Russell
Archie Shepp
Sam Snead
Bruce Springsteen
Jack Valenti
Mike Wallace
Hal Wallis
Raquel Welch
Herman Wouk

Edible, adj.: good to eat and wholesome to digest,
as a worm to a toad, a toad to a snake, a snake to a pig, a pig to a man,
and a man to a worm. — Ambrose Bierce

THE SIX/SIX SET AFFINITIES

THE SIX/SIX NUMBERS ARE: 3 6 6

ODD NUMBERS: 3 EVEN NUMBERS: 6 6

SET INTERVAL: 0 (Double 6)

FAMILY NUMBER: 3

THE SIX/SIXES REPRESENT 0.8 PERCENT OF THE POPULATION.

PEOPLE I KNOW WHO ARE SIX/SIXES:

_____   _____
_____   _____
_____   _____
_____   _____
_____   _____
_____   _____

MY SIX/SIX OBSERVATIONS:

_____
_____
_____
_____
_____
_____
_____

DISPOSITION

— FAMILY ORIENTED — FIERY — COMPANIONABLE —

— HOT AND COLD — SELF-EDUCATORS —

— STYLISH — CREATIVE —

— INTRACTABLE —

"Home is both the heart and start of the journey."

SIX/SIX

*The three days of the year
that would make you a SIX/SIX are:*

*June 6
June 15
June 24*

For Six/Sixes, everything is related, and one thing leads to the next in a great revolving cycle. Their life and identity reside in family or family-type relationships. Their level of personal confidence determines the scope of these relationships, which can be as expansive as the universal family, or as limited as the nuclear family. Their temperament fluctuates between hot and cold, happy and sad — and their actions and humor can range from the mundane to the outrageous. Six/Sixes are either innovative and unconventional or conventional and mired in responsibilities. They are studies in motion and rhythm, but not distance, as they tend to take only a few steps forward, then several back.

Six/Sixes never want to be left out of anything. They require social interaction with others — the hustle and bustle of crowds and continuous streams of conversation are an inspiration for their extraperceptive eyes and ears. Yet they walk an emotional tightrope and are not always easy to understand. Their delusion of unworthiness feeds an inner nervousness that they hide with their cool, collected, friendly exterior. They are not anxious to leave the warmth and comfort of the hearth for the cold unknown, but if they do sever their umbilical cords, they may roam far from home.

Six/Sixes are fiery and impulsive, and always want to do things their own way. They are competitive by nature, but will mask this quality from others. Their tendency to suppress and internalize their anger and frustration can have disastrous effects on their health. They have a strong personal need for balance and are particularly aware of subtle nuances of discord that others often miss. They stay around people only as long as they feel comfortable and interested. If they are bored or turned off, they may withdraw physically or mentally.

Six/Sixes tend to be self-educators, and are always involved in some form of learning and exploring. With their strong sense of both attachment and detachment, they need to work intimately with others while maintaining a safe distance — they make great baby-sitters, for example. They are naturally creative, with a good eye for design and style. Their internal sense of harmony tends to give them exceptional abilities in music. Six/Sixes frequently go through life on a merry-go-round, open to whatever opportunities they chance to encounter.

Nancy Allen
Yuri Andropov
Dusty Baker
Jeff Beck
Jim Belushi
Ambrose Bierce
Bjorn Borg
Jack Carter
Billy Casper
Claude Chabrol
John Ciardi
Norman Cousins
Mario Cuomo
Jack Dempsey
George Deukmejian
Bill Dickey
Erroll Garner
Chief Dan George
Domenico Guidi
Nathan Hale
Pete Hamill
Phil Harris
William Inge
Rachel Jackson
Waylon Jennings
Kirk Kerkorian
Henry King
Harry Langdon
Michele Lee
Janet Lennon
Ted Lewis
Thomas Mann
Maria Montez
Harry Partch
Aleksandr Pushkin
David Rose
Michael Rysbrack
David Scott
John Trumbull
Morris Udall
Diego Velázquez
Sinclair Weeks

All animals are equal,
but some animals are more equal than others. — George Orwell

THE SIX/SEVEN SET AFFINITIES

THE SIX/SEVEN NUMBERS ARE: 1 4 6 7

ODD NUMBERS: 1 7   EVEN NUMBERS: 4 6

SET INTERVAL: 1

FAMILY NUMBER: 4

THE SIX/SEVENS REPRESENT 1.6 PERCENT OF THE POPULATION.

PEOPLE I KNOW WHO ARE SIX/SEVENS:

_____   _____
_____   _____
_____   _____
_____   _____
_____   _____

MY SIX/SEVEN OBSERVATIONS:

_____
_____
_____
_____
_____
_____
_____

DISPOSITION

— WORKAHOLICS — INTENSE PLAYERS —

— CONVENTIONALLY UNCONVENTIONAL —

— DUTIFUL — ENTREPRENURIAL — ZEALOUS —

— FORERUNNERS —

"Is life a playground, an occupation, or a battlefield?'

SIX/SEVEN

*The six days of the year
that would make you a SIX/SEVEN are:*

June 7   June 25   July 6   July 15
June 16   July 24

Deep inside, Six/Sevens always know they are special — but they are not sure why. This uncertainty is transformed into a driving need to find themselves through their work, their family, and their relationships. Probably the most conventionally unconventional of all the sets, they are in constant battle with a powerful foe — themselves. They need to understand that they, themselves, are the "Big Brother" they sense watching them as they see-saw between their need for order and stability, and their happy dream of escape to the land of joy and play. They are strongly connected to the comfort and pleasure of home and family, but they are also drawn to spiritual odysseys or adventures into the unusual.

Six/Sevens always seem to be fighting a battle between work and play. Unless they find an occupation that allows them to express both sides of their nature, they will bury themselves in their work, and dream incessantly of their eventual freedom. Six/Sevens need to find their salvation inside of their work, rather than outside. Work is an important key to understanding them. It is the cradle of their stability and the basis of their personal identity. To Six/Sevens, work is defined as who they are and what they do: if they are mothers, that is their occupation; if they are loafers, that is their work.

Six/Sevens are workaholics, and are deeply committed to their beliefs. They have high standards, demand much from themselves and others, and need to be rewarded for their efforts. They work well with others and make loyal mates and steadfast friends. Some form of play or recreation is essential for them. Their personality at work and their personality at play can take on almost a Dr. Jekyll and Mr. Hyde difference. On closer examination, however, they simply approach play with the same compulsive intensity that serves them so well in their work.

It is amazing how many creative solutions Six/Sevens can come up with to solve their quest for both stability and adventure. Although they have strong qualities of leadership, they are also excellent as seconds-in-command or employees. Their mark is that, whatever their occupation or focus, they are fully committed — 200 percent.

Bella Abzug
Jack Albertson
Ned Beatty
Simón Bolivar
Elizabeth Bowen
Thomas Bulfinch
Ruth Buzzi
Lynda Carter
Jim Dine
Alexandre Dumas
Amelia Earhart
Mick Fleetwood
Antonio Gaudí
Paul Gauguin
Robert Graves
Rocky Graziano
Merv Griffin
Tom Jones
Alex Katz
Stan Laurel
Janet Leigh
June Lockhart
Sidney Lumet
John D. MacDonald
George Michael
Iris Murdoch
Joyce C. Oates
George Orwell
Irving Penn
Beatrix Potter
Prince
Nancy Reagan
Willis Reed
Della Reese
Rembrandt van Rijn
Linda Ronstadt
Chris Sarandon
Eric Segal
Carly Simon
Sylvester Stallone
Jessica Tandy
Jamie Wyeth

Make 'em laugh; make 'em cry;
make 'em wait. — Charles Reade

THE SIX/EIGHT SET AFFINITIES

THE SIX/EIGHT NUMBERS ARE: 2 5 6 8

ODD NUMBERS: 5 EVEN NUMBERS: 2 6 8

SET INTERVAL: 2

FAMILY NUMBER: 5

THE SIX/EIGHTS REPRESENT 1.6 PERCENT OF THE POPULATION.

PEOPLE I KNOW WHO ARE SIX/EIGHTS:

_____   _____
_____   _____
_____   _____
_____   _____
_____   _____
_____   _____

MY SIX/EIGHT OBSERVATIONS:

_____
_____
_____
_____
_____
_____
_____
_____

DISPOSITION

— HELPFUL — RISK TAKERS — ACTIVE —

— INDEPENDENT — INTUITIVE — HAPPY —

— STUBBORN — METICULOUS —

— INNOVATORS —

Pushing the frontier from the inside out.

SIX/EIGHT

The six days of the year
that would make you a SIX/EIGHT are:

June 8	June 26	August 6	August 15
June 17			August 24

Bil Baird
Lucille Ball
Ethel Barrymore
Ralph Bellamy
Thomas Hart Benton
Napoleon Bonaparte
Jorge Luís Borges
Pearl S. Buck
Julia Child
Walter Crane
James Darren
Abner Doubleday
Charles Eames
Edna Ferber
Alexander Fleming
Hoot Gibson
Jill Haworth
John Hersey
Wendy Hiller
Durwood Kirby
Lawrence of Arabia
Peter Lorre
Barry Manilow
Dean Martin
John Millias
Robert Mitchum
Alphonse Mucha
Leroy Neiman
Eleanor Parker
Louella Parsons
Oscar Peterson
Ella Raines
Lillian Ross
Janice Rule
Boz Scaggs
Walter Scott
Nancy Sinatra
Alexis Smith
Alfred Lord Tennyson
Andy Warhol
Frank Lloyd Wright
Marguerite Yourcenar

Continuous activity is the mark of Six/Eights. They tend to be physically quick and agile, and their life is filled with diversity and unusual adventure. They are independent, do not like to feel obligated to others, and do not appreciate hand-outs. They are also stubborn and tend to push situations to extremes. They can let their pride impede their ability to compromise; often they suffer in silence and let their resentment build until it explodes. Natural risk takers with strong intuition, they are not frightened by change or danger. They quickly accept new ideas, and find that their gambles usually pay off.

Six/Eights have a basically busy, happy, helpful nature. While they sometimes seem haughty and aloof, they have an inner sympathetic self. They enjoy doing things for others, but there is always one string attached: it is essential that their actions be appreciated. They see a lack of appreciation from others as a slap in the face. To have given their all and not have it be appreciated makes Six/Eights feel resentful and alienated — and when they feel alienated, they are quick to act. In personal relationships, it is important for them to feel that they are number one, but, because they have difficulty verbalizing their feelings, it is often easier for them to move on than to work on a relationship that is damaged.

Six/Eights are meticulous and exacting, and enjoy planning and organizing. They like to be in charge or share leadership, and tend to relate to others as equals — be they king or criminal. Although this works well for them when they associate with superiors, it can be a problem for them if they fall in with the wrong crowd. They have a particularly strong need for attachments to family, groups, or organizations that can help them to validate their identity, yet they relate best to others on an intimate, one-to-one basis.

Six/Eights can be successful in any area where their efforts are appreciated. If allowed to develop their natural independence, they will often gravitate to pioneering fields or unusual occupations. They make good public speakers once they get over their initial shyness. They can produce imaginative fiction and be excellent reporters. With their inquiring minds and powerful memories, they are good at puzzles and can solve mysteries quickly.

So we beat on, boats against the current,
borne back ceaselessly into the past. — *F. Scott Fitzgerald*

THE SIX/NINE SET AFFINITIES

THE SIX/NINE NUMBERS ARE: 3 6 6 9

ODD NUMBERS: 3 9   EVEN NUMBERS: 6 6

SET INTERVAL: 3

FAMILY NUMBER: 6

THE SIX/NINES REPRESENT 1.6 PERCENT OF THE POPULATION.

PEOPLE I KNOW WHO ARE SIX/NINES:

_____   _____
_____   _____
_____   _____
_____   _____
_____   _____
_____   _____

MY SIX/NINE OBSERVATIONS:

_____
_____
_____
_____
_____
_____
_____
_____

DISPOSITION

— PERPETUAL STUDENTS — SOUL SEARCHERS —

— LOST LAMBS — INDECISIVE — RESTLESS —

— CAPABLE — AMBITIOUS —

— INDEPENDENT — SOLITARY —

An endless quest for self-knowledge.

SIX/NINE

*The six days of the year
that would make you a SIX/NINE are:*

June 9	June 27	September 6	September 15
June 18			September 24

Creighton Abrams
Jane Addams
Cannonball Adderly
Isabelle Adjani
Bruce Babbitt
Eva Bartok
Robert Benchley
Richard Boone
Lou Brock
Ettore Bugatti
Sammy Cahn
Ian Carmichael
Agatha Christie
Jackie Cooper
James Fenimore Cooper
Gary Crosby
Robert Cummings
F. Scott Fitzgerald
Michael J. Fox
Philip Guston
Jim Henson
Buddy Holly
Tommy Lee Jones
Kay Kyser
Helen Keller
Joseph Kennedy, Sr.
Marquis de Lafayette
Peter Lawford
Margaret Lockwood
Jeanette MacDonald
E. G. Marshall
Paul McCartney
Anthony Newley
Peter the Great
Cole Porter
Jean Renoir
Billy Rose
Bobby Short
Franz Joseph Strauss
Blanche Sweet
William Howard Taft
Horace Walpole

Six/Nines are characterized by an endless quest for self-discovery. Typically, they start off in one career for which they are eminently qualified, then suddenly change their minds and go off on something else. Their spirits vacillate between the desire to stay home and be comfortable, and the restless urge to tear off the fetters and leave. Many times they change just on a challenge or whim, and if their needs are unfulfilled, they can spend a lifetime ricocheting from one pursuit to another. For the most part, however, they are straightforward, solitary individuals, with a touch of mystery.

Six/Nines avoid being categorized or locked into things by others. Nothing seems to impede them more than the desire of others to change them. They want direction only from those who agree with them, and will act only on the basis of their inner voice. They can be tied to family or other relationships, and, at the same time, they can wander off on some idealistic, universal duty or quest. Drugs and alcohol can sometimes play a part in this. Six/Nines have a deep need for personal relationships, but cannot always fill it because of their upbringing, their outspokenness, their self-indulgence, or their vagabond souls. Examining the relationships that have been important in their lives can be illuminating for them.

Six/Nines are ambitious, and concerned about how their actions appear to others. They have a natural indecisiveness, but rather than appear uncertain, they will point to other factors. Although capable of mastering anything, they may have problems finding the proper arena for their many talents. They can become so lost in their quest to find themselves that others will become completely frustrated with them. Once their minds are set on a goal, however, they pursue it with great resolution.

Most Six/Nines are attracted to vocations that symbolize family relationships — the military, large corporations, family-run businesses, or social or political causes — and they can become overly attached to an employer or employee. Then again, many Six/Nines simply take off and begin traveling. They are frequently professional students, and the arts hold a magical appeal for them.

Jesus of Nazareth was the most scientific man that ever trod the globe.
He plunged beneath the material surface of things,
and found the spiritual cause. — Mary Baker Eddy

THE SEVEN/SEVEN SET AFFINITIES

THE SEVEN/SEVEN NUMBERS ARE: 5 7 7

ODD NUMBERS: 5 7 7 EVEN NUMBERS: None

SET INTERVAL: 0 (Double 7)

FAMILY NUMBER: 5

THE SEVEN/SEVENS REPRESENT 0.8 PERCENT OF THE POPULATION.

PEOPLE I KNOW WHO ARE SEVEN/SEVENS:

_____ _____
_____ _____
_____ _____
_____ _____
_____ _____
_____ _____

MY SEVEN/SEVEN OBSERVATIONS:

_____
_____
_____
_____
_____
_____
_____
_____

DISPOSITION

— SEEKERS — MYSTERIOUS —

— MOVERS — LEADERS — FAMILY ORIENTED —

— SPECIALISTS — INTENSE —

— EMOTIONALLY PROTECTIVE — INGENIOUS

"Change for the thrill, change for the movement, change for the challenge."

SEVEN/SEVEN

*The three days of the year
that would make you a SEVEN/SEVEN are:*

July 7
July 16
July 25

Seven/Sevens are at the same time earthy pragmatists and idealistic dreamers. They want to experience the ebb and flow of life, and to search for its mystery and meaning in their cultural past, their family, and their spiritual studies. They are nostalgic in their outlook and are never content with how things are; they want to orchestrate their lives and everything that goes on around them. Often filled with a vague restlessness, they can be attracted to the unconventional and unusual. They tend to be great self-educators and avid readers, and lead fruitful lives full of personal change.

Seven/Sevens may have a missionary zeal. They are compelled to be busy, and often set aside forethought in order to jump into action. Their impulsive behavior may land them in situations that they really do not want to be in, causing them frustration and anger. Usually precocious as children, their especially vivid memory of insensitive treatment by adults gives them a strong affinity for the rights and needs of children. They are particularly attached to their home turf, very territorial about all aspects of their life, and extremely unhappy when anything intrudes on their sense of domain. To protect themselves, they carefully buffer their emotions and place many layers of armor around their heart.

Seven/Sevens pay great attention to details and can easily fall in love with hard work. They need independence and control, and their temperament is not suited to compromise. They want their own way, and tend to impose their own ethics or ideas. Seven/Sevens may have more than their share of problems in personal relationships, and sometimes function best on their own or with a mate who serves as a disciple. Yet they are not hermits, and would secretly love to have a fan club of adoring servants and acolytes.

Seven/Sevens seek out careers that let them control their environment, express their uniqueness, and satisfy their need for glory and approval. They tend to choose arenas where they can pursue their endeavors without the intervention of others. Their autocratic nature makes it difficult for them to shine in politics. Science and religion offer great outlets for their dynamics, and an extraordinarily high number of Seven/Sevens are attracted to music and the arts.

Alexander the Great
David Belasco
Ruben Blades
Walter Brennan
Pierre Cardin
Marc Chagall
Frank Church
Jean Baptiste Corot
George Cukor
Alan J. Dixon
Thomas Eakins
Mary Baker Eddy
Vince Edwards
Mary Ford
Sam Francis
Jack Gilford
Camillo Golgi
Steve Goodman
Adnan Khashoggi
Anna Harrison
Henry VIII
Eric Hoffer
Trygve H. Lie
José López Portillo
Charlie Louvin
Gustav Mahler
Janet Margolin
Gian-Carlo Menotti
Bess Myerson
Satchel Paige
Maxfield Parrish
Walter Payton
Joshua Reynolds
Ginger Rogers
Andrea del Sarto
Doc Severinson
Charles Sheeler
Barbara Stanwyck
Ringo Starr
Cal Tjader
Sonny Tufts
Pinchas Zukerman

People are always blaming their circumstances for what they are. I don't believe in circumstances. The people who get on in this world are people who get up and look for the circumstances they want, and, if they can't find them, make them. — *George Bernard Shaw*

THE SEVEN/EIGHT SET AFFINITIES

THE SEVEN/EIGHT NUMBERS ARE: 1 6 7 8

ODD NUMBERS: 1 7   EVEN NUMBERS: 6 8

SET INTERVAL: 1

FAMILY NUMBER: 6

THE SEVEN/EIGHTS REPRESENT 1.6 PERCENT OF THE POPULATION.

PEOPLE I KNOW WHO ARE SEVEN/EIGHTS:

_____   _____
_____   _____
_____   _____
_____   _____
_____   _____

MY SEVEN/EIGHT OBSERVATIONS:

_____
_____
_____
_____
_____
_____
_____

DISPOSITION

— INTELLECTUAL — INQUISITIVE —

— POMPOUS — RESTLESS — POWERFUL —

— INDEPENDENT — EGO-BOUND — SELF-CRITICAL —

— ZEALOUS —

"Think, know, and act — rain or shine, right or wrong."

SEVEN/EIGHT

*The six days of the year
that would make you a SEVEN/EIGHT are:*

| July 8 | July 26 | August 7 | August 16 |
| July 17 | | | August 25 |

Seven/Eights create their own situations in life. Their attitudes and beliefs diverge so frequently from those of their parents and siblings that they often feel they were born into the wrong family. They are very sensitive to the moods, likes, and dislikes of others, and tend to be trendsetters with a good eye for fashion. They enjoy traveling and are generally extremely well read and well informed. They sometimes mask their quick intellect and mental precision by playing dumb and asking foolish questions, but they ultimately express their uniqueness with a rational approach, rather than an emotional one.

Seven/Eights are attracted to fame and power. They need to question everything, and are marked by their innate good sense and logic. They are formidable opponents: they quickly sort through their ideas, make up their minds, and take off running. Their main weakness is that they often let their logical quickness override their intuition. They can also be too self-critical or too egotistical, sometimes rapidly switching between the two extremes. When they do not take themselves too seriously, however, they have a wonderful sense of humor. Their strong independent spirit and private inner self make it easier for them to live alone than for most.

Although Seven/Eights tend to be experts or leaders in their particular fields, they are also quite content working for others. They usually make their choices from a wide variety of options, rather than from a narrow perspective. They do not mind changing careers, but do so because of their orientation to growth and success, not because of boredom. They have a built-in capacity for hard work and conscientious detail, and are often attracted to unusual causes. They are not afraid to take unpopular stances, and can often be found among the avant-garde. Because of their preoccupation with work and detail, they do not always make attentive spouses, but they are loyal to their friends, especially those of the same sex.

Seven/Eights, with their supertalents, can reach the top in many fields. Their ability to ferret out and draw logical conclusions from undisclosed details and private information makes them excellent researchers, interviewers, lawyers, and spies. Their thinking is shaped by their strong feel for the pulse of their time, and they are able to use their anticipation of popular tastes to successful commercial advantage.

Berenice Abbott
Gracie Allen
Anne Archer
Luci Arnaz
John Jacob Astor
Menachem Begin
Leonard Bernstein
Ralph Bunche
Billie Burke
Julius Caesar
James Cagney
Diahann Carroll
Sean Connery
Elvis Costello
Robert Culp
Phyllis Diller
Mel Ferrer
Frederick Forsyth
Erle Stanley Gardner
Eydie Gorme
Robert Graves
George Grosz
Monty Hall
Bret Harte
Aldous Huxley
Mick Jagger
Carl Jung
Ruby Keeler
Rahsaan Roland Kirk
Kathë Kollwitz
Steve Lawrence
Art Linkletter
Madonna
Mata Hari
George Meany
Emil Nolde
Fess Parker
John D. Rockefeller
Nelson A. Rockefeller
George Bernard Shaw
Donald Sutherland
Ferdinand Von Zeppelin

Committing yourself is a way of finding out who you are.
A man finds his identity by identifying. — Robert Terwilliger

THE SEVEN/NINE SET AFFINITIES

THE SEVEN/NINE NUMBERS ARE: 2 7 7 9

ODD NUMBERS: 7 7 9   EVEN NUMBERS: 2

SET INTERVAL: 2

FAMILY NUMBER: 7

THE SEVEN/NINES REPRESENT 1.6 PERCENT OF THE POPULATION.

PEOPLE I KNOW WHO ARE SEVEN/NINES:

_____   _____
_____   _____
_____   _____
_____   _____
_____   _____
_____   _____

MY SEVEN/NINE OBSERVATIONS:

_____
_____
_____
_____
_____
_____
_____
_____

DISPOSITION

— ELITISTS — EXACTING —

— RESPONSIBLE — COMMITTED —

— WORLDLY — COLLABORATORS — ARTISTIC —

— SENSITIVE —

"Life is fluid — with long gliding steps, intricate movements and poses. It takes two to tango..."

SEVEN/NINE

*The six days of the year
that would make you a SEVEN/NINE are:*

July 9	July 27	September 7	September 16
July 18			September 25

Seven/Nines are natural collaborators. Whether motivated by great humanitarian aims, the desire for social position, gut-level survival, or artistic expression, they find their identity through their association with someone or something else: an idea, a group, a goal, a cause, or a career. They are fearless and will stare the tiger right in the eye, but they are not loners and tend to shun isolated greatness. They carry an air of superiority and condescension, yet their elitist thinking is modulated by their sensitivity and sincere concern for others. They are very exacting, not attracted to the mundane, and will reject any proposal that does not fit into their life scheme. Still, they are worldly in their outlook, and open to new and different ideas.

Seven/Nines see themselves as "me, the great artist," or "me, the great doctor." It is essential for them to have a personal association with something they care about — their identity absolutely depends on it. How their words, actions, and dress appear to others is very important to them, although not in the conventional sense. They specifically seek the approval of their peers and loved ones over that of society at large. They are attracted to power, and, if they cannot achieve it personally, they will attach themselves to a group or person who has it. They are serious in their relationships with others, and are usually committed mates.

Seven/Nines are, by nature, responsible individuals. They can, however, take on too much responsibility for the actions and feelings of others. They will stifle their natural expression of anger or frustration in order to maintain a pleasant appearance. Because of their deep, intuitive sensitivity, their physical health can be directly affected by their emotional well-being. They have a tendency to believe that they, personally, have done something wrong when things that are quite beyond their control go astray.

Seven/Nines usually undergo an interesting eclectic search when they try to find their appropriate career. Once they find it, though, they commit themselves to it with a discipline and persistence that lasts for a lifetime. They make fine doctors, artists, architects, and therapists.

Ed Ames
Jean Arp
Lauren Bacall
Hilaire Belloc
Corbin Bernson
Susan Blakely
James Brolin
Charlie Byrd
Barbara Cartland
Hume Cronyn
Richard Dix
Michael Douglas
Alexandre Dumas (fils)
Leo Durocher
Peter Falk
William Faulkner
Anne Francis
Allen Funt
Bobbie Gentry
John Glenn, Jr.
Glenn Gould
Mark Hamill
S. I. Hayakawa
David Hockney
Daniel K. Inouye
Roscoe Karns
Elia Kazan
B. B. King
Alexander Korda
Norman Lear
Grandma Moses
Clifford Odets
J. C. Penney
Aldo Ray
Christopher Reeve
Mark Rothko
Dimitri Shostakovich
O. J. Simpson
Edith Sitwell
Red Skelton
William M. Thackeray
Barbara Walters

I make the most of all that comes
and the least of all that goes. — Sara Teasdale

THE EIGHT/EIGHT SET AFFINITIES

THE EIGHT/EIGHT NUMBERS ARE: 7 8 8

ODD NUMBERS: 7   EVEN NUMBERS: 8 8

SET INTERVAL: 0 (Double 8)

FAMILY NUMBER: 7

THE EIGHT/EIGHTS REPRESENT 0.8 PERCENT OF THE POPULATION.

PEOPLE I KNOW WHO ARE EIGHT/EIGHTS:

_____   _____
_____   _____
_____   _____
_____   _____
_____   _____

MY EIGHT/EIGHT OBSERVATIONS:

_____
_____
_____
_____
_____
_____
_____

DISPOSITION

— CONTROLLING —

— ENERGETIC — LOYAL — CHALLENGING —

— JUDGMENTAL — KEEN BUSINESS PEOPLE — GAMBLERS —

— PURPOSEFUL —

*"Take a look into my eyes and
tell me who you see."*

EIGHT/EIGHT

*The three days of the year
that would make you an EIGHT/EIGHT are:*

*August 8
August 17
August 26*

Eight/Eights want to rule the domain. They take particular pride in controlling all they survey, and see themselves as the godfather or godmother of those who share their environment. Eight/Eights are the ones in charge, the ones who do the giving, the ones who make the decisions for others. They are fiery pillars who stand in relation to others as commanding, yet loving figures. Their independent, challenging spirit makes them want to climb the highest mountain — their own way. They must get their hands dirty, experience life, show others, and prove themselves.

Eight/Eights, whether born into poverty or power, are driven by an inner need to pay their dues. The "buck" may not stop with them, but they will always find out where it should. They tend to do things the hard way, and will expend so much energy on their endeavors that they can burn out unless they force themselves to follow a program of rest and relaxation. Eight/Eights are loyal, self-appointed caretakers of others. Family ties are all-important to them, and weaker members of their family — or extended family — can always rely on them for protection.

Eight/Eights are never satisfied with how things are and always want more. Their hobby is hard work, and they pursue it with vigor. Their tools are precision, exactness, and persistence, and nothing will stop them when they focus their attention on an endeavor. Although they are judgmental, they are seldom narrowly so. They first take a long hard look at a situation, and then make up their minds. Once they decide, though, they will not budge from their position. They can be unrelentingly ruthless if they — or individuals they consider "family" members — are attacked or criticized by others.

Eight/Eights have a great love for gambling, and although they enjoy the risks they are seldom foolish. They have the keenest business sense of all the sets and, from childhood on, the world of commerce is open to them. They have a lifelong association with money — like the tide, it seems to flow naturally in and out of their lives. Their ability to accept change and embrace risk, coupled with their natural resiliency during times of hardship, makes them successful in any challenge or endeavor.

*Prince Albert
Guillaume Apollinaire
Ben Bradlee
John Buchan
Charles Bulfinch
Rory Calhoun
Keith Carradine
Davy Crockett
Vic Dana
Jim Davenport
Dino De Laurentiis
Robert De Niro
Kenny Dryden
Geraldine Ferraro
Llewellyn George
Arthur J. Goldberg
Samuel Goldwyn
Louis Gottschalk
Peggy Guggenheim
Dustin Hoffman
Harry Hopkins
Christopher Isherwood
Joan Mondale
V. S. Naipaul
Maureen O'Hara
Sean Penn
Francis Gary Powers
David Ragen
Chita Rivera
Larry Rivers
Jimmy Rushing
William French Smith
Connie Stevens
Sylvia Sidney
Maxwell Taylor
Joe Tex
Melvin Tillis
Mae West
John Hay Whitney
Esther Williams
Monty Woolley
Cole Younger*

Beware the fury of
a patient man. — John Dryden

THE EIGHT/NINE SET AFFINITIES

THE EIGHT/NINE NUMBERS ARE: 1 8 8 9

ODD NUMBERS: 1 9   EVEN NUMBERS: 8 8

SET INTERVAL: 1

FAMILY NUMBER: 8

THE EIGHT/NINES REPRESENT 1.6 PERCENT OF THE POPULATION.

PEOPLE I KNOW WHO ARE EIGHT/NINES:

_____   _____
_____   _____
_____   _____
_____   _____
_____   _____
_____   _____

MY EIGHT/NINE OBSERVATIONS:

_____
_____
_____
_____
_____
_____
_____

DISPOSITION

— WILLFUL — BENEVOLENT — ACQUISITIVE —

— CAPTAINS — EMOTIONAL —

— SELF-ASSURED — DEBONAIR —

— CAPABLE OF MANY VOCATIONS —

Understated intensity and a need for control.

EIGHT/NINE

*The six days of the year
that would make you an EIGHT/NINE are:*

August 9	August 27	September 8	September 17
August 18			September 26

Eight/Nines are understated autocrats who enjoy attention. They are instinctive experts in back-room politics, as well as sharp bargainers interested in material success. They tend to be very generous to their friends and family, showering them with money and possessions. Intense and courageous, Eight/Nines have active imaginations and usually appear to be in complete control of themselves and their situation. They can be relied upon in an emergency — their benevolent natures respond to the cries of the needy. Yet they have a very short emotional fuse and a strong attraction to the dramatic, tragic, and traumatic.

Eight/Nines like everything detailed and structured. Although they can be impulsive, spontaneity is not a strong characteristic — planning is. They are capable of tremendous organization and are not put off by detail work. They have a particularly strong need to maintain the appearance of calm control, and they would not go into battle unprepared, or take a trip without making careful plans. Extremely persistent, they tend to make it on their own efforts, go to great lengths to prove a point, and never give up unless their public or self-image is threatened.

Eight/Nines have great willpower and endurance. They are vigilant, hard workers who tenaciously pursue success, power, and public attention. They like to be in the driver's seat and enjoy giving directions to others. Although they are not narrow-minded, they constantly monitor the responses of others and can be quite judgmental and candid in assessing their actions. Eight/Nines can forgive, but they will seldom forget. They need to learn how to modulate their tendency to get overinvolved in the experiences of others. They are able to place their personal relationships on a back burner and let work become the focus in their lives, yet their involvement with their loved ones can be so profound that the trauma of being hurt may drive Eight/Nines to sever the relationship.

Eight/Nines have a broad spectrum of interests and the ability to be successful in a wide variety of occupations. Many of them can even maintain several different careers simultaneously. While they need to learn that they cannot live others' lives for them, they thrive in situations where they are the experts.

Melissa Sue Anderson
Johnny Appleseed
Barbara Bach
Anne Bancroft
Anne Beattie
George Blanda
Sid Caesar
Theodore Dreiser
T. S. Eliot
Sam Elliott
Max Factor
Marshall Fields
George Gershwin
Melanie Griffith
Pee-wee Herman
Whitney Houston
Hurricane Jackson
Lyndon B. Johnson
Rafer Johnson
Ken Kesey
Rod Laver
Roddy McDowall
Martin Mull
Olivia Newton-John
Ken Norton
Patrick O'Neal
Roman Polanski
Man Ray
Martha Raye
Robert Redford
Harry Reems
John Ritter
Tommy Sands
Peter Sellers
Robert Shaw
David Steinberg
Mother Teresa
Ben Turpin
Tuesday Weld
William Carlos Williams
Shelley Winters
Lester Young

When one has made a mistake, one says:
"Next time I shall really know what to do." What one should say is:
"I already know what I shall really do next time." — Cesare Pavese

THE NINE/NINE SET AFFINITIES

THE NINE/NINE NUMBERS ARE: 9 9 9

ODD NUMBERS: 9 9 9 EVEN NUMBERS: None

SET INTERVAL: 0 (Double 9)

FAMILY NUMBER: 9

THE NINE/NINES REPRESENT 0.8 PERCENT OF THE POPULATION.

PEOPLE I KNOW WHO ARE NINE/NINES:

_____   _____
_____   _____
_____   _____
_____   _____
_____   _____
_____   _____

MY NINE/NINE OBSERVATIONS:

_____
_____
_____
_____
_____
_____
_____

DISPOSITION

— PRECISE — SPECIALISTS —

— CONSISTENT — SELF-CONTAINED — ELITISTS —

— SELF-CREATING — VERSATILE —

— METICULOUS —

Lovers of detail, searching for perfection.

NINE/NINE

*The three days of the year
that would make you a NINE/NINE are:*

*September 9
September 18
September 27*

Nine/Nines carry themselves with an attitude of self-containment and aloofness. Sureness and confidence permeate their every action. They always call things as they see them, and having the last, definitive word on a subject seems to come naturally to them. They are very tenacious but seldom jealous of the possessions or achievements of others. Usually optimistic, idealistic, and broad-minded, they are good-natured, witty, enlightened autocrats.

Nine/Nines tend to the habitual and need to maintain a uniform appearance and follow a consistent pattern in their personal lifestyle. They are not risk takers and flakiness is not a trait of theirs. They are perfectionists who must analyze everything and avoid situations that make them appear incompetent or foolish. They prefer to conduct their lives out of the public limelight — the last thing in the world Nine/Nines want to do is create a scene in public. Yet they thrive on the approval of others and are reluctant to leave the spotlight if it is focused on their success.

Nine/Nines quickly grasp the "big picture," but instantly refine its focus to the area they wish to pursue and master. They become successful specialists and experts, but their success can be their curse. They are so welded to their success in a specific field that they can limit themselves by their unwillingness to move or grow into other areas. They sense when something is out of place or someone is out of step, and they spot errors of all types, particularly unnecessary waste. They can easily become self-appointed guardians of correctness. Very meticulous and exacting individuals, they have little patience with those who fail. They seldom bear grudges, however, and prefer to distance themselves from those with whom they experience conflict.

Although Nine/Nines have an incredible range of interests, they are drawn to areas that have clearly defined elements and strong structures. They make excellent architects, with their love for detail and form, and they have a particularly good ear for music, which attracts them with its rules of harmony. They can also be drawn to politics, but, because of their autocratic natures and sometimes elitist ideas, they seldom attract much public support. Many Nine/Nines excel in sports, happy with the regulations and the rewards for achievement.

Samuel Adams
Eddie (Rochester) Anderson
Louis Auchincloss
Frankie Avalon
Robert Blake
Rossano Brazzi
Shaun Cassidy
William Conrad
George Cruikshank
Agnes De Mille
Sam Ervin
Greta Garbo
Samuel Johnson
Elvin Jones
Michael Keaton
Alfred Landon
Joseph E. Levine
Sol Lewitt
Catherine Marshall
Kristy McNichol
Jayne Meadows
Sylvia Miles
Thomas Nast
Kathleen Nolan
Arthur H. Penn
Charles H. Percy
Bud Powell
Billy Preston
George Raft
Otis Redding
Max Reinhardt
Cardinal Richelieu
Cliff Robertson
Jimmie F. Rodgers
Cyril Scott
Joe Theismann
Cheryl Tiegs
Leo Tolstoy
Topol
Jack Warden
Vincent M. Youmans

PART II

YOUR NUMERIC IDENTITY

The Mathematics of the Forty-five Sets

Adam Bourgeois, a brilliant Chicago attorney with a long-standing interest in numerology, first introduced me to the idea that there are forty-five diverse groups of personalities that can be described and interrelated on the basis of numerical patterns. Initially, I rejected his idea because of my lifelong disinterest in anything connected to mathematics. To me, math and numbers represented useless, dull exercises in abstraction that bore no relationship to life. As an artist, my interest always lay in what I felt to be the concrete shapes and forces of the universe, the underlying patterns in the cosmos that influence life.

I began to look more closely at the aesthetics of the ancient Greeks, Chinese, Japanese, Egyptians, Persians, Africans, and pre-Columbians. I discovered that in each of these cultures, the point, the line, the triangle, the square, the circle, and the hexagon were the tools of the architect, artisan, builder, and priest. These simple geometric elements were used as symbols to communicate the underlying order and rhythm of life, and to describe the relationship of humanity to the cosmos. I realized then that I was becoming a devotee of geometric form. In a flash of insight, I understood that numbers were not the abstractions that I feared and avoided. Instead, I realized, numbers were the vocabulary of a universal language that could be used to communicate the form, structure, and function of the universe. Once I grasped the concept of numbers as vocabulary, I became fascinated by their symbolic representations in many aspects of human life.

To understand ourselves and our fellow beings, we first need a frame of reference. The fact that each of us was born in a certain month (a number from one to twelve) on a certain day (a number from one to thirty-one) supplies such a framework — a framework of numbers. I set out to explore numbers as keys to personal relationships, using them to define the subtle elements that make our lives uniquely individual and yet similar to one another — each on a distinct path and yet each referring to a collectively created map of humanity for direction.

To make my task manageable, I focused on the simplest numeric vocabulary, the single-digit numbers one through nine. I reduced the multiple-digit numbers (up to the number thirty-one, the maximum possible number of days in a month) to single digits by adding their individual digits together. Therefore:

10 becomes 1 + 0,
    which reduces to 1;

11 becomes 1 + 1,
    which reduces to 2;

12 becomes 1 + 2,
    which reduces to 3;

13 becomes 1 + 3,
    which reduces to 4;

14 becomes 1 + 4,
    which reduces to 5;

15 becomes 1 + 5,
    which reduces to 6;

16 becomes 1 + 6,
    which reduces to 7;

17 becomes 1 + 7,
    which reduces to 8;

18 becomes 1 + 8,
    which reduces to 9;

19 becomes 1 + 9,
    which equals 10,
    which reduces to 1;
20 becomes 2 + 0,
    which reduces to 2;
21 becomes 2 + 1,
    which reduces to 3;
22 becomes 2 + 2,
    which reduces to 4;

23 becomes 2 + 3,
    which reduces to 5;
24 becomes 2 + 4,
    which reduces to 6;
25 becomes 2 + 5,
    which reduces to 7;
26 becomes 2 + 6,
    which reduces to 8;
27 becomes 2 + 7,
    which reduces to 9;

28 becomes 2 + 8,
    which equals 10,
    which reduces to 1;
29 becomes 2 + 9,
    which equals 11,
    which reduces to 2;
30 becomes 3 + 0,
    which reduces to 3;
31 becomes 3 + 1,
    which reduces to 4.

At first, I was stymied when I viewed these numbers linearly, beginning with one and ending with nine, since they seemed to represent life as a static, unchanging thing, not the pulsing, dynamic force I knew it to be. How, then, could numbers be used as symbols of the mutable forces in life?

The solution was both profound and simple. The key lay in perceiving life not as a linear sequence, but as an infinite circle of cyclical energies. When I looked at the numbers one through nine from this perspective, placing them on a circle where nine was not only next to eight but also next to one, everything fell into place. Suddenly no one number was greater or more important than another. Each was different and unique, but each had equal stature and was in a relationship of dynamic exchange with all the other numbers. Once I grasped this simple insight, riddle after riddle about numbers and relationships evaporated, and the patterns of the numeric personality began to emerge.

As it turns out, my flash of insight into the cyclical nature of life and numbers is very elegant mathematically. First of all, if you add one to each number in the numeric sequence of one through nine, you get the next number in the sequence. In other words, you get the number seven if you add one to the number six, the number eight if you add one to the number seven, and so forth. It follows, then, that adding one to the number nine will give you the next number in the sequence: ten. However, since you are working only with single-digit numbers, you reduce ten to a single digit: one. Voilá! The number that follows nine is not ten, but one, so the sequence is indeed cyclical.

When describing dates as numbers, January 1 becomes One/One, July 4 becomes Seven/Four, December 2 becomes Three/Two (remember: December, which is 12, reduces to 1 + 2, which is 3), and so forth. For the sake of mathematical purity, the smaller of the two numbers is always expressed first. July 4 (Seven/Four), then, is expressed as Four/Seven and December 2 as Two/Three. Using this technique, every day in the year converts into one of forty-five combinations (see Numeric Personality Set Calendar, pages 11 and 12).

As I became more engrossed in this method for mapping personality types, I noticed that the number forty-five had some interesting properties. If you reduce it to a single-digit number, that number is nine (4 + 5), which happens to be our largest single digit and the point at which one cycle converts into the next. Furthermore, forty-five turns out to be the sum of each of the single-digit numbers (1 + 2 + 3 + 4 + 5 + 6 + 7 + 8 + 9 = 45).

As I studied the forty-five different mathematical combinations along with the people born on the dates that form the forty-five combinations, or sets, I saw archetypical personality patterns take form.

Everyone has specific numbers that can be calculated and analyzed within three basic groups: set numbers, family numbers, and set intervals. Your *set number* is a two-digit combination determined by the number of the month of your birth and the number of the day of your birth. Your *family number* is calculated by adding together your set number (see Set Numbers and Their Family Numbers, page 122). Your *set interval* is the difference between the smaller and the larger of the numbers that make up your set number (see Set Numbers and their Intervals, page 120).

Each of these numbers represents a multiplicity of effects in your life and personality. The numbers reflect the orderly, sequential cycles in life and your interrelationship with these energies. Your birth numbers connect you to specific patterns of perception, action, and personality. Ultimately, it does not matter whether your numeric identity derives its power from heavenly bodies, geomagnetic fields, genetic codes, or any other source. What matters is that you understand your position and

One/One	= 2.2%	Two/Eight	= 2.7%	Five/Five	= 0.8%
One/Two	= 4.3%	Two/Nine	= 2.7%	Five/Six	= 1.6%
One/Three	= 4.3%	Three/Three	= 2.2%	Five/Seven	= 1.6%
One/Four	= 3.3%	Three/Four	= 3.3%	Five/Eight	= 1.6%
One/Five	= 2.7%	Three/Five	= 2.7%	Five/Nine	= 1.6%
One/Six	= 2.7%	Three/Six	= 2.7%	Six/Six	= 0.8%
One/Seven	= 2.7%	Three/Seven	= 2.7%	Six/Seven	= 1.6%
One/Eight	= 2.7%	Three/Eight	= 2.7%	Six/Eight	= 1.6%
One/Nine	= 2.7%	Three/Nine	= 2.7%	Six/Nine	= 1.6%
Two/Two	= 2.2%	Four/Four	= 0.8%	Seven/Seven	= 0.8%
Two/Three	= 4.1%	Four/Five	= 1.9%	Seven/Eight	= 1.6%
Two/Four	= 2.7%	Four/Six	= 1.6%	Seven/Nine	= 1.6%
Two/Five	= 2.7%	Four/Seven	= 1.9%	Eight/Eight	= 0.8%
Two/Six	= 2.7%	Four/Eight	= 1.9%	Eight/Nine	= 1.6%
Two/Seven	= 2.7%	Four/Nine	= 1.6%	Nine/Nine	= 0.8%

THE INDIVIDUAL SETS AS A PERCENTAGE OF THE POPULATION

role in the pattern that makes up our universe.

No one set or numeric personality is more or less important than any other, and members of a particular set are not identical clones. When you look at the sets, remember that they show the relative interplay of forces that are affecting your unique traits, talents, and characteristics. Each set represents no more than 4.3 percent of the total population, and each set is an indispensable element in the cosmic energy that generates the life force.

THE FORTY-FIVE SETS AS A MAGIC TRIANGLE

```
                    1/1
                 2/2   1/2
              3/3   2/3   1/3
           4/4   3/4   2/4   1/4
        5/5   4/5   3/5   2/5   1/5
     6/6   5/6   4/6   3/6   2/6   1/6
  7/7   6/7   5/7   4/7   3/7   2/7   1/7
8/8  7/8  6/8  5/8  4/8  3/8  2/8  1/8
9/9  8/9  7/9  6/9  5/9  4/9  3/9  2/9  1/9
```

The Number Sets seem to arrange themselves naturally into an equal-sided triangle. By studying this arrangement closely, a number of patterns and relationships between the sets becomes evident. Some of the simplest, most easily apparent patterns are:

1. From left to right, each row shows set numbers whose set intervals increase by 1;

2. From right to left, each row shows set numbers whose family numbers increase by 1;

3. From top to bottom, left to right, each diagonal row contains set numbers whose set intervals and family numbers increase by 1; and

4. From top to bottom, right to left, each diagonal row contains set numbers with identical set intervals, and each diagonal row alternates family numbers by odd or even groups.

These are just a few of the possible patterns; there are many others. For example: If you add up the set intervals in a horizontal row, then add that number to the number of set numbers found in the row, you can predict the sum of the set intervals in the next row down. In other words, if you look at the row that begins with the set number 4/4, you will see that the set intervals for the set numbers in that row are 0, 1, 2, and 3. Added together, they equal 6. The row has four set numbers in it. The numbers 6 + 4 equal 10, which reduces to 1. The next row, which begins with the set number 5/5, has the set intervals 0, 1, 2, 3, and 4. Added together, they equal 10, which reduces to 1, just as you predicted mathematically.

See if you can find a few patterns on your own — they will open doors to your perceptions. I have been studying this triangle for some time and I am still making new discoveries.

Numbers and Their Energy: One Through Nine

Each of the numbers one through nine has a unique character and energy associated with it — its *numeressence*. Each numeressence is a force or power that is relative to all the other numeressences. As you become familiar with the energies of the various numbers, you will begin to understand in detail the many internal forces that help shape the forty-five personality types. You will also begin to recognize which number energies you or the people you interact with are emphasizing, and how to best respond to them.

Below, the characteristics of each number are described, along with a list of the sets that incorporate those characteristics in some way. For each set listed, the numeressence can come from one of the set numbers; it can come from the family number; and/or it can come from the set interval number. A set can resonate with several numeressences, and may also have a multiple dose of a single numeressence.

— ONE —

One is the number of creation: the beginning, the light that pierces darkness, and the voice that breaks silence. The strongest of the odd, or active numbers, it encompasses the dualities of finite/infinite and selfless/selfish. Its numeressence is one of action and logic. It can be geometrically represented by the point, and it represents the nucleus and the ego that relates everything to itself.

The number one is characteristic of the initiator, the leader, and the pioneer. It has the energies of self-discipline, ambition, and independence. One symbolizes the desire to dominate all situations, the struggle to overcome obstacles and complete tasks, and the ability to accomplish tremendous deeds. As the number of aggressiveness and willpower, one represents concentration that cannot be broken and stubbornness that will not be coerced. It is the essence of pride and the need for praise, the reluctance to take orders from others and the profound depth of conviction that inspires others to act. It stands for the law unto itself — the confidence of rightness in belief and action that leads to decisions without regard for the consequences. It typifies the practical rather than the emotional outlook, the tendency to regard romance as a frill rather than a necessity. As a result, the number one encapsulates the energy of the loner traveling a self-made path through life.

The twenty sets that resonate with ONE energy are:

• 1/1 • 1/2 • 1/3 • 1/4 • 1/5 • 1/6 • 1/7 • 1/8 • 1/9 • 2/3 • 2/8 •
• 3/4 • 3/7 • 4/5 • 4/6 • 5/5 • 5/6 • 6/7 • 7/8 • 8/9 •

— TWO —

Two is the number of reception: the connection, the audience that sees the light in the darkness and hears the voice in the silence. The mate of the number one, it is the weakest of the even, or reactive numbers. Two encompasses the dualities of constancy/change and devotion/fickleness. Its numeressence is one of dependence and emotion. It can be geometrically represented by the line and acts as the bridge or connection that spans the emptiness between opposite sides.

Two is the most sensitive and romantic of all the numbers. It is the essence of being in love with love and other such ideals, rather than facing the realities of daily life. It is the number of the rhythmic and the artistic, and it embodies gentleness, adaptability, charm, cooperation, and diplomacy. Resonating with a powerful sense of what might be, the number two represents the essence of the dreamer and visionary. Its focus is internal, rather than external, as it seeks harmony and balance in life.

Two energy is the enemy of rigidity and exactness, and the lover of ease and comfort. It is the preference for working with or for others, even in obscurity, rather than striking out alone. It is the need to be connected or attached to someone or something at all times, and it represents the jealous spirit unwilling to share the source of its attachment since, without it, it ceases to exist.

The nineteen sets that resonate with TWO energy are:

• 1/1 • 1/2 • 1/3 • 2/2 • 2/3 • 2/4 • 2/5 • 2/6 • 2/7 • 2/8 • 2/9 •
• 3/5 • 3/8 • 4/6 • 4/7 • 5/6 • 5/7 • 6/8 • 7/9 •

— THREE —

Three is the number of combination: the new structure, the force that combines with one and two to make the elemental geometric shape of the triangle, which creates an infinite source of new forms when cloned and combined. Three symbolizes the stability and security of the family and society. It encompasses the dualities of kindness/ruthlessness and follower/leader. Its numeressence is that of the desire for consensus in all things from all people, and the perpetual search for the proper forum for its dynamics.

The three energy is one of rule by the heart, not the head, of reliance on emotion and deep feelings rather than intellect. It represents the craving for friends and popularity, and the love of entertaining and bringing good times to all. It is the number of sensuality and flirtation, but its strength resides in faithfulness. It is the symbol of social concern and the wish to make everyone happy.

Three is the number of the artistic, dramatic, and boldly expressive. It resonates with pride in showing off skills and abilities, and extravagance in gestures, things, and ideas. It is the energy that is quick to move when faced with discouragement or failure, and that has no patience with people or things that block its path. Three represents the need to make a game out of life, to write and rewrite the rules. to suit the situation.

The eighteen sets that resonate with THREE energy are:
• 1/2 • 1/3 • 1/4 • 2/3 • 2/5 • 3/3 • 3/4 • 3/5 • 3/6 • 3/7 •
• 3/8 • 3/9 • 4/7 • 4/8 • 5/7 • 5/8 • 6/6 • 6/9 •

— FOUR —

Four is the number of organization: the structure that governs and the boundary that defines limits. It encompasses the dualities of directing/serving and innovating/preserving. It can be geometrically represented by the cross and the square, and its numeressence is that of work, order, and practicality.

The four energy is one of respectability, solidity, and even, at times, rigidity. It is staunch and pragmatic, and it seeks its identity in what it does. It is very material rather than spiritual in its orientation, with a deep love for the tangible and the definable. The number four represents the primal sense of territory, with its desire for clearly delineated borders, as well as power and mastery over all people or situations within them. It is the number of wanting to be the innovator and resenting innovation from others.

Four resonates with patience and exactness in all things, even following orders. Its energy is that of the home-loving and the patriotic, and it operates from the principle that what is good for the four is good for all. It is the number of the dynamic that revels in details, loves harmony and regularity, and views chaos as its archenemy.

The seventeen sets that resonate with FOUR energy are:
• 1/3 • 1/4 • 1/5 • 2/2 • 2/4 • 2/6 • 3/4 • 3/7 • 4/4 • 4/5 •
• 4/6 • 4/7 • 4/8 • 4/9 • 5/8 • 5/9 • 6/7 •

— FIVE —

Five is the number of modulation: of transformation, influence, and change. It is the number in the middle and encompasses the dualities of logic/emotion and influencing/being influenced. It can be geometrically represented by the pentagon. Five's numer-essence is the most difficult to isolate, since it is in a constant state of fluctuation, but it revolves around resourcefulness, resilience, and change.

Five is the energy of the elusiveness of wind, with freedom from all restraints in all directions. Being its own master, it symbolizes the gambler, resistance to routine and detail, and avoidance of responsibility. It also represents cleverness and versatility, with pleasure and sociability as its aim. It resonates with the need to seek variety and experience everything. It is the number of opportunity and the quest for the new, different, unusual, strange, adventurous, and mysterious.

The five energy injects new ideas into all it touches, and adapts and mingles with any condition, environment, or culture. Once it has absorbed the essence of an experience, it moves on, unhampered by the conventions or opinions of others. It represents the force that jolts people to action; then, once they think they have grasped it, it departs, leaving them in a state of puzzled bewilderment.

The seventeen sets that resonate with FIVE energy are:
• 1/4 • 1/5 • 1/6 • 2/3 • 2/5 • 2/7 • 3/5 • 3/8 • 4/5 •
• 4/9 • 5/5 • 5/6 • 5/7 • 5/8 • 5/9 • 6/8 • 7/7 •

— SIX —

Six is the number of association: of joining, of the group and the network. It can be geometrically represented by the hexagon and the six-pointed star, and is the only number divisible by both an odd and an even number. Six stands for the force that encompasses the dualities of weakness/power and elitism/idealism. The six numeressence is that of harmony, domesticity, and affiliation.

The six energy is the essence of alliance and dependence. It finds its power through linking with others. Alone, without a collective focus, it is the most neutral of all the numbers, lifeless and without strength. The range of sources for its identity, however, is infinite. It may come from social causes, political movements, religious or philosophical systems, occupations, friends, or family, and it is limited only by its own creativity and sense of adventure. The six energy strives for balance and symmetry. It moves from nothing to consensus, to the powerful roar of the crowd.

The sixteen sets that resonate with SIX energy are:
• 1/5 • 1/6 • 1/7 • 2/4 • 2/6 • 2/8 • 3/3 • 3/6 • 3/9 • 4/6 •
• 5/6 • 6/6 • 6/7 • 6/8 • 6/9 • 7/8 •

— SEVEN —

Seven is the number of orchestration: of the director, the arranger, and the conductor. It can be geometrically represented by a triangle superimposed on a square. It is the orphan number and the symbol of unresolved feelings about the past, the present, and the future. Its numeressence is that of a force to be responded to without question, rather than understood, and it encompasses the dualities of gentleness/harshness and coaxing/demanding.

The number seven symbolizes seeing what should be done, then doing it. It is the energy of searching, sorting, and relating a number of different elements, then organizing and directing them. Seven represents the urge to lead and govern, and the reluctance to take a backseat to anything or anyone else. It is the voice of authority, and it expects those who hear it to jump to its commands.

The seven energy is one of emotion modulated by a pristine desire for order. It resists argument, dislikes explaining itself, and is uncomfortable with sudden change and the unknown. It maintains a precarious position between the spiritual and the material worlds and is never completely at ease on either plane.

The fifteen sets that resonate with SEVEN energy are:
• 1/6 • 1/7 • 1/8 • 2/5 • 2/7 • 2/9 • 3/4 • 3/7 • 4/7 • 5/7 •
• 6/7 • 7/7 • 7/8 • 7/9 • 8/8 •

— EIGHT —

Eight is the number of domination: of power, authority, and judgment. It can be geometrically represented by the rectangle, the double square, and the symbol of infinity, and it is the strongest of the even, or reactive numbers. It encompasses the duality of astounding success/resounding failure, and its numeressence is one of self-reliance, impatience, and the endless quest for worldly accomplishment.

The number eight symbolizes practicality, dependability, and the instinctive gravitation toward sources of power. It represents the need to direct, the ability for great achievement, and the struggle for success as the ultimate goal. Yet, since eight resonates with an underlying current of dissatisfaction and a sense of never having enough, each goal it achieves merely fuels its desire for more. Eight typifies the force that acts as an inspiration for others as it continually collects, amasses, combines, sorts, ponders, and restructures its environment and possessions.

Eight energy is one of multifaceted ambition, high standards and expectations of itself and others, and an intolerance for foolishness. It places seriousness and responsibility first, and lets laughter enter only at rare and appropriate moments. It is opinionated, but not small-minded; dominating and exact in its requirements; and,

114

when it wants something, it must have it without delay.

The fourteen sets that resonate with EIGHT energy are:
• 1/7 • 1/8 • 1/9 • 2/6 • 2/8 • 3/5 • 3/8 • 4/4 • 4/8 • 5/8 •
• 6/8 • 7/8 • 8/8 • 8/9 •

— NINE —

Nine is the number of interpretation: of the mirror, the teacher, the artist, the executive, and the scientist. It is the most universal of all the numbers and rests next to one in the circle of life. It can be geometrically represented by the nine-pointed star whose rays shine in all directions, offering new beginnings, and it encompasses the duality of wanting to give to the world/needing to receive from the world. Its numeressence is one of high mental and spiritual achievement combined with the desire for personal recognition and social approval.

Nine energy wants to share its wisdom, intuition, knowledge, experience, and broadness of mind with everyone. It sees itself as an interpreter for the masses of all the greatness to be found in life. Nine resonates with the feeling of belonging to all the world. It symbolizes the urge to serve the causes of humanity, often placing social commitments and responsibilities well before personal relationships.

The number nine holds the capability for great achievement in any field. It represents a combination of the physical energy of the doer with the mental energy of the visionary and the dreamer. Nine has an active energy that rapidly changes to dissatisfaction and frustration when it is limited to merely dreaming about doing or accomplishing something.

The thirteen sets that resonate with NINE energy are:
• 1/8 • 1/9 • 2/7 • 2/9 • 3/6 • 3/9 • 4/5 • 4/9 • 5/9 •
• 6/9 • 7/9 • 8/9 • 9/9 •

The Effects of Odd and Even Numbers

Since ancient times, pairs of opposites have been used to define the structure of the universe and the nature of life. Pairs such as male and female, positive and negative, day and night, and odd and even underlie the philosophical systems of cultures the world over, from the mathematical theories of Pythagoras to the metaphysical structure of the *I Ching* (*The Book of Change*). This Chinese classic, handed down over thousands of years, uses the odd/even relationship as its foundation. Its principles of polarity have guided millions in their daily lives and have inspired leaders, scientists, politicians, mathematicians, and philosophers.

In each of the forty-five set descriptions in Part I, you will notice a listing of odd and even numbers on the left-hand page. These odd and even numbers are derived from your set number, family number, and set interval. They reveal detailed information about your numeric dynamics and can give you greater insight into why you do or feel the things you do. In effect, they are important operative factors in your unique personality type.

The terms *action* and *reaction* describe the basic dynamics of odd and even numbers in personal energies. Odd numbers are the forces of action and even numbers are the forces of reaction. The forces of action are the instigators, the originators, and the bringers of change, while the forces of reaction are the balancers, the consolidators, and the adapters of new energies. Neither is more important than the other; each is merely a state of being that incorporates different perceptions, approaches, and tactics.

In the Set Number Odd and Even Combinations chart, page 117, you will find three sets that contain only odd numbers, four that contain only even numbers, and fourteen that contain an equal number of both. The remaining sets contain a combination of the two, some sets with more odd numbers, some with more even numbers. At the same time, the relative strengths of these numbers vary in intensity. The Scale of Relative Active-Reactive Intensities for the Odd and Even Numbers, below, shows that the number one is the most active odd number, while the number nine is the least active; the number eight is the most reactive of the even numbers, while the number two is the least reactive. One way to analyze any set is to look at the proportion of odd numbers to even numbers, then compare the relative strengths of these numbers to determine the active or reactive tendencies.

Individuals with all odd numbers tend to approach life from a very active, direct

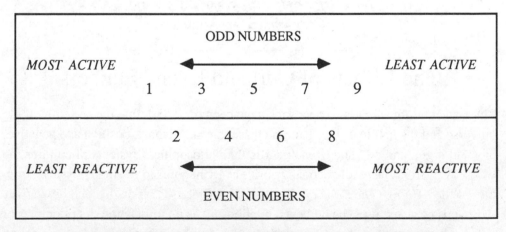

SCALE OF RELATIVE ACTIVE-REACTIVE INTENSITIES
FOR THE ODD AND EVEN NUMBERS

SET NUMBER	ODD NUMBERS	EVEN NUMBERS	ODD/EVEN COMBINATION
One/One	1 1	2	Two Odd — One Even
One/Two	1 1 3	2	Three Odd — One Even
One/Three	1 3	2 4	Two Odd — Two Even
One/Four	1 3 5	4	Three Odd — One Even
One/Five	1 5	4 6	Two Odd — Two Even
One/Six	1 5 7	6	Three Odd — One Even
One/Seven	1 7	6 8	Two Odd — Two Even
One/Eight	1 7 9	8	Three Odd — One Even
One/Nine	1 1 9	8	Three Odd — One Even
Two/Two	—	2 2 4	Three Even
Two/Three	1 3 5	2	Three Odd — One Even
Two/Four	—	2 2 4 6	Four Even
Two/Five	3 5 7	2	Three Odd — One Even
Two/Six	—	2 4 6 8	Four Even
Two/Seven	5 7 9	2	Three Odd — One Even
Two/Eight	1	2 6 8	One Odd — Three Even
Two/Nine	7 9	2 2	Two Odd — Two Even
Three/Three	3 3	6	Two Odd — One Even
Three/Four	1 3 7	4	Three Odd — One Even
Three/Five	3 5	2 8	Two Odd — Two Even
Three/Six	3 3 9	6	Three Odd — One Even
Three/Seven	1 3 7	4	Three Odd — One Even
Three/Eight	3 5	2 8	Two Odd — Two Even
Three/Nine	3 3 9	6	Three Odd — One Even
Four/Four	—	4 4 8	Three Even
Four/Five	1 5 9	4	Three Odd — One Even
Four/Six	1	2 4 6	One Odd — Three Even
Four/Seven	3 7	2 4	Two Odd — Two Even
Four/Eight	3	4 4 8	One Odd — Three Even
Four/Nine	5 9	4 4	Two Odd — Two Even
Five/Five	1 5 5	—	Three Odd
Five/Six	1 5	2 6	Two Odd — Two Even
Five/Seven	3 5 7	2	Three Odd — One Even
Five/Eight	3 5	4 8	Two Odd — Two Even
Five/Nine	5 5 9	4	Three Odd — One Even
Six/Six	3	6 6	One Odd — Two Even
Six/Seven	1 7	4 6	Two Odd — Two Even
Six/Eight	5	2 6 8	One Odd — Three Even
Six/Nine	3 9	6 6	Two Odd — Two Even
Seven/Seven	5 7 7	—	Three Odd
Seven/Eight	1 7	6 8	Two Odd — Two Even
Seven/Nine	7 7 9	2	Three Odd — One Even
Eight/Eight	7	8 8	One Odd — Two Even
Eight/Nine	1 9	8 8	Two Odd — Two Even
Nine/Nine	9 9 9	—	Three Odd

SET NUMBER ODD AND EVEN COMBINATIONS

perspective. Those with all even numbers tend to be reactive, subtle, and indirect in their approach. Those with an equal number of odd and even numbers tend to have balanced numeric dynamics (depending on the relative intensity of their numbers), while those with varying proportions of odd and even numbers tend to be more active if they have more odd numbers and more reactive if they have more even numbers (again, the relative intensity of the numbers must be considered).

My set number is Two/Eight and my personal odd/even makeup is one odd number and three even numbers. This makes my personal nature more reactive than active, which means that I am less likely to instigate actions and more likely to respond to them. Therefore, I tend to manipulate situations indirectly rather than directly, and, although the end results may be the same as those of a very direct manipulator, my tactics and approach are quite different. For example, when I play chess, I prefer to have the second rather than the opening move, but I still intend to play a very aggressive offensive game. At the same time, in personal relationships, I have always been attracted to sets with three odd numbers and one even number. Those who possess the exact reverse polarity are very fulfilling to me emotionally.

Although it seems easy to divide everyone into a series of paired energies, gender bias can cause confusion. It is possible to fall into the trap of thinking that "active" is a male characteristic and "reactive" is a female characteristic. In reality, few males are purely active and few females are purely reactive. The traits that most cultures tacitly assign to gender behavior often have nothing at all to do with an individual's personal energies, and may, in fact, distort or even damage them. For example, many traditionally assigned gender traits dictate that males are aggressive and direct, while females are passive and subtle. Males who are inherently giving and sensitive or females who are inherently energetic and direct can find themselves in emotional conflict when they try to suppress their natural tendencies for the sake of their perceived social roles. It is important not to confuse physical makeup or gender with your true number dynamics. These must be brought into a harmonic balance both within the self and with the help of a mate or partner who possesses complementary energies.

Set Intervals and Their Meanings

The set interval is the numeric key to a set's range of interests. Just as different camera lenses take in details at different distances and widths, different individuals approach life from different perspectives. Some individuals focus closely, while others focus distantly; some focus narrowly and others broadly. The set interval represents the way a set focuses on both personal concerns and outside interests, and the way this is expressed. Generally, sets with smaller intervals have more intense and deeper interests, while sets with greater intervals have a wider and more diverse range of interests. No specific set interval is more meaningful or important than any other; each is appropriate to the personality represented by that set.

You can determine your set interval in one of two ways. You can look up your set number on the chart, Set Numbers and Their Intervals, page 120; or you can calculate your set interval mathematically. To do this, simply subtract the smaller of your set numbers from the larger one. If your set number is Four/Five, for example, subtract four from five. The resulting number, one, is your set interval. Once you have determined your set interval, you will want to refer to its numeressence in the earlier chapter, "Numbers and Their Energy: One Through Nine," beginning on page 110. While your interval number describes the scope of your interests — broad or narrow, diverse or intense — the numeressence of your interval number elaborates on your approach to life within that scope.

If you belong to one of the nine double set numbers (One/One, Two/Two, Three/Three, Four/Four, Five/Five, Six/Six, Seven/Seven, Eight/Eight, and Nine/Nine), you will find that they have a set interval of zero. This does *not* mean that these sets lack a range of interests or a numeressence. Instead, it means that each of these sets has a set interval represented by one of its numbers, and that this number resonates with a double dose of its numeressence. In other words, the numeressence for One/One is one, for Two/Two is two, for Three/Three is three, and so forth, but each has

SET NUMBERS THAT SHARE INTERVALS AND ATTRIBUTES

SET INTERVAL		
0	1/1 2/2 3/3 4/4 5/5 6/6 7/7 8/8 9/9	All Interests Are Deep and Intense
1	1/2 2/3 3/4 4/5 5/6 6/7 7/8 8/9	Most Interests Are Deeply Focused
2	1/3 2/4 3/5 4/6 5/7 6/8 7/9	Interests Tend To Be Deep
3	1/4 2/5 3/6 4/7 5/8 6/9	Interests Can Easily Be Focused at Will
4	1/5 2/6 3/7 4/8 5/9	Simultaneously Focused and Widespread
5	1/6 2/7 3/8 4/9	Interests Can Easily Be Extended at Will
6	1/7 2/8 3/9	Interests Tend To Be Widespread
7	1/8 2/9	Most Interests Are Widely Extended
8	1/9	All Interests Are Extremely Widespread

The single-digit numbers in the left-hand column represent the set interval. The set numbers to the right of them share that set interval and its characteristic energy. Remember: Set numbers with a set interval of zero are double-energy numbers and highly intensify the numeressence of their double number. Refer to "Numbers and Their Energy: One Through Nine," page 110, to further analyze the characteristics of the interval numbers.

SET NUMBER	MATH	SET INTERVAL	NUMERESSENCE QUALITY
One/One	1 - 1	0 (Double 1)	1 — Creativity & Action
One/Two	2 - 1	1	1 — Creativity & Action
One/Three	3 - 1	2	2 — Receptivity & Emotion
One/Four	4 - 1	3	3 — Combining & Consensus
One/Five	5 - 1	4	4 — Organizing & Stability
One/Six	6 - 1	5	5 — Transformation & Adventure
One/Seven	7 - 1	6	6 — Joining & Affiliation
One/Eight	8 - 1	7	7 — Orchestrating & Command
One/Nine	9 - 1	8	8 — Authority & Power
Two/Two	2 - 2	0 (Double 2)	2 — Receptivity & Emotion
Two/Three	3 - 2	1	1 — Creativity & Action
Two/Four	4 - 2	2	2 — Receptivity & Emotion
Two/Five	5 - 2	3	3 — Combining & Consensus
Two/Six	6 - 2	4	4 — Organizing & Stability
Two/Seven	7 - 2	5	5 — Transformation & Adventure
Two/Eight	8 - 2	6	6 — Joining & Affiliation
Two/Nine	9 - 2	7	7 — Orchestrating & Command
Three/Three	3 - 3	0 (Double 3)	3 — Combining & Consensus
Three/Four	4 - 3	1	1 — Creativity & Action
Three/Five	5 - 3	2	2 — Receptivity & Emotion
Three/Six	6 - 3	3	3 — Combining & Consensus
Three/Seven	7 - 3	4	4 — Organizing & Stability
Three/Eight	8 - 3	5	5 — Transformation & Adventure
Three/Nine	9 - 3	6	6 — Joining & Affiliation
Four/Four	4 - 4	0 (Double 4)	4 — Organizing & Stability
Four/Five	5 - 4	1	1 — Creativity & Action
Four/Six	6 - 4	2	2 — Receptivity & Emotion
Four/Seven	7 - 4	3	3 — Combining & Consensus
Four/Eight	8 - 4	4	4 — Organizing & Stability
Four/Nine	9 - 4	5	5 — Transformation & Adventure
Five/Five	5 - 5	0 (Double 5)	5 — Transformation & Adventure
Five/Six	6 - 5	1	1 — Creativity & Action
Five/Seven	7 - 5	2	2 — Receptivity & Emotion
Five/Eight	8 - 5	3	3 — Combining & Consensus
Five/Nine	9 - 5	4	4 — Organizing & Stability
Six/Six	6 - 6	0 (Double 6)	6 — Joining & Affiliation
Six/Seven	7 - 6	1	1 — Creativity & Action
Six/Eight	8 - 6	2	2 — Receptivity & Emotion
Six/Nine	9 - 6	3	3 — Combining & Consensus
Seven/Seven	7 - 7	0 (Double 7)	7 — Orchestrating & Command
Seven/Eight	8 - 7	1	1 — Creativity & Action
Seven/Nine	9 - 7	2	2 — Receptivity & Emotion
Eight/Eight	8 - 8	0 (Double 8)	8 — Authority & Power
Eight/Nine	9 - 8	1	1 — Creativity & Action
Nine/Nine	9 - 9	0 (Double 9)	9 — Teaching & Vision

To find your set interval, look down the first column until you find your set number.
The column next to it shows the mathematical process for determining the set interval,
the third column lists the set interval, and the last column shows the numeressence of the
interval number. Refer to "Numbers and Their Energy: One Through Nine," page 110,
for a discussion of the individual numeressence characteristics.

a range of interest and an approach that is very deeply focused, more so than any other set.

When you study a set number, do not overlook the dynamics of the set interval. Not only can it give you clues as to how a set approaches life in general, but its numeressence, or number energy, can also help define those areas in which different sets have characteristics in common. For example, on the "Set Numbers That Share Intervals and Attributes" chart, page 119, the sets One/Seven, Two/Eight, and Three/Nine each have a set interval of six, so they all tend to have widespread interests and all share a six numeressence. By looking up the numeressence for the number six, you can deduce that they will all have a similar inclination to join with others to fulfill their personal goals. The set Six/Six also has the same six numeressence, but because the set interval is zero, the six energy is extremely concentrated, and they are even more dependent on affiliations with others. For this reason, double-set number personalities are more profoundly affected by their numeressence.

Family Numbers and Their Characteristics

The family number represents the way members of particular sets can best express their numeric dynamics in order to achieve their goals and fulfill their dreams. It pinpoints the areas in life that should be concentrated on for the sake of self-realization and personal growth. In addition, the family number resonates with the energy, or numeressence, of specific dates, and thus it draws together and connects groups of sets along destiny lines.

Generally, sets with the same family number get along well with one another. They often ally themselves with each other because they are traveling a similar path through life. The "Set Numbers That Share a Family Number" chart, page 122, shows which family number contains which sets. Within each family number, certain sets are more closely connected to one another. The sets within your family number that are to the left and right of your set number are the ones that have the strongest complementary energy to yours. For example, if you are a Four/Five, your family number is nine. When you look up the other sets that share this number, you will see that Three/Six and Nine/Nine are on either side of you. Although you would also be drawn to One/Eight or Two/Seven, you will tend to be more intensely connected to Three/Six and Nine/Nine. Remember to think about these numbers cyclically, rather than linearly. For example, the sets with family number two are shown as One/One, Two/Nine, Three/Eight, Four/Seven, and Five/Six. If these sets were placed in a circle, Five/Six would be located between Four/Seven and One/One —

SET NUMBER	MATH	FAMILY NUMBER
One/One	1 + 1	2
One/Two	1 + 2	3
One/Three	1 + 3	4
One/Four	1 + 4	5
One/Five	1 + 5	6
One/Six	1 + 6	7
One/Seven	1 + 7	8
One/Eight	1 + 8	9
One/Nine	1 + 9	10, which reduces to 1
Two/Two	2 + 2	4
Two/Three	2 + 3	5
Two/Four	2 + 4	6
Two/Five	2 + 5	7
Two/Six	2 + 6	8
Two/Seven	2 + 7	9
Two/Eight	2 + 8	10, which reduces to 1
Two/Nine	2 + 9	11, which reduces to 2
Three/Three	3 + 3	6
Three/Four	3 + 4	7
Three/Five	3 + 5	8
Three/Six	3 + 6	9
Three/Seven	3 + 7	10, which reduces to 1
Three/Eight	3 + 8	11, which reduces to 2
Three/Nine	3 + 9	12, which reduces to 3
Four/Four	4 + 4	8
Four/Five	4 + 5	9
Four/Six	4 + 6	10, which reduces to 1
Four/Seven	4 + 7	11, which reduces to 2
Four/Eight	4 + 8	12, which reduces to 3
Four/Nine	4 + 9	13, which reduces to 4
Five/Five	5 + 5	10, which reduces to 1
Five/Six	5 + 6	11, which reduces to 2
Five/Seven	5 + 7	12, which reduces to 3
Five/Eight	5 + 8	13, which reduces to 4
Five/Nine	5 + 9	14, which reduces to 5
Six/Six	6 + 6	12, which reduces to 3
Six/Seven	6 + 7	13, which reduces to 4
Six/Eight	6 + 8	14, which reduces to 5
Six/Nine	6 + 9	15, which reduces to 6
Seven/Seven	7 + 7	14, which reduces to 5
Seven/Eight	7 + 8	15, which reduces to 6
Seven/Nine	7 + 9	16, which reduces to 7
Eight/Eight	8 + 8	16, which reduces to 7
Eight/Nine	8 + 9	17, which reduces to 8
Nine/Nine	9 + 9	18, which reduces to 9

SET NUMBERS AND THEIR FAMILY NUMBERS

To find your family number in the chart on the left, look down the first column until you find your set number. The column next to it shows the mathematical process for determining the family number, and the third column lists the family number itself.

SET NUMBERS THAT SHARE A FAMILY NUMBER

FAMILY NUMBER		
1	1/9 2/8 3/7 4/6 5/5
2	1/1 2/9 3/8 4/7 5/6
3	1/2 3/9 4/8 5/7 6/6
4	1/3 2/2 4/9 5/8 6/7
5	1/4 2/3 5/9 6/8 7/7
6	1/4 2/4 3/3 6/9 7/8
7	1/6 2/5 3/4 7/9 8/8
8	1/7 2/6 3/5 4/4 8/9
9	1/8 2/7 3/6 4/5 9/9

To discover which set numbers share the same family number, look at the chart above. The single-digit numbers in the left-hand column represent the family number. The set numbers to the right of them share that family number. Although all set numbers that share a family number follow similar paths, neighboring set numbers tend to be more closely aligned. First and last set numbers in rows are considered neighbors.

the sets to which it is most intensely connected.

Your family number gives you clues for your direction in life and hints at the work you must do in order to achieve personal completeness. The family numbers of others lets you know who shares your path, and can help you understand the paths that others must travel. No one path is better or more important than any other. Each is different, and knowing the "rules of the road" for each makes everybody's journey easier and more pleasant.

Although your family number will tell you a great deal about where your numeric dynamics can take you, it does not assure you of a specific outcome. It is up to you to determine how far you can go in your process of self-realization. You alone will determine how much you want to understand about yourself, and decide how thoroughly you wish to develop the potential that you have.

You can find out which family number you belong to in one of two ways. You can refer to the "Set Numbers and Their Family Numbers" chart, page 122, or you can calculate your family number mathematically. To do this, simply add together the two single digits that make up your set number. For set number Three/Four, for example, add together three and four to get seven: the family number. If the digits in your set number add up to a double digit, reduce it to a single digit. For example, if your set number is Five/Six, add together five and six. The resulting number, eleven, reduces to the number two, which is your family number. Here is a brief description of the family number destiny paths:

Individuals with a family number of ONE (set numbers One/Nine, Two/Eight, Three/Seven, Four/Six, Five/Five) must develop their creative energies. They need an appreciative audience and a sense of self-importance to succeed.

Individuals with a family number of TWO (set numbers One/One, Two/Nine, Three/Eight, Four/Seven, and Five/Six) must develop their personal relationships. They need intimate, personal interactions with others to realize their dreams.

Individuals with a family number of THREE (set numbers One/Two, Three/Nine, Four/Eight, Five/Seven, Six/Six) must develop their sense of social purpose and social recognition. They need to know they have a place in society to feel secure.

Individuals with a family number of FOUR (set numbers One/Three, Two/Two, Four/Nine, Five/Eight, and Six/Seven) must develop skills in organization and leadership. To fulfill themselves, they need to be in control, and they will define their identity through their work.

Individuals with a family number of FIVE (set numbers One/Four, Two/Three, Five/Nine, Six/Eight, and Seven/Seven) must follow a path of transformation that allows them to make dramatic changes in their lives. They need constant movement and change — in any direction — to find themselves.

Individuals with a family number of SIX (set numbers One/Five, Two/Four, Three/Three, Six/Nine, and Seven/Eight) must seek association and affiliation for their personal validation. For fulfillment, they need identification, alignment, and validation through a group, family, or organization.

Individuals with a family number of SEVEN (set numbers One/Six, Two/Five, Three/Four, Seven/Nine, and Eight/Eight) must develop skills in the orchestration of ideas, people, services, or performances. To achieve their potential, they need to sort, arrange, and oversee tasks, collections, or groups.

Individuals with a family number of EIGHT (set numbers One/Seven, Two/Six, Three/Five, Four/Four, and Eight/Nine) must dominate their worldly surroundings. To find fulfillment, they need to overcome challenges, acquire material possessions, attract followers, and establish themselves in positions of personal power.

Individuals with a family number of NINE (set numbers One/Eight, Two/Seven, Three/Six, Four/Five, and Nine/Nine) must serve others by reinterpreting and reflecting the diversity that surrounds them. To achieve their true potential, they need to be appreciated and to attract an approving audience.

Special Days and Their Number Energy

Each day of the year resonates with the numeric energies of one of the forty-five different day and month combinations that define a numeric personality. In the same way that the set numbers give you insight into your personal dynamics and your interactions with others, they can help you understand why certain dates are more important to you than others.

In Part I, each set description is preceded with a list of dates that share that set number. These dates have a special importance for members of that set. As a member of the Two/Eight set, I look upon the ten days of the year that are Two/Eight days (February 8, 17, and 26; August 2, 11, 20, and 29; and November 8, 17, and 26) as special days that are particularly harmonious for me. I also find that the dates corresponding to the sets that are the most compatible to mine are also interesting days for me (see "Tables of Numeric Compatibility Between Sets," page 132).

A day's numeressence can give you insight into the general trends that prevail on that particular day. You can apply your awareness of the energies of the various days of the year to predict what you can expect and plan your approach to your daily concerns. The calendar date February 6, for example, is a Two/Six day. Its numeressence, as derived from its family number, is that of the number eight. (See "Set Numbers and Their Family Numbers," page 122, to calculate a numeressence.) By looking up the meaning of an eight numeressence in "Numbers and Their Energy: One Through Nine," pages 110 through 115, it is clear that an eight day is ideal for making important decisions or resolutions and taking on challenges. If you happen to share a number in common with the numbers of this date (two, six, or eight), particularly if that number is an eight, then this is an especially good day for you to take a deep breath and reach out toward your goal or dream.

When analyzing the numeressence of dates, remember: days with a ONE energy are good for creative activities and self-involvement. Those with a numeressence of TWO are days for working on and enjoying relationships. Days with a THREE energy are days of fulfilling social interaction, while those with a FOUR energy are excellent for accomplishing work and completing tasks. Days with a FIVE numeressence are good for personal changes and new ventures. Days with a SIX energy are fruitful for alliances and affiliations, and days with a SEVEN energy are ideal for organizing and rearranging people or things. Days with an EIGHT numeressence are best for self-reliance, dealing with power, and meeting challenges, while days with a NINE numeressence are especially good for mental and spiritual achievements and reflections.

Once you understand the relationship between dates and their numeressences, you can use your creativity to expand on their infinite possibilities. You can analyze the numeric energy of a pet you are considering adopting, select the best starting date for a project, or choose the right day to shower that special someone with attention. The possibilities are endless. You can even determine the numeric personality of a country, city, organization, or movement that you belong to, since each has a starting date.

For example, the United States has a "birthday" of July 4, which makes it a Four/Seven country; France, which celebrates its modern birth on Bastille Day (July 14), is a Five/Seven country; and Los Angeles, which was founded on September 4, is a Four/Nine city. Each of these places has numeric dynamics that can either be harmoniously aligned with your own energy or disruptive to your personal development. As you pursue your dreams and ambitions, it is important to consider the role the numeric energy of your location may play in your life and to try to place your uniqueness where it best belongs. If your development is stifled where you live now, do not hesitate to move on. You are fortunate to live at a time of remarkable mobility, which is to your great advantage in the pursuit of personal fulfillment.

PART III

YOUR NUMERIC COMPATIBILITY WITH OTHERS

Compatibility and Conflict Among the Sets

Individually, we all possess different patterns of need, thought, sensitivity, and behavior, which are reflected in our set numbers, set interval, and family number. The dynamic forces that each number symbolizes directly affects our perceptions, values, actions, and relationships to others. These forces manifest both in how we perceive our roles in life and in how we perceive the roles of others. By analyzing the interplay between different number energies, we can better understand ourselves and others.

When you combine the numeric identity of any two individuals, there is a dynamic interconnection between their sets. These interconnections are *compatible* when the sets share identical numbers that represent a sociability and receptivity toward others, or when they have differing numbers that supplement or complement each other. The interconnections are *conflicting* when the sets share identical numbers that represent a competition for power and control over others, or when they have differing numbers that misunderstand or misperceive each other.

The dynamics of each set number point both to areas of compatibility and areas of potential conflict, and their numeressences establish the types of interactions they are most likely to have. Each numeric personality has a predictable style of sociability that influences its personal and social interactions. For example, some sets are only comfortable in intimate, one-on-one relationships, whereas others may shy away from such intimate personal exchanges or approach them as confrontations.

Generally, the set numbers are the primary determinants of compatibility, with the family number and set interval following. Some individuals, however, do not seem to belong to their sets. When you encounter such people, look carefully at their family number and set interval, to see which numeressence is the dominant influence. These secondary numbers can sometimes be stronger than set numbers. Typically, a Three/Seven emphasizes the three and seven set number energies. However, in Three/Sevens with certain backgrounds, you might find that their family number "one" energy or their set interval "four" energy is the dominant numeressence. As a result, the normally strong sense of social purpose carried by Three/Sevens may be overpowered by their "one" energy ego and individuality, or by their "four" energy interest in material goods.

Furthermore, characteristics you might expect to find in certain individuals may be hidden or repressed. A member of a set supposedly strongly connected to family relationships may seem to be quite the opposite — usually in reaction to some unpleasant event in the past. Or, the characteristics you expect may simply manifest themselves in unexpected ways. Executive ability, for example, is not limited to the office. It is present in such divergent situations as parenting and athletics. You could miss important details about an individual's numeric dynamics if you limit your interpretation of executive ability to the business world, rather than understanding its more fundamental dynamic: the need to control and lead others.

Overall, sets that share two or more numbers in common with yours tend to attract you. In many cases, sets that have numbers in common with those of your parents may also attract you. My Three/Four mother and my Three/Seven wife, for example, both have the numbers one, three, four, and seven in common. Their numbers predict that they have very similar dynamics (which I can assure you they do), and that I would tend to be attracted to them (I was attracted enough to my Three/Seven to marry her). As a Two/Eight, the important numbers for me are one, two, six, and eight, so my wife and I only have the number one in common, which we share as a family number, but her odd number "three" and "seven" energies complement my even number "two" and "eight" energies to the extent that we have had a long and very happy marriage.

The need for balance between active and reactive forces is one of nature's basic dynamics. You will find that the same dynamic is important in relationships. For example, my important numbers (one, two, six, and eight) form the combination of one odd and three even numbers. In my most important relationships with the opposite sex, I find that, almost instinctively, I have always been attracted to individuals with a three odd and one even combination — the exact opposite, but complementary polarity to mine. My Three/Seven wife, with her three odd and one even number combination, provides the necessary complementary energy to make our relationship a balanced one.

Look carefully at the Set Number Odd and Even Combinations chart, page 117. If your numbers are primarily active (odd numbers) or reactive (even numbers), you'll be most complemented by a mate whose numeressence is your polar opposite. If your numbers are equally balanced between odd and even, you will find an easy compatibility with someone who has complementary numeric energies to your own.

As a rule, the strongest relationships are between sets that share some numbers in common and also have complementary odd and even energies. Be alert, however, to qualitative differences: although members of a set may have shared personality characteristics, how they manifest these characteristics frequently varies. For example, as an experimental, opinionated, bright One/Three, Woody Allen uses his role as an actor and filmmaker to explore and reveal (and also spoof) the variety of human personality types, while Hermann Goering, also a One/Three, used his role as a military leader and politician in Nazi Germany to deny and stifle any human variety that did not fit his plan.

As you begin to grasp how unique you are as an individual, you will realize why you might encounter difficulties in relationships with certain different personality types. As a rule, you will tend to get along well with about two thirds of the sets, and encounter some conflict with the rest. Most conflicts with others will be due to three factors: competition, expectations in behavior, and differences in sensory perceptions. By anticipating these three areas where you are most likely to encounter problems with other sets, you can become skilled in defusing or avoiding conflict with them.

Competition is healthy when it is used to develop your full potential. When it is used for the sake of satisfying questionable expectations, however, or when it is used as a means to control and manipulate others, it can be disastrous. As you look at the numeric personalities of the forty-five sets, you will notice that some sets are deeply involved with the struggle for power and control. If you are a member of one of these sets or if you are attracted to members of one of these sets, bear in mind that mastery of the self is is the ultimate power and control in life.

Expectations regarding the behavior of others can cause great difficulty in your personal life. When you fail to take into account the relative differences among individuals and their priorities, you put yourself unnecessarily into situations of frustration, disappointment, anger, and conflict. Repeated difficulties in this area suggest a very basic and unresolvable incompatibility between individuals.

Differences in sensory perceptions inevitably lead to misunderstandings between individuals. One of the most common errors that you can make with others is to assume that their senses of hearing, smell, taste, touch, sight, and intuition are the same as yours. In fact, the senses are very selective and individual. Some people hear the emotional expression in the rhythms of jazz, while others only hear a jumbled series of discordant tones. Some people rely more on the words they hear than on the actions they see to understand a situation, while others may only look at actions and fail to hear the explanation of those actions. When you are aware of the inevitable differences in the perceptions of others, you can learn to communicate more effectively. For example, Six/Sixes are sensitive to visual stimulation, so pictures and gestures are more useful than words or sounds when interacting with them.

As you uncover the underlying dynamics in your own relationships, you will be able to improve their quality, both among casual acquaintances and intimates. The ideal numeric relationship is one that has similar dynamics to yours as well as differing energies that complement and enhance the areas where your forces are weak.

Numeric Compatibility Numbers and Their Meanings

The nine numeric compatibility numbers represent the types of relationships that tend to exist between the forty-five different sets. No one numeric compatibility number is inherently better or suggests a more compatible relationship than any other. A numeric compatibility number simply describes one of the nine basic relationship paths.

To find the numeric compatibility between yourself and another, refer to the "Tables of Numeric Compatibility Between Sets," page 132. Each of the nine tables represents the relationships between the five sets in a particular number family and all the different sets. Locate your family number and set number in the top panel of one of the nine tables. Next, locate the line in the box below that contains the set number you are interested in. The numbers one through nine running down the left-hand column will be your numeric compatibility number. It symbolizes the type of relationship that tends to exist between the two of you.

To derive your numeric compatibility number mathematically, add the family number of your set to the family number of the set you are curious about. The resulting sum is the numeric compatibility number. If the sum is a double-digit number, reduce it to a single digit. For example, if your family number is five, and the individual you are interested in has a family number of seven, your numeric compatibility number will be three (the sum of five plus seven, or twelve, which reduces to three).

Once you know your numeric compatibility number, you can read the descriptions below to discover the type of relationship you can expect.

— ONE —

A numeric compatibility of one represents a relationship of unity. It emphasizes a strong meaningful connection with a sense of agreement and completeness. Creativity and individuality can flourish in this relationship, yet its overall energy is one of merging together with a harmony of purpose.

— TWO —

A numeric compatibility of two represents a relationship of polarity. Opposite, complementary energies can be stimulating and attractive, and they can generate creative power in both individuals. When they work at cross purposes, opposite energies can pull the relationship apart, but when they are harmonious, these energies can bring tremendous balance and satisfaction to the relationship.

131

TABLES OF NUMERIC COMPATIBILITY BETWEEN SETS

FAMILY NUMBER: 1
Set Numbers:

	1/9	2/8	3/7	4/6	5/5
1	1/8	2/7	3/6	4/5	9/9
2	1/9	2/8	3/7	4/6	5/5
3	1/1	2/9	3/8	4/7	5/6
4	1/2	3/9	4/8	5/7	6/6
5	1/3	2/2	4/9	5/8	6/7
6	1/4	2/3	5/9	6/8	7/7
7	1/5	2/4	3/3	6/9	7/8
8	1/6	2/5	3/4	7/9	8/8
9	1/7	2/6	3/5	4/4	8/9

FAMILY NUMBER: 2
Set Numbers:

	1/1	2/9	3/8	4/7	5/6
1	1/7	2/6	3/5	4/4	8/9
2	1/8	2/7	3/6	4/5	9/9
3	1/9	2/8	3/7	4/6	5/5
4	1/1	2/9	3/8	4/7	5/6
5	1/2	3/9	4/8	5/7	6/6
6	1/3	2/2	4/9	5/8	6/7
7	1/4	2/3	5/9	6/8	7/7
8	1/5	2/4	3/3	6/9	7/8
9	1/6	2/5	3/4	7/9	8/8

FAMILY NUMBER: 3
Set Numbers:

	1/2	3/9	4/8	5/7	6/6
1	1/6	2/5	3/4	7/9	8/8
2	1/7	2/6	3/5	4/4	8/9
3	1/8	2/7	3/6	4/5	9/9
4	1/9	2/8	3/7	4/6	5/5
5	1/1	2/9	3/8	4/7	5/6
6	1/2	3/9	4/8	5/7	6/6
7	1/3	4/9	5/8	2/2	6/7
8	1/4	2/3	5/9	6/8	7/7
9	1/5	2/4	3/3	6/9	7/8

FAMILY NUMBER: 4
Set Numbers:

	1/3	2/2	4/9	5/8	6/7
1	1/5	2/4	3/3	6/9	7/8
2	1/6	2/5	3/4	7/9	8/8
3	1/7	2/6	3/5	4/4	8/9
4	1/8	2/7	3/6	4/5	9/9
5	1/9	2/8	3/7	4/6	5/5
6	1/1	2/9	3/8	4/7	5/6
7	1/2	3/9	4/8	5/7	6/6
8	1/3	2/2	4/9	5/8	6/7
9	1/4	2/3	5/9	6/8	7/7

FAMILY NUMBER: 5
Set Numbers:

	1/4	2/3	5/9	6/8	7/7
1	1/4	2/3	5/9	6/8	7/7
2	1/5	2/4	3/3	6/9	7/8
3	1/6	2/5	3/4	7/9	8/8
4	1/7	2/6	3/5	4/4	8/9
5	1/8	2/7	3/6	4/5	9/9
6	1/9	2/8	3/7	4/6	5/5
7	1/1	2/9	3/8	4/7	5/6
8	1/2	3/9	4/8	5/7	6/6
9	1/3	2/2	4/9	5/8	6/7

FAMILY NUMBER: 6
Set Numbers:

	1/5	2/4	3/3	6/9	7/8
1	1/3	2/2	4/9	5/8	6/7
2	1/4	2/3	5/9	6/8	7/7
3	1/5	2/4	3/3	6/9	7/8
4	1/6	2/5	3/4	7/9	8/8
5	1/7	2/6	3/5	4/4	8/9
6	1/8	2/7	3/6	4/5	9/9
7	1/9	2/8	3/7	4/6	5/5
8	1/1	2/9	3/8	4/7	5/6
9	1/2	3/9	4/8	5/7	6/6

FAMILY NUMBER: 7
Set Numbers:

	1/6	2/5	3/4	7/9	8/8
1	1/2	3/9	4/8	5/7	6/6
2	1/3	2/2	4/9	5/8	6/7
3	1/4	2/3	5/9	6/8	7/7
4	1/5	2/4	3/3	6/9	7/8
5	1/6	2/5	3/4	7/9	8/8
6	1/7	2/6	3/5	4/4	8/9
7	1/8	2/7	3/6	4/5	9/9
8	1/9	2/8	3/7	4/6	5/5
9	1/1	2/9	3/8	4/7	5/6

FAMILY NUMBER: 8
Set Numbers:

	1/7	2/6	3/5	4/4	8/9
1	1/1	2/9	3/8	4/7	5/6
2	1/2	3/9	4/8	5/7	6/6
3	1/3	2/2	4/9	5/8	6/7
4	1/4	2/3	5/9	6/8	7/7
5	1/5	2/4	3/3	6/9	7/8
6	1/6	2/5	3/4	7/9	8/8
7	1/7	2/6	3/5	4/4	8/9
8	1/8	2/7	3/6	4/5	9/9
9	1/9	2/8	3/7	4/6	5/5

FAMILY NUMBER: 9
Set Numbers:

	1/8	2/7	3/6	4/5	9/9
1	1/9	2/8	3/7	4/6	5/5
2	1/1	2/9	3/8	4/7	5/6
3	1/2	3/9	4/8	5/7	6/6
4	1/3	2/2	4/9	5/8	6/7
5	1/4	2/3	5/9	6/8	7/7
6	1/5	2/4	3/3	6/9	7/8
7	1/6	2/5	3/4	7/9	8/8
8	1/7	2/6	3/5	4/4	8/9
9	1/8	2/7	3/6	4/5	9/9

Find the table that has your set number and family number. The numbers 1 through 9 on the left side indicate the numeric compatibility between the set numbers shown across from them and your set number.

— THREE —

A numeric compatibility of three represents a relationship that joins together for the sake of accomplishment. It emphasizes the combining of passions and energies to achieve goals, fulfill common purposes, or reap the rewards of mutual efforts. Working together on tasks and projects — including long-term ones such as life — is what makes this relationship succeed.

— FOUR —

A numeric compatibility of four represents a relationship of definition. Each individual has a specific role to play and functions best working within that role. Hard work and dedication will make this relationship prosper and grow. Emotion plays only a small part in it, and logic controls most actions.

— FIVE —

A numeric compatibility of five represents a relationship of change. Roles and rules shift constantly, which can sometimes cause adversarial or competitive attitudes to develop. If this occurs, conflicts can arise as plans are made and unmade. Otherwise, the relationship frequently passes from one state of being to another, offering tremendous variety and generating great energy.

— SIX —

A numeric compatibility of six represents a relationship of equilibrium. It emphasizes harmony and working together. Generally, individuals in this kind of relationship are surprisingly in tune with each other. Each is able to take on the feelings and energy of the other, sharing a comfortable consensus.

— SEVEN —

A numeric compatibility of seven represents a relationship of inner development. Both individuals find compatibility by sharing their spiritual and moral insights, and exploring their intimate feelings about everything. They seek to understand and establish their connections to the past, present, and future.

— EIGHT —

A numeric compatibility of eight represents a relationship of possessiveness and power. It emphasizes sensuality and the physical comforts in life. Wealth and the accumulation of material possessions can be predominant factors in this relationship.

Pragmatism and a constant desire for more are the basis of its motivation and growth.

— NINE —

A numeric compatibility of nine represents a relationship of universality and completion. It is all-embracing, and fosters both spiritual development and personal achievement. The versatility of interests and abilities in this relationship gives it a well-rounded and solidly grounded feeling.

At the back of the book, you will find several copies of the "Numeric Personality Chart," where you can list the names of the people in your life. You can use the chart for quick reference to an individual's set number, set interval, and family number. As you fill it in, you will start to notice certain repeating numeric patterns among family members, friends, and coworkers. If you wish, you can add your numeric compatibility numbers to this chart under each row's family number. Your numeric compatibility number will be the same for each member of a particular number family.

Social Roles and Their Numeric Dynamics

When you study the number energies at work in any social interaction, you can develop great insight into the roles of others and how your own numeric personality will interact with them. The range in individual dynamics is a broad one, from pious to arrogant, disinterested to zealous, generous to selfish, withdrawn to outgoing. Yet, within families, groups, or organizations, the individuals involved tend to share common and complementary numeric dynamics. These complementary dynamics define and influence social roles and interactions. For example, my wife is an outgoing Three/Seven who shines in social situations, while as a withdrawn Two/Eight, I tend to be a silent observer in the same situations. At the same time, we share the family number, one, and my even set numbers, two and eight, complement her odd set numbers, three and seven. Furthermore, my one-odd-and-three-even number combination perfectly complements her three-odd-and-one-even combination. As a result, although we present ourselves to the world in very different ways, our numeric dynamic is such that we are extremely well suited to each other.

Although numeric dynamics influence social interactions, or relationships between individuals, bear in mind that the relationships themselves often determine which dynamic is emphasized and how it is expressed. For example, the image that an individual presents to the outside world is frequently influenced by the degree of personal success and self-confidence that the individual has achieved. A ruler who has power and privilege will be more confident about revealing and expressing personal dynamics than a powerless dependent might be. In addition, a certain amount of personal style is involved in the way individuals express their numeric dynamics. For example, Elvis Presley and Al Capone, both power-seeking One/Eights, pursued very different paths: Presley chose music and entertainment as a means to capture public attention, while Capone chose crime.

There are four main social roles that are shaped and influenced by numeric dynamics: family relationships; friendly relationships, which includes close friends and intimates; professional relationships, which includes partners, employers, employees, clients, and vendors; and general relationships, which includes day-to-day interactions with casual acquaintances and strangers.

Family relationships are primarily based on shared environments, experiences, and values. Although interactions between family members may undergo changes over the years, the basic numeric dynamics that influence these interactions are present from the start. When you look at family histories, you will often find shared numeric patterns overall, and widely divergent numeric dynamics between close relations. One of the first things you are likely to discover is that, as you perhaps suspected, mothers and fathers do not necessarily love and interact with all their children in the same way, and children do not necessarily love and interact with both parents in the same way. A parent may feel close to one child and view another almost as a stranger, while a child may feel very close to one parent and quite distant from the other, or perhaps distant from both of them. Furthermore, although parents and their children may truly love each other, they may not necessarily share the same interests or instinctive dynamics. How many times does the phrase "I love you, but I just *don't* understand why you..." come up in family discussions?

Generally, different sets express their emotions in different ways and need different levels of attention from others. When you study the number energies that exist between you and your parents or your children, you will understand more clearly how and why you interact the way you do, and how you can enhance the positive interactions while defusing the negative ones. Behavior that can cause a great deal of pain between you and your parents or children can evaporate when you can understand its underlying motivation. For example, my daughter and I have an excellent rapport with each other, but for years we had problems and misunderstandings, the source of which we could not pin down. When we studied the energies of our numeric personalities, however, it became clear to us that our problems were rooted in our different levels of need for my wife's affection, and our need to be the dominant recipient of that affection. Once we understood that our problems were actually due to this unnecessary competition between us, we were able to defuse and eliminate the tension that it created.

Friendly relationships, including intimate ones, are based on real or imagined common interests and experiences. The intensity of these shared interests is one of the most important deciding factors in the strength of the bonds between friends. Intimate relationships are also based on shared interests, but these interests are enhanced by mutual feelings of deep love, and the desire and ability of each individual to meet the emotional, social, and physical needs of the other. By studying the number energies that exist between you and your friends, and between you and your intimate partners, you will find areas that each of you share with or complement in each other, as well as areas that tend to generate tension or friction between you. You will suddenly see why some friends only call you when they want something from you, why some only call when they have something they want to share with you, and why some call for no other reason than to connect with you in friendship.

Generally, analyzing the number energies between you and others can help you better understand the particular dynamics that attract you to them, the levels of attention that you need in your friendly interactions, and the types of attention that your friends need from you. In effect, you can make more informed choices about pursuing certain friendly relationships, or perhaps developing some relationships into more intimate ones.

When you study the influences of numeric dynamics in friendly relationships, be careful to look beyond socially defined stereotypes that may be misleading or inappropriate. For example, if you are a female in one of the sets where strong, active odd numbers predominate, such as One/One, and you hope for the stereotypic dominant male to sweep you off your feet, you may be courting a personal emotional disaster. Many times, alliances between equally dominant individuals can lead to clashing wills and constant competition, rather than harmony and nurturing.

Professional relationships can be greatly enhanced by analyzing the numeric dynamics at work within them. The best business partners — besides being responsible, reliable individuals — are those who have complementary energies to yours, supporting your weak areas and enhancing your strengths. A creative Five/Five textile designer, for example, with neither a background nor a deep interest in the ins and outs of sales, distribution, and accounting, would probably do well to find a disciplined, socially active Two/Four partner. Two/Fours understand the importance of style and creativity, and have the ability to turn a creative effort into a solid business venture.

When you study the numeric personalities of your clients and vendors, you can learn to make your interactions with them more satisfying and successful. Exploring the number energies of your clients can be preliminary market research that will help you target their needs and motivations. Vendors provide the resources that you need in order to satisfy your clients. Understanding the number energies of your vendors enhances your ability to select specialists and consultants with the skills, motivation, and personal dynamics you require.

It is very common for executives to hire employees who share their numeric dynamics, or even belong to their set. As an executive or a boss, you will find that understanding these underlying numeric dynamics can help you enhance your rapport with your employees while defusing disruptive or counterproductive conflicts. You can use your awareness of the numeric personalities to praise or criticize constructively in order to bring out the best in your employees. In return, they will bring out the best in you and your company.

If you are an employee, you can explore the numeric personalities of your boss and your coworkers to discover how they think and where their expectations lie. Thus, you can alert yourself to possible areas of conflict — and avoid them. You will also find areas where you can share and complement their energies to your mutual benefit and advancement.

Be especially careful to look beyond stereotypic roles in professional relationships. The clerk in the mailroom may just turn out to have the perfect numeric dynamics to become a manager in the company. If you, as an employer, fail to see this because you view this person as a clerk, you will deprive yourself and your company of an important asset. Conversely, if you, as the mailroom clerk, fail to go the extra mile to express your talents, you will deprive yourself of a great opportunity.

Satisfaction in your professional relationships ultimately depends on how well your numeric dynamics are suited to your profession and to your role in that profession. Do you prefer to work alone? Do you take direction well? Does change frighten you, or does it excite you? You can use your numbers to help sort these things out, and determine where your talents and skills can flourish and succeed. After all, work is a pleasure when it is something that you really love to do. Two/Sixes, for example, love attention. They are very good communicators and they have a dramatic dynamic that has wide appeal. As a result, they are drawn to storytelling and acting, fields that they shine in, and they are happiest when performing for an audience.

General relationships with casual acquaintances and in day-to-day human encounters may never develop into deeper friendly or professional interactions. Instead of relating blindly to these individuals, however, you can use your knowledge of the forty-five numeric personalities to explore the people you encounter in your life and expand your intuitive understanding and appreciation of the rich diversity of humanity that exists in your world.

Discovering Yourself and Others Through Set Archetypes

The individuals who possess the distinctive traits and personality characteristics of a particular set are its archetypes. When you examine the well-known archetypes who share your set number, you will see many different and creative ways that your numeric energies can be expressed. The more you learn of the brilliance and the folly of the members of your set in their various endeavors, the more clearly you will begin to understand yourself.

Consider the roles that the actors and actresses in your set tend to play, for example. If you are a member of the Four/Five set, look at the dynamics of your fellow Four/Fives Laurence Olivier and Bette Davis to see yourself in action. Whether in their film roles or in real life, these two performers are fond of dramatic effect, and have inevitable conflicts in conventional family relationships. They play to win, but will fight only if winning is assured. They think of themselves as romantics.

Read books or letters written by authors who belong to your set. If you are a Two/Three, feast on the cornucopia of self-examination by Two/Three Anais Nin, or lose yourself in the voluminous journals of Two/Three Winston Churchill. Both of these individuals lived with a constant need for change and drama in their lives, and both suffered from the conflict caused by the desire to be personally successful while being of service to others at the same time.

If you are a One/Nine with an interest in music, listen to your fellow set members Wolfgang Amadeus Mozart and John Lennon. In their exceptional music and in their lives, these people were innovators rather than imitators. Very disciplined in their field (although it may not seem that way to some observers), they functioned from a strong ethical viewpoint and found it difficult to accept personal weakness in themselves.

Exploring your set archetypes and the set archetypes of your friends and family members can also lead you to a greater awareness of the harmonies and conflicts in your relationships. If, for example, you find yourself in constant conflict with your One/Eight father, look at the Rev. Jesse Jackson and performer David Bowie. These men use very different arenas to express their individuality, but they share a strong desire to lead. As One/Eights, they need to control situations, and are dramatic and demanding in their expectations of others. They like to give orders — not take them — and will take great personal or professional risk to have things done their way. By understanding the qualities these men share, you will begin to see more clearly the motivations and desires that are expressed in your relationship with your father.

If you are having emotional conflicts with your mate or partner, try reading novels written by members of that set. If your partner is a Six/Seven, for example, look at the writings of Alexandre Dumas, Iris Murdock, Joyce Carol Oates, and John D. MacDonald. Through the characters they create and the social observations that they make, these writers reveal the dynamics of individuals who constantly strive for a sense of identity, who use their work as their salvation, and who are engaged in a lifelong battle with one of their most powerful foes — themselves.

Television is one of our richest and most readily available sources for the direct observation of the different sets in action. Consider such performers as the One/Five Johnny Carson, who takes risks with his monologues and uses his skill in judging character to bring out the best (or worst) in his guests. Or observe One/Ones Oprah Winfrey and Dolly Parton, who act with conviction and responsibility to their personal ideals, and have clearly gained strength from their struggles with adversity.

When you study the archetypes of each set, look for the underlying motivation at work in each. For example, Ronald Reagan, a conservative political leader, is a Two/Six. Actor Ed Asner, a liberal political activist, is also a Two/Six. If you allow their differing political stances to throw you, you will miss the important Two/Six dynamics that they share. These include a love of power, an absolute conviction in their personal beliefs, a strong sense of personal responsibility for the well-being of humanity, and a tendency to be ruled by feelings over reason.

An enhanced numeric awareness of yourself and others will compel you to adopt a larger viewpoint in your perceptions. You will become more conscious of interpersonal opportunities in your relationships, and more resilient in dealing with adversity and temporary setbacks. Use your own set archetypes as a foundation for developing your full potential.

Part IV of this book, which follows this chapter, contains an extensive alphabetical list of famous (and, in some cases, infamous) individuals. You may want to use some of the names on this list along with one of the numeric personality charts in the Appendix to create a constellation of individuals who excel in occupations to which you aspire, or for whom you have an affinity or likeness-of-mind. The number patterns that result from this kind of experiment can tell you a great deal about yourself and about the directions you might explore in your relationships in order to fulfill your dreams in life.

PART IV

THE NUMERIC PERSONALITIES OF 4,022 FAMOUS AND NOTABLE INDIVIDUALS

NAME	FIELD	SET	MONTH	DAY	YEAR
Aaron, Hank	Sports	2/5	2	5	1934
Abbado, Claudio	Music	6/8	6	26	1923
Abbott, Berenice	Visual Arts	7/8	7	17	1898
Abbott, Bud	Film	1/2	10	2	1895
Abbott, George	Dramatic Arts	6/7	6	25	1887
Abdnor, James	Politics	2/4	2	13	1923
Abdul-Jabbar, Kareem	Sports	4/7	4	16	1947
Abel, Walter	Dramatic Arts	6/6	6	6	1898
Abernathy, Ralph	Politics	2/3	3	11	1926
Abrahams, Mort	Dramatic Arts	3/8	3	26	1916
Abrams, Creighton W.	Military	6/9	9	6	1914
Abrams, Elliott	Politics	1/6	1	24	1948
Abzug, Bella	Politics	6/7	7	24	1920
Acconci, Vito	Visual Arts	1/6	1	24	1940
Ace, Goodman	Entertainment	1/6	1	15	1899
Ace, Jane	Entertainment	2/2	11	11	1900
Acheson, Dean	Politics	2/4	4	11	1893
Adams, Abigail Smith	Politics	2/5	11	23	1744
Adams, Ansel	Visual Arts	2/2	2	20	1902
Adams, Don	Television	1/4	4	19	1927
Adams, Edie	Television	4/7	4	16	1927
Adams, Henry	Literature	2/7	2	16	1838
Adams, Joey	Television	1/6	1	6	1911
Adams, John	President	1/3	10	30	1735
Adams, John Quincy	President	2/7	7	11	1776
Adams, Louisa Catherine	Politics	2/3	2	12	1775
Adams, Maud	Dramatic Arts	2/3	2	12	1945
Adams, Nick	Film	1/7	7	10	1931
Adams, Samuel	Politics	9/9	9	27	1722
Adams, Sherman	Politics	1/8	1	8	1899
Addams, Charles	Visual Arts	1/7	1	7	1912
Addams, Jane	Politics	6/9	9	6	1860
Adderley, Herb	Sports	6/8	6	8	1939
Adderley, Julian (Cannonball)	Music	6/9	9	6	1928
Adelman, Kenneth	Politics	6/9	6	9	1946
Adenauer, Konrad	Politics	1/5	1	5	1876
Adjani, Isabelle	Film	6/9	6	27	1955
Adler, Buddy	Film	4/6	6	22	1909
Adler, Luther	Dramatic Arts	4/5	5	4	1903
Adler, Mortimer J.	Letters	1/3	12	28	1902

NAME	FIELD	SET	MONTH	DAY	YEAR
Adler, Stella	Dramatic Arts	1/2	2	10	1902
Agee, James	Literature	2/9	11	27	1909
Agnew, Spiro	Politics	2/9	11	9	1918
Agronsky, Martin	Television	1/3	1	12	1915
Aherne, Brian	Film	2/5	5	2	1902
Ahn, Philip	Film	2/3	3	29	1911
Aiello, Danny	Film	2/6	6	20	1933
Aiken, Conrad	Literature	5/8	8	5	1889
Aiken, George	Politics	2/8	8	20	1892
Ailey, Alvin	Dance	1/5	1	5	1931
Aimee, Anouk	Film	4/9	4	27	1932
Akins, Claude	Film	5/7	5	25	1918
Akins, Zoë	Literature	1/3	10	30	1886
Albee, Edward	Dramatic Arts	3/3	3	12	1928
Albeniz, Isaac	Music	2/5	5	29	1860
Alberghetti, Anna Maria	Film	5/6	5	15	1936
Albers, Anni	Visual Arts	3/6	6	12	1899
Albers, Josef	Visual Arts	1/3	3	19	1888
Albert, Eddie	Film	4/4	4	22	1908
Albert, Edward	Film	2/2	2	20	1951
Albertson, Jack	Film	6/7	6	16	1910
Albinoni, Tomaso	Music	5/6	6	14	1674
Albright, Lola	Television	2/7	7	20	1924
Alcott, Louisa May	Literature	2/2	11	29	1832
Alda, Alan	Television	1/1	1	28	1936
Aldrin, Edwin (Buzz)	Exploration	1/2	1	20	1930
Alessandri, Jorge	Politics	1/5	5	19	1896
Alexander, Ben	Television	5/8	5	26	1911
Alexander, Grover C.	Sports	2/8	2	26	1887
Alexander, Jane	Film	1/1	10	28	1939
Alexander, Kermit	Sports	1/4	1	4	1941
Alexander, Shana	Letters	1/6	10	6	1925
Alexander the Great	Military	7/7	7	16	B.C. 356
Alfven, Hannes Olof Gösta	Sciences	3/5	5	30	1908
Alger, Horatio	Literature	1/4	1	13	1834
Algren, Nelson	Literature	1/3	3	28	1909
Ali, Muhammad	Sports	1/9	1	18	1942
Alioto, Joseph	Law	2/3	2	12	1916
Allen, Dick	Sports	3/8	3	8	1942
Allen, Ethan	Politics	1/1	1	10	1738

NAME	FIELD	SET	MONTH	DAY	YEAR
Allen, Fred	Entertainment	4/5	5	31	1894
Allen, George H.	Sports	2/4	4	29	1922
Allen, Gracie	Television	7/8	7	26	1899
Allen, Karen	Film	1/5	10	5	1951
Allen, Marcus	Sports	3/8	3	26	1960
Allen, Marty	Entertainment	3/5	3	23	1922
Allen, Mel	Television	2/5	2	14	1913
Allen, Nancy	Film	6/6	6	24	1950
Allen, Peter	Music	1/2	2	10	1944
Allen, Steve	Television	3/8	12	26	1921
Allen, William P.	Business	1/9	9	1	1900
Allen, Woody	Film	1/3	12	1	1935
Allison, Bobby	Sports	2/3	12	2	1937
Allison, Fran	Television	2/2	11	20	1907
Allison, Mose	Music	2/2	11	11	1927
Allman, Gregg	Music	3/7	12	7	1947
Allyson, June	Film	1/7	10	7	1917
Alma-Tadema, Lawrence	Visual Arts	1/8	1	8	1836
Alonso, Alicia	Dance	3/3	12	21	1921
Alpert, Herb	Music	3/4	3	31	1935
Alsop, Joseph W., Jr.	Letters	1/2	10	11	1910
Alsop, Stewart J.	Letters	5/8	5	17	1914
Altman, Robert	Film	1/2	2	28	1922
Alvarez, Luís W.	Sciences	4/6	6	13	1911
Alworth, Lance	Sports	3/8	8	3	1940
Alzado, Lyle	Sports	3/4	4	3	1949
Amado, Jorge	Literature	1/8	8	10	1912
Ambler, Eric	Literature	1/6	6	28	1909
Amdahl, Gene Myron	Sciences	2/7	11	16	1922
Ameche, Don	Film	4/5	5	31	1908
Ames, Ed	Music	7/9	7	9	1927
Ames, Gene	Music	2/4	2	13	1925
Ames, Joe	Music	3/5	5	3	1924
Ames, Leon	Film	1/2	1	20	1903
Ames, Vic	Music	2/5	5	20	1926
Amis, Kingsley	Literature	4/7	4	16	1922
Amory, Cleveland	Litcrature	2/9	9	2	1917
Ampère, Andre M.	Sciences	1/4	1	22	1775
Amsterdam, Morey	Television	3/5	12	14	1914
Anders, William A.	Exploration	1/8	10	17	1933

NAME	FIELD	SET	MONTH	DAY	YEAR
Andersen, Hans Christian	Literature	2/4	4	2	1805
Anderson, Broncho Billy	Film	3/3	3	21	1882
Anderson, Donny	Sports	3/4	4	3	1949
Anderson, Eddie (Rochester)	Television	9/9	9	18	1905
Anderson, Eric	Music	2/5	2	14	1943
Anderson, Ian	Music	1/8	8	10	1947
Anderson, Jack	Letters	1/1	10	19	1922
Anderson, Judith	Dramatic Arts	1/2	2	10	1898
Anderson, Ken	Sports	2/6	2	15	1949
Anderson, Laurie	Dramatic Arts	5/6	6	5	1947
Anderson, Marian	Music	2/8	2	17	1902
Anderson, Maxwell	Literature	3/6	12	15	1888
Anderson, Melissa Sue	Television	8/9	9	26	1962
Anderson, Robert	Literature	4/6	6	4	1917
Anderson, Sherwood	Literature	4/9	9	13	1876
Anderson, Sparky	Sports	2/4	2	22	1934
Andersson, Bibi	Film	2/2	11	11	1935
Andress, Ursula	Film	1/3	3	19	1936
Andretti, Mario	Sports	1/2	2	28	1940
Andrews, Dana	Film	1/1	1	1	1909
Andrews, Julie	Film	1/1	10	1	1935
Andrews, LaVerne	Music	6/7	7	6	1916
Andrews, Maxene	Music	1/3	1	3	1918
Andrews, Patti	Music	2/7	2	16	1920
Andropov, Yuri	Politics	6/6	6	15	1914
Angeles, Victoria de los	Music	1/2	11	1	1924
Angeli, Pier	Film	1/6	6	19	1932
Angelou, Maya	Literature	4/4	4	4	1928
Ångström, Anders	Sciences	4/8	8	13	1814
Anka, Paul	Music	3/7	7	30	1941
Ann-Margret	Film	1/4	4	28	1941
Annabella	Film	5/7	7	14	1912
Anouilh, Jean	Literature	5/6	6	23	1910
Ansermet, Ernest	Music	2/2	11	11	1883
Ant, Adam	Music	2/3	11	3	1954
Anthony, Earl	Sports	4/9	4	27	1938
Anthony, Ray	Music	1/2	1	20	1922
Anthony, Susan B.	Politics	2/6	2	15	1920
Anton, Susan	Film	1/3	10	12	1950
Antonioni, Michelangelo	Film	2/9	9	29	1912

NAME	FIELD	SET	MONTH	DAY	YEAR
Apollinaire, Guillaume	Literature	8/8	8	26	1880
Appel, Karel	Visual Arts	4/7	4	25	1921
Appleseed, Johnny	Exploration	8/9	9	26	1774
Appling, Luke	Sports	2/4	4	2	1907
Aquino, Corazon	Politics	1/7	1	25	1933
Arbuckle, Fatty	Film	3/6	3	24	1887
Arcaro, Eddie	Sports	1/2	2	19	1916
Archer, Anne	Film	7/8	8	25	1950
Archerd, Army	Letters	1/4	1	13	1919
Arden, Elizabeth	Business	3/4	12	31	1891
Arden, Eve	Film	3/4	4	30	1912
Arendt, Chris	Sports	4/5	5	13	1961
Ariosto, Lodovico	Literature	8/9	9	8	1474
Ariyoshi, George	Politics	3/3	3	12	1926
Arkin, Alan	Film	3/8	3	26	1934
Arkoff, Samuel Z.	Film	3/6	6	12	1918
Arlen, Harold	Music	2/6	2	15	1905
Arlen, Richard	Film	1/9	9	1	1898
Arliss, George	Film	1/4	4	1	1868
Armstrong, Bess	Dramatic Arts	2/3	12	11	1953
Armstrong, Herbert W.	Religion	4/7	7	31	1892
Armstrong, Louis	Music	4/7	7	4	1900
Armstrong, Neil	Exploration	4/8	8	4	1930
Arnaz, Desi	Television	2/3	3	2	1917
Arnaz, Desi, Jr.	Television	1/1	1	19	1953
Arnaz, Lucie	Television	7/8	7	17	1951
Arness, James	Television	5/8	5	26	1923
Arno, Peter	Visual Arts	1/8	1	8	1904
Arnold, Benedict	Military	1/5	1	14	1741
Arp, Jean	Visual Arts	7/9	9	16	1887
Arquette, Cliff	Television	1/3	12	28	1905
Arquette, Rosanna	Film	1/8	8	10	1959
Arrau, Claudio	Music	2/6	2	6	1903
Arthur, Beatrice	Television	4/5	5	13	1926
Arthur, Chester A.	President	1/5	10	5	1830
Arthur, Ellen	Politics	3/8	8	30	1837
Arthur, Jean	Film	1/8	10	17	1905
Asch, Sholem	Literature	1/2	11	1	1880
Ashe, Arthur	Sports	1/7	7	10	1943
Ashkenazy, Vladimir	Music	6/7	7	6	1937

NAME	FIELD	SET	MONTH	DAY	YEAR
Ashley, Elizabeth	Film	3/8	8	30	1939
Asimov, Isaac	Literature	1/2	1	2	1920
Asner, Ed	Television	2/6	11	15	1929
Aspin, Leslie, Jr.	Politics	3/7	7	21	1938
Assante, Armand	Television	1/4	10	4	1949
Astaire, Adele	Dance	1/9	9	10	1897
Astaire, Fred	Film	1/5	5	10	1899
Astin, John	Television	3/3	3	30	1930
Astin, Patty Duke	Film	3/5	12	14	1947
Astor, John Jacob	Business	7/8	7	17	1763
Astor, Mary	Film	3/5	5	3	1906
Ates, Roscoe	Film	1/2	1	20	1892
Atkins, Chet	Music	2/6	6	20	1924
Atlas, Charles	Sports	1/3	10	30	1893
Attenborough, Richard	Film	2/8	8	29	1923
Attlee, Clement	Politics	1/3	1	3	1883
Atwill, Lionel	Film	1/3	3	1	1885
Atwood, Donna	Dance	2/5	2	14	1923
Auberjonois, Rene	Dramatic Arts	1/6	6	1	1940
Auchincloss, Louis	Literature	9/9	9	27	1917
Auden, W. H.	Literature	2/3	2	21	1907
Audubon, John J.	Sciences	4/8	4	26	1785
Auer, Mischa	Film	2/8	11	17	1905
Aumont, Jean-Pierre	Film	1/5	1	5	1913
Austen, Jane	Literature	3/7	12	16	1775
Austin, Stephen F.	Politics	2/3	11	3	1793
Austin, Tracy	Sports	2/3	12	2	1962
Autry, Gene	Film	2/9	9	29	1907
Avalon, Frankie	Music	9/9	9	18	1939
Avery, Milton	Visual Arts	3/7	3	7	1893
Avogadro, Amedeo	Sciences	6/9	6	9	1776
Axton, Hoyt	Film	3/7	3	25	1938
Ayatola Ruholla Khomeini	Politics	5/8	5	17	1900
Aykroyd, Dan	Film	1/7	7	1	1952
Ayres, Lew	Film	1/3	12	28	1908
Ayres, Mitchell	Music	3/6	12	24	1910
Aznavour, Charles	Music	4/5	5	22	1924
Baba, Meher	Literature	2/7	2	25	1894
Babashoff, Shirley	Sports	1/4	1	31	1957
Babbage, Charles	Sciences	3/8	12	26	1792

NAME	FIELD	SET	MONTH	DAY	YEAR
Babbitt, Bruce	Politics	6/9	6	27	1938
Bacall, Lauren	Film	7/9	9	16	1924
Bach, Barbara	Film	8/9	8	27	1949
Bach, Carl P. E.	Music	3/8	3	8	1714
Bach, Catherine	Film	1/3	3	1	1954
Bach, Johann Christian	Music	5/9	9	5	1735
Bach, Johann Sebastian	Music	3/3	3	21	1685
Bacharach, Burt	Music	3/5	5	12	1929
Backus, Jim	Television	2/7	2	25	1913
Bacon, Francis	Visual Arts	1/1	10	28	1909
Bacon, Francis	Literature	1/4	1	22	1561
Baddeley, Hermione	Dramatic Arts	2/4	11	13	1906
Baer, Max, Jr.	Television	3/4	12	4	1937
Baer, Max, Sr.	Sports	2/2	2	11	1909
Baez, Joan	Music	1/9	1	9	1941
Bagnold, Enid	Literature	1/9	10	27	1889
Bailey, F. Lee	Law	6/9	6	18	1933
Bailey, Pearl	Music	2/3	3	29	1918
Bain, Barbara	Television	2/4	2	4	1923
Bainter, Fay	Film	3/7	3	7	1892
Baio, Scott	Television	4/9	9	22	1961
Baird, Bil	Entertainment	6/8	8	15	1904
Baker, Carroll	Film	1/5	5	28	1931
Baker, Diane	Film	2/7	2	25	1938
Baker, Dusty	Sports	6/6	6	15	1949
Baker, Howard H., Jr.	Politics	2/6	11	15	1925
Baker, James A.	Politics	5/8	8	14	1925
Baker, Joe Don	Film	2/3	2	12	1936
Baker, Josephine	Entertainment	3/6	6	3	1906
Baker, Kenny	Music	3/9	9	30	1912
Baker, Samuel Aaron	Politics	2/7	11	7	1874
Baker, Stanley	Film	1/2	2	28	1927
Bakker, Jim	Religion	1/2	1	2	1940
Bakst, Léon	Visual Arts	1/5	5	10	1866
Balanchine, George	Dance	1/9	1	9	1904
Baldwin, Faith	Literature	1/1	10	1	1893
Baldwin, James	Literature	2/8	8	2	1924
Ball, George W.	Politics	3/3	12	21	1909
Ball, Lucille	Television	6/8	8	6	1910
Balla, Giacomo	Visual Arts	6/7	7	24	1871

NAME	FIELD	SET	MONTH	DAY	YEAR
Ballard, Kaye	Dramatic Arts	2/2	11	20	1926
Ballard, Robert	Exploration	3/6	6	30	1942
Balsam, Martin	Film	2/4	11	4	1919
Balthus	Visual Arts	2/2	2	29	1908
Balzac, Honoré de	Literature	2/5	5	20	1799
Bancroft, Anne	Dramatic Arts	8/9	9	17	1931
Bancroft, George	Film	3/9	9	30	1882
Bankhead, Tallulah	Dramatic Arts	1/4	1	31	1902
Banks, Ernie	Sports	1/4	1	31	1931
Banky, Vilma	Film	1/9	1	9	1898
Bara, Theda	Film	2/7	7	20	1890
Barber, Red	Television	2/8	2	17	1908
Barber, Samuel	Music	3/9	3	9	1910
Bardot, Brigitte	Film	2/9	9	29	1933
Barenboim, Daniel	Music	2/6	11	15	1942
Bari, Lynn	Film	3/9	12	18	1917
Barker, Bob	Television	3/3	12	12	1923
Barker, Lex	Film	5/8	5	8	1919
Barlach, Ernst	Visual Arts	1/2	1	2	1870
Barnard, Christiaan	Sciences	1/8	10	8	1922
Barnes, Djuna	Literature	3/6	6	12	1892
Barnet, Will	Visual Arts	5/7	5	25	1911
Barnum, P. T.	Entertainment	5/7	7	5	1810
Barrett, Rona	Letters	1/8	10	8	1936
Barrie, Barbara	Film	5/5	5	23	1931
Barrie, James M.	Literature	5/9	5	9	1860
Barrie, Mona	Film	3/9	12	18	1909
Barrie, Wendy	Dramatic Arts	4/8	4	8	1912
Barrow, Clyde	Crime	3/6	3	24	1909
Barry, Gene	Television	4/6	6	4	1922
Barry, Jack	Television	2/3	3	20	1918
Barry, Rick	Sports	1/3	3	28	1944
Barrymore, Diana	Film	3/3	3	3	1921
Barrymore, Ethel	Film	6/8	8	15	1879
Barrymore, John	Film	2/6	2	15	1882
Barrymore, John Drew	Film	6/6	6	24	1932
Barrymore, Lionel	Film	1/4	4	28	1878
Barthelme, Donald	Literature	4/7	4	7	1931
Bartholomew, Freddie	Film	1/3	3	28	1924
Bartók, Béla	Music	3/7	3	25	1881

NAME	FIELD	SET	MONTH	DAY	YEAR
Bartok, Eva	Film	6/9	6	18	1929
Barton, Clara	Sciences	3/7	12	25	1821
Barty, Billy	Film	1/7	10	25	1924
Baryshnikov, Mikhail	Dance	1/1	1	28	1948
Basehart, Richard	Film	4/8	8	31	1914
Basie, William (Count)	Music	3/8	8	21	1904
Basinger, Kim	Film	3/8	12	8	1953
Bassey, Shirley	Music	1/8	1	8	1937
Bateman, Jason	Television	1/5	1	14	1969
Bateman, Justine	Television	1/2	2	19	1966
Bates, Alan	Film	2/8	2	17	1930
Batista, Fulgencio	Politics	1/7	1	16	1901
Baudelaire, Charles	Literature	4/9	4	9	1821
Bauer, Hank	Sports	4/7	7	31	1922
Baum, L. Frank	Literature	5/6	5	15	1856
Bausch, Pina	Dance	7/9	7	27	1940
Baxter, Anne	Film	5/7	5	7	1923
Baxter, Warner	Film	2/3	3	29	1889
Baylor, Elgin	Sports	8/9	9	17	1934
Beach, Sylvia	Literature	3/5	3	14	1887
Beamon, Bob	Sports	2/8	8	2	1946
Bean, Orson	Entertainment	4/7	7	22	1928
Beard, James	Letters	5/5	5	5	1903
Beardsley, Aubrey	Visual Arts	3/8	8	21	1872
Beaton, Cecil	Visual Arts	1/5	1	14	1904
Beattie, Ann	Literature	8/9	9	8	1947
Beatty, Clyde	Entertainment	1/6	6	10	1903
Beatty, Ned	Film	6/7	7	6	1937
Beatty, Warren	Film	3/3	3	30	1937
Beaumarchais, Pierre A. C. de	Literature	1/6	1	24	1732
Beauvoir, Simone de	Literature	1/9	1	9	1908
Bechet, Sidney	Music	5/5	5	14	1947
Beck, Jeff	Music	6/6	6	24	1944
Becker, Boris	Sports	2/4	11	22	1967
Beckett, Samuel	Literature	4/4	4	13	1906
Beckmann, Max	Visual Arts	2/3	2	12	1884
Bedelia, Bonnie	Film	3/7	3	25	1948
Bedford, Brian	Dramatic Arts	2/7	2	16	1935
Beebe, William	Exploration	2/7	7	29	1877
Beerbohm, Max	Literature	6/8	8	24	1872

NAME	FIELD	SET	MONTH	DAY	YEAR
Beery, Noah, Jr.	Film	1/8	8	10	1916
Beery, Wallace	Film	2/4	4	11	1881
Beethoven, Ludwig van	Music	3/7	12	16	1770
Begin, Menachem	Politics	7/8	8	16	1913
Begley, Ed	Film	3/7	3	25	1901
Begley, Ed, Jr.	Film	7/9	9	16	1949
Behrens, Hildegard	Music	2/9	2	9	1937
Bel Geddes, Barbara	Film	1/4	10	31	1922
Belafonte, Harry	Music	1/3	3	1	1927
Belanger, François	Visual Arts	3/4	4	12	1744
Belasco, David	Dramatic Arts	7/7	7	25	1854
Bell, Alexander Graham	Sciences	3/3	3	3	1847
Bell, Rex	Film	1/7	10	16	1905
Bellamy, Ralph	Film	6/8	6	17	1904
Beller, Kathleen	Dramatic Arts	1/2	2	10	1955
Belli, Melvin M.	Law	1/7	7	19	1907
Belloc, Hilaire	Literature	7/9	7	27	1870
Bellow, Saul	Literature	1/6	6	10	1915
Belmondo, Jean-Paul	Film	4/9	4	9	1933
Belushi, Jim	Film	6/6	6	15	1954
Belushi, John	Film	1/6	1	24	1948
Ben-Gurion, David	Politics	3/7	12	16	1886
Benatar, Pat	Music	1/1	1	10	1953
Bench, Johnny	Sports	3/7	12	7	1947
Benchley, Peter	Literature	5/8	5	8	1940
Benchley, Robert	Literature	6/9	9	15	1889
Bendix, William	Film	1/5	1	14	1906
Benèt, Stephen Vincent	Literature	4/7	7	22	1898
Benjamin, Richard	Film	4/5	5	22	1938
Bennett, Constance	Film	1/4	10	22	1904
Bennett, Joan	Film	2/9	2	27	1910
Bennett, Michael	Dramatic Arts	4/8	4	8	1943
Bennett, Robert Russell	Music	6/6	6	15	1894
Bennett, Tony	Music	3/8	8	3	1926
Benny, Jack	Television	2/5	2	14	1894
Benson, George	Music	3/4	3	22	1943
Benson, Robby	Film	1/3	1	21	1956
Bentley, John	Television	2/3	12	2	1916
Benton, Barbi	Entertainment	1/1	1	28	1950
Benton, Thomas Hart	Visual Arts	6/8	8	15	1889

NAME	FIELD	SET	MONTH	DAY	YEAR
Berenson, Marisa	Film	2/6	2	15	1948
Berg, Alban	Music	2/9	2	9	1885
Bergen, Candice	Film	5/9	5	9	1946
Bergen, Edgar	Entertainment	2/7	2	16	1903
Bergen, Polly	Television	4/7	7	4	1930
Berger, Helmut	Film	2/5	5	29	1944
Bergman, Ingmar	Film	5/7	7	14	1918
Bergman, Ingrid	Film	3/8	8	21	1915
Berle, Milton	Television	3/7	7	12	1908
Berlin, Irving	Music	2/5	5	11	1888
Berman, Lazar	Music	2/8	2	26	1930
Berman, Shelley	Entertainment	2/3	2	3	1924
Bernardi, Herschel	Dramatic Arts	1/1	10	28	1922
Bernsen, Corbin	Television	7/9	9	7	1951
Bernstein, Elmer	Music	4/4	4	4	1922
Bernstein, Leonard	Music	7/8	8	25	1918
Berra, Yogi	Sports	3/5	5	12	1925
Berrigan, Daniel	Religion	5/9	5	9	1921
Berrigan, Philip	Religion	1/5	10	5	1923
Berry, Chuck	Music	1/9	10	18	1926
Bertinelli, Valerie	Television	4/5	4	23	1960
Bessemer, Henry	Sciences	1/1	1	19	1813
Beymer, Richard	Film	2/3	2	21	1939
Bhutto, Benazir	Politics	3/6	6	21	1953
Biaggi, Mario N.	Politics	1/8	10	26	1917
Biberman, Abner	Film	1/4	4	1	1909
Bickford, Charles	Film	1/1	1	1	1889
Biden, Joseph R., Jr.	Politics	2/2	11	20	1942
Bieber, Owen	Politics	1/3	12	28	1929
Bierce, Ambrose	Letters	6/6	6	24	1842
Bierstadt, Albert	Visual Arts	1/7	1	7	1830
Bikel, Theodore	Music	2/5	5	2	1924
Biletnikoff, Frederick	Sports	2/5	2	23	1943
Bill, Tony	Film	5/8	8	23	1940
Billingsley, Barbara	Television	3/4	12	22	1922
Billingsley, Sherman	Business	1/3	3	10	1900
Binet, Alfred	Sciences	1/9	10	18	1911
Bird, Larry	Sports	3/7	12	7	1956
Birney, David	Television	4/5	4	23	1939
Bishop, Elizabeth	Literature	2/8	2	8	1911

NAME	FIELD	SET	MONTH	DAY	YEAR
Bishop Fulton Sheen	Religion	5/8	5	8	1885
Bishop, Joey	Entertainment	2/3	2	3	1918
Bismarck, Otto von	Military	1/4	4	1	1815
Bisset, Jacqueline	Film	4/9	9	13	1944
Bixby, Bill	Television	1/4	1	22	1934
Bizet, Georges	Music	1/7	10	25	1838
Black, Karen	Film	1/7	7	1	1942
Blackmun, Henry	Politics	2/3	11	12	1908
Blades, Ruben	Music	7/7	7	16	1948
Blaine, Vivian	Film	2/3	11	21	1932
Blair, Janet	Film	4/5	4	23	1921
Blair, Linda	Film	1/4	1	22	1959
Blake, Amanda	Television	2/2	2	20	1931
Blake, Eubie	Music	2/7	2	7	1883
Blake, Robert	Film	9/9	9	18	1933
Blake, William	Visual Arts	1/2	11	28	1757
Blakelock, Ralph	Visual Arts	1/6	10	15	1847
Blakely, Susan	Television	7/9	9	7	1948
Blakey, Art	Music	1/2	10	11	1919
Blanc, Mel	Entertainment	3/5	5	30	1908
Blanda, George	Sports	8/9	9	17	1927
Blass, Bill	Design	4/6	6	22	1922
Bleyer, Archie	Business	3/6	6	12	1909
Bloch, Ray	Music	3/8	8	3	1902
Blocker, Dan	Television	1/3	12	10	1932
Blondell, Joan	Film	3/8	8	30	1909
Bloom, Claire	Dramatic Arts	2/6	2	15	1931
Bloomingdale, Alfred	Business	4/6	4	15	1916
Blount, Mel	Sports	1/4	4	10	1948
Blue, Ben	Film	3/9	9	12	1901
Blue, Vida	Sports	1/7	7	28	1949
Blyth, Ann	Film	7/8	8	16	1928
Bobo, Willie	Music	1/2	2	28	1934
Boccherini, Luigi	Music	1/2	2	19	1743
Boesak, Allan	Politics	2/5	2	23	1945
Bogan, Louise	Literature	2/8	8	11	1897
Bogarde, Dirk	Film	1/3	3	28	1920
Bogart, Humphrey	Film	1/5	1	23	1899
Bogdanovich, Peter	Film	3/7	7	30	1939
Boggs, Wade	Sports	6/6	6	15	1958

NAME	FIELD	SET	MONTH	DAY	YEAR
Böhm, Karl	Music	1/8	8	28	1894
Bohr, Niels	Sciences	1/7	10	7	1885
Boles, John	Film	1/9	10	27	1895
Bolger, Ray	Dance	1/1	1	10	1904
Bolívar, Simón	Military	6/7	7	24	1783
Bols, Ferdinand	Visual Arts	6/6	6	24	1616
Bonaparte, Josephine	Politics	5/6	6	23	1763
Bonaparte, Napoleon	Military	6/8	8	15	1769
Bond, Julian	Politics	1/5	1	14	1940
Bond, Ward	Film	4/9	4	9	1903
Bondi, Beulah	Film	3/5	5	3	1892
Bonet, Lisa	Television	2/7	11	16	1967
Bonheur, Rosa	Visual Arts	3/7	3	16	1822
Bonnard, Pierre	Visual Arts	1/3	10	3	1867
Bonney, William (Billy the Kid)	Crime	2/5	11	23	1859
Bono, Sonny	Music	2/7	2	16	1935
Boole, George	Sciences	2/2	11	2	1815
Boone, Debby	Music	4/9	9	31	1956
Boone, Pat	Music	1/6	6	1	1934
Boone, Randy	†elevision	1/8	1	17	1942
Boone, Richard	Television	6/9	6	18	1916
Boorman, John	Film	1/9	1	18	1933
Booth, John Wilkes	Crime	1/5	5	10	1838
Booth, Shirley	Dramatic Arts	3/8	8	30	1907
Borg, Bjorn	Sports	6/6	6	6	1956
Borge, Victor	Entertainment	1/3	1	3	1908
Borges, Jorge Luís	Literature	6/8	8	24	1899
Borgnine, Ernest	Film	1/6	1	24	1915
Borman, Frank	Exploration	3/5	3	14	1928
Borodin, Aleksandr	Music	2/3	11	12	1834
Bosley, Tom	Television	1/1	10	1	1927
Bossey, Mike	Sports	1/4	1	22	1957
Boston, Ralph	Business	5/9	5	9	1939
Bostwick, Barry	Television	2/6	2	24	1945
Boswell, Connee	Music	3/3	12	3	1907
Boswell, James	Literature	1/2	10	29	1740
Bottoms, Joseph	Film	4/4	4	22	1954
Bottoms, Sam	Film	1/8	10	17	1955
Bottoms, Timothy	Film	3/8	8	30	1954
Boucher, François	Visual Arts	2/9	9	29	1703

NAME	FIELD	SET	MONTH	DAY	YEAR
Bouguereau, Adolphe William	Visual Arts	2/3	11	30	1825
Bourke-White, Margaret	Visual Arts	5/6	6	14	1906
Bowen, Elizabeth	Literature	6/7	6	7	1899
Bowen, Otis	Politics	2/8	2	26	1918
Bowie, David	Music	1/8	1	8	1947
Bowles, Chester	Politics	4/5	4	5	1901
Bowman, Lee	Film	1/3	12	28	1914
Boy George	Music	5/6	6	14	1961
Boyd, Jimmy	Music	1/9	1	9	1940
Boyd, William	Film	5/6	6	5	1895
Boyer, Charles	Film	1/8	8	28	1899
Boyle, Peter	Film	1/9	10	18	1933
Boyle, Robert	Sciences	1/7	1	25	1627
Bracken, Eddie	Film	2/7	2	7	1920
Bradlee, Ben	Publishing	8/8	8	26	1921
Bradley, Bill	Politics	1/7	7	28	1943
Bradley, Omar	Military	2/3	2	12	1893
Bradley, Tom	Politics	2/3	12	29	1917
Bradshaw, Terry	Sports	2/8	8	2	1948
Brady, Jane E.	Literature	1/5	5	19	1941
Brady, Scott	Film	4/9	9	13	1924
Brahe, Tycho	Sciences	3/5	12	14	1546
Brahms, Johannes	Music	5/7	5	7	1883
Braille, Louis	Sciences	1/4	1	4	1809
Brancusi, Constantin	Visual Arts	2/3	2	21	1876
Brand, Neville	Film	4/8	8	13	1921
Brand, Oscar	Music	2/7	2	7	1920
Brando, Marlon	Film	3/4	4	3	1924
Brandt, Willy	Politics	3/9	12	18	1913
Braque, Georges	Visual Arts	4/5	5	13	1882
Brazzi, Rossano	Film	9/9	9	18	1916
Brecht, Bertolt	Dramatic Arts	1/2	2	10	1898
Brennan, Eileen	Dramatic Arts	3/9	9	3	1935
Brennan, Walter	Film	7/7	7	25	1894
Brenner, David	Entertainment	2/4	2	4	1945
Brett, George	Sports	5/6	5	15	1953
Brett, Jeremy	Dramatic Arts	2/3	11	3	1935
Brewer, Teresa	Music	5/7	5	7	1931
Breytenbach, Breyten Poe	Politics	7/9	9	16	1939
Brezhnev, Leonid	Politics	1/3	12	19	1906

NAME	FIELD	SET	MONTH	DAY	YEAR
Brian, David	Television	5/8	8	5	1914
Brice, Fanny	Entertainment	1/2	10	29	1891
Bridges, Beau	Film	3/9	12	9	1941
Bridges, Jeff	Film	3/4	12	4	1949
Bridges, Lloyd	Television	1/6	1	15	1913
Bridges, Styles	Politics	9/9	9	9	1898
Brinkley, David	Television	1/7	7	10	1920
Britten, Benjamin	Music	2/4	11	22	1913
Broca, Paul	Sciences	1/6	6	28	1824
Brock, Lou	Sports	6/9	6	18	1939
Brokaw, Tom	Television	2/6	2	6	1940
Brolin, James	Television	7/9	7	18	1942
Bronson, Charles	Film	2/3	11	3	1921
Brontë, Anne	Literature	1/8	1	17	1820
Brontë, Charlotte	Literature	3/4	4	21	1861
Brontë, Emily	Literature	3/7	7	30	1818
Brook, Clive	Dramatic Arts	1/6	6	1	1886
Brooke, Rupert	Literature	3/8	8	3	1887
Brooks, Albert	Film	4/7	7	22	1947
Brooks, Gwendolyn	Literature	6/8	6	17	1917
Brooks, Mel	Film	1/6	6	28	1926
Brothers, Joyce	Psychology	1/2	10	20	1928
Browder, Earl	Politics	2/5	5	2	1891
Brown, Georgia	Dramatic Arts	1/3	10	21	1933
Brown, Helen Gurley	Publishing	2/9	2	18	1922
Brown, James	Music	3/5	5	3	1928
Brown, Jerry	Politics	4/7	4	7	1938
Brown, Jim	Sports	2/8	2	17	1935
Brown, Joe E.	Film	1/7	7	28	1891
Brown, John	Politics	5/9	5	9	1800
Brown, Johnny Mack	Film	1/9	9	1	1904
Brown, Les	Music	3/5	3	14	1912
Brown, Pat	Politics	3/4	4	21	1905
Brown, Paul	Sports	7/9	7	9	1908
Browne, Jackson	Music	1/9	10	9	1950
Browning, Elizabeth Barrett	Literature	3/6	3	6	1806
Browning, Robert	Literature	5/7	5	7	1812
Brubeck, Dave	Music	3/6	12	6	1930
Bruce, Lenny	Entertainment	1/4	10	13	1925
Bruch, Max	Music	1/6	1	6	1838

NAME	FIELD	SET	MONTH	DAY	YEAR
Bruckner, Anton	Music	4/9	9	4	1824
Bryan, William Jennings	Politics	1/3	3	19	1860
Bryant, Anita	Music	3/7	3	25	1940
Bryant, Paul (Bear)	Sports	2/9	9	11	1913
Bryant, W. C.	Literature	2/3	11	3	1794
Buber, Martin	Philosophy	2/8	2	8	1878
Buchan, John	Literature	8/8	8	26	1875
Buchanan, Edgar	Film	3/3	3	21	1902
Buchanan, James	President	3/3	4	23	1791
Buchholz, Horst	Film	3/4	12	4	1933
Buchwald, Art	Letters	1/2	10	20	1925
Buck, Pearl S.	Literature	6/8	6	26	1892
Buckley, William F.	Letters	2/6	11	24	1925
Buffett, Jimmy	Music	3/7	12	25	1946
Bugatti, Ettore	Design	6/9	9	15	1881
Bugliosi, Vincent T.	Law	8/9	8	18	1934
Bujold, Genevieve	Film	1/7	7	1	1942
Bulfinch, Charles	Visual Arts	8/8	8	8	1763
Bulfinch, Thomas	Letters	6/7	7	15	1796
Bumbry, Grace	Music	1/4	1	4	1937
Bunche, Ralph	Politics	7/8	8	7	1904
Bundy, McGeorge	Politics	3/3	3	30	1919
Bunker, Ellsworth	Politics	2/5	5	11	1894
Bunsen, Robert von	Sciences	3/3	3	21	1811
Buñuel, Luis	Film	2/4	2	22	1900
Bunyan, John	Literature	2/9	11	27	1628
Burbank, Luther	Sciences	3/7	3	7	1849
Burchfield, Charles	Visual Arts	4/9	4	9	1893
Burgess, Anthony	Literature	2/7	2	25	1917
Burgess, Thornton	Literature	1/4	1	4	1874
Burke, Arleigh	Military	1/1	10	19	1901
Burke, Billie	Film	7/8	8	7	1884
Burne-Jones, Edward	Visual Arts	1/8	8	28	1833
Burnett, Carol	Television	4/8	4	26	1933
Burns, George	Entertainment	1/2	1	20	1896
Burns, Robert	Literature	1/7	1	25	1759
Burr, Aaron	Politics	2/6	2	6	1756
Burr, Raymond	Television	3/3	3	21	1917
Burroughs, Edgar Rice	Literature	1/9	9	1	1875
Burroughs, William S.	Literature	2/5	2	5	1914

NAME	FIELD	SET	MONTH	DAY	YEAR
Burrows, Abe	Entertainment	3/9	12	18	1910
Burstyn, Ellen	Film	3/7	12	7	1932
Burton, LeVar	Film	2/7	2	16	1957
Burton, Richard	Film	1/2	11	10	1925
Burton, Sir Richard F.	Exploration	1/3	3	19	1821
Busch, August Anheuser	Business	1/3	3	28	1899
Busch, Mae	Film	1/2	1	20	1891
Busey, Gary	Film	2/6	6	29	1944
Bush, George	Politics	3/6	6	12	1924
Bushman, Francis X.	Film	1/1	1	10	1883
Bushmiller, Ernie	Visual Arts	5/8	8	23	1905
Butkus, Dick	Sports	3/9	12	9	1942
Butterfield, William	Visual Arts	7/9	9	7	1814
Buttons, Aaron (Red)	Entertainment	2/5	2	5	1919
Buzzi, Ruth	Television	6/7	7	24	1936
Byington, Spring	Television	1/8	10	17	1892
Byrd, Charlie	Music	7/9	9	16	1925
Byrd, Richard E.	Exploration	1/7	10	25	1888
Byrne, David	Music	5/5	5	14	1952
Byron, George Gordon, Lord	Literature	1/4	1	22	1788
Caan, James	Film	3/8	3	26	1939
Cabell, James Branch	Literature	4/5	4	14	1879
Cabot, Bruce	Film	2/4	4	20	1904
Cabot, Sebastian	Television	6/7	7	6	1918
Cadmus, Paul	Visual Arts	3/8	12	17	1904
Caesar, Julius	Military	7/8	7	8	B.C. 102
Caesar, Sid	Television	8/9	9	8	1922
Cage, John	Music	5/9	9	5	1912
Cagney, James	Film	7/8	7	17	1904
Cahn, Sammy	Music	6/9	6	18	1913
Cain, James M.	Literature	1/7	7	1	1892
Caine, Michael	Film	3/5	3	14	1933
Calder, Alexander	Visual Arts	4/7	7	22	1898
Calder, Nigel	Literature	3/6	3	24	1931
Caldwell, Erskine	Literature	3/8	12	17	1903
Caldwell, Taylor	Literature	7/9	9	7	1900
Caldwell, Zoe	Dramatic Arts	5/9	9	14	1933
Calhern, Louis	Film	1/2	2	19	1895
Calhoun, John	Politics	3/9	3	18	1782
Calhoun, Rory	Film	8/8	8	8	1922

NAME	FIELD	SET	MONTH	DAY	YEAR
Callas, Maria	Music	3/3	12	3	1923
Calleia, Joseph	Film	4/8	8	4	1897
Calloway, Cab	Music	3/7	12	25	1907
Calvert, Phyllis	Film	2/9	2	18	1915
Calvin, John	Religion	1/7	7	10	1509
Cambridge, Godfrey	Entertainment	2/8	2	26	1933
Cameron, Kirk	Television	1/3	10	12	1970
Cameron, Rod	Film	3/7	12	7	1910
Campanella, Roy	Sports	1/2	11	19	1921
Campbell, Glen	Music	4/4	4	22	1936
Camus, Albert	Literature	2/7	11	7	1913
Candy, John	Film	1/4	10	31	1951
Caniff, Milton	Visual Arts	1/2	2	28	1907
Cannon, Dyan	Film	1/4	1	4	1929
Canova, Judy	Film	2/2	11	20	1916
Cantinflas (Mario Moreno)	Film	3/8	8	12	1911
Cantor, Eddie	Entertainment	1/4	1	31	1892
Canutt, Yakima	Film	2/2	11	29	1895
Capehart, Homer	Politics	6/6	6	6	1897
Capone, Alphonse (Scarface)	Crime	1/8	1	17	1899
Capote, Truman	Literature	3/9	9	30	1924
Capp, Al	Visual Arts	1/9	9	28	1909
Capra, Frank	Film	5/9	5	18	1897
Capucine	Film	1/6	1	6	1933
Cara, Irene	Dance	3/9	3	18	1959
Caravaggio, Michelangelo da	Visual Arts	1/9	9	28	1573
Cardin, Pierre	Design	7/7	7	7	1922
Cardinal Richelieu	Religion	9/9	9	9	1585
Cardinal Spellman	Religion	4/5	5	4	1889
Cardinale, Claudia	Film	4/6	4	15	1939
Carew, Rod	Sports	1/1	10	1	1945
Carey, Harry	Film	1/7	1	16	1878
Carey, Harry, Jr.	Film	5/7	5	16	1921
Carey, Macdonald	Television	3/6	3	15	1913
Carey, Philip	Literature	6/7	7	15	1922
Carlin, George	Entertainment	3/5	5	12	1937
Carlisle, Belinda	Music	8/8	8	17	1958
Carlisle, Kitty	Television	3/9	9	3	1915
Carlisle, Mary	Film	2/3	2	3	1912
Carlson, Richard	Film	2/4	4	29	1912

NAME	FIELD	SET	MONTH	DAY	YEAR
Carlyle, Thomas	Literature	3/4	12	4	1795
Carmichael, Hoagy	Music	2/4	11	22	1899
Carmichael, Ian	Film	6/9	6	18	1920
Carmichael, Stokely	Politics	2/6	6	29	1941
Carne, Judy	Television	4/9	4	27	1939
Carnegie, Andrew	Business	2/7	11	25	1835
Carnegie, Dale	Business	2/6	11	24	1888
Carney, Art	Television	2/4	11	4	1918
Caron, Leslie	Film	1/7	7	1	1931
Carpenter, John	Film	1/7	1	16	1948
Carpenter, Karen	Music	2/3	3	2	1950
Carpenter, Richard	Music	1/6	10	15	1946
Carpenter, Scott	Exploration	1/5	5	1	1925
Carr, Vikki	Music	1/7	7	19	1941
Carradine, David	Film	3/8	12	8	1936
Carradine, John	Film	2/5	2	5	1906
Carradine, Keith	Film	8/8	8	8	1949
Carrillo, Leo	Film	6/8	8	6	1881
Carroll, Diahann	Entertainment	7/8	7	17	1935
Carroll, Leo G.	Film	1/7	10	25	1892
Carroll, Lewis (Chas. Dodgson)	Literature	1/9	1	27	1832
Carroll, Madeleine	Film	2/8	2	26	1906
Carroll, Pat	Entertainment	5/5	5	5	1927
Carson, Jack	Film	1/9	10	27	1910
Carson, Johnny	Television	1/5	10	23	1925
Carson, Kit	Exploration	3/6	12	24	1809
Carson, Rachel	Letters	5/9	5	27	1907
Carson, Sunset	Sports	2/3	11	12	1922
Carter, Amy	Politics	1/1	10	19	1967
Carter, Betty	Music	5/7	5	16	1929
Carter, Billy	Business	2/3	3	29	1937
Carter, Jack	Entertainment	6/6	6	24	1923
Carter, Jimmy	President	1/1	10	1	1924
Carter, June	Music	5/6	6	23	1929
Carter, Lillian	Politics	6/8	8	15	1898
Carter, Lynda	Television	6/7	7	24	1951
Carter, Ron	Music	4/5	5	4	1937
Carter, Rosalynn	Politics	8/9	8	18	1927
Cartland, Barbara	Literature	7/9	7	9	1901
Caruso, Enrico	Music	2/7	2	25	1873

NAME	FIELD	SET	MONTH	DAY	YEAR
Carver, George Washington	Sciences	3/7	7	12	1861
Cary, Joyce	Literature	3/7	12	7	1888
Casals, Pablo	Music	2/3	12	29	1876
Casanova, Giovanni	Letters	2/4	4	2	1725
Cash, Johnny	Music	2/8	2	26	1932
Casper, Billy	Sports	6/6	6	24	1931
Cass, Peggy	Television	3/5	5	21	1924
Cassatt, Mary	Visual Arts	4/5	5	22	1845
Cassavetes, John	Film	3/9	12	9	1929
Cassidy, Butch	Crime	4/6	4	6	1866
Cassidy, David	Music	3/4	4	12	1950
Cassidy, Shaun	Television	9/9	9	27	1958
Cassini, Oleg	Design	2/4	4	11	1913
Castle, Irene	Dance	4/7	4	7	1893
Castle, Vernon	Dance	2/5	5	2	1887
Castro, Fidel	Politics	4/8	8	13	1927
Cather, Willa	Literature	3/7	12	7	1873
Catherine de Medicis	Royal	3/6	6	21	1519
Catherine the Great	Royal	2/5	5	2	1729
Caulfield, Joan	Film	1/6	6	1	1922
Cauthen, Steve	Sports	1/5	5	1	1960
Cavendish, Henry	Sciences	1/1	10	10	1731
Cavett, Dick	Television	1/2	11	19	1936
Cayce, Edgar	Philosophy	3/9	3	18	1877
Cerf, Bennett	Letters	5/7	5	25	1898
Cervantes, Miguel de	Literature	2/9	9	29	1547
Cézanne, Paul	Visual Arts	1/1	10	19	1839
Chabrol, Claude	Film	6/6	6	24	1930
Chagall, Marc	Visual Arts	7/7	7	7	1887
Chamberlain, Richard	Television	3/4	3	31	1935
Chamberlain, Wilt	Sports	3/8	8	21	1936
Champion, Gower	Dance	4/6	6	22	1920
Champion, Marge	Dance	2/9	9	2	1923
Chancellor, John	Television	5/7	7	14	1927
Chandler, Jeff	Film	3/6	12	15	1918
Chandler, Otis	Politics	2/5	11	23	1927
Chandler, Raymond	Literature	5/7	7	23	1888
Chandrasekhar, Subrahmanyan	Sciences	1/1	10	19	1910
Chanel, Coco	Design	1/8	8	19	1883
Channing, Carol	Entertainment	1/4	1	31	1923

NAME	FIELD	SET	MONTH	DAY	YEAR
Channing, Stockard	Film	2/4	2	13	1944
Chapin, Harry	Music	3/7	12	7	1942
Chaplin, Charlie	Film	4/7	4	16	1889
Chaplin, Geraldine	Film	4/7	7	31	1944
Chaplin, Sydney	Dramatic Arts	3/4	3	31	1926
Chapman, Lonny	Dramatic Arts	1/1	10	1	1920
Charisse, Cyd	Dance	3/8	3	8	1923
Charles, Mary Eugenia	Politics	5/6	5	15	1919
Charles, Ray	Music	5/9	9	23	1930
Charo	Entertainment	1/6	1	15	1951
Chase, Barrie	Dance	1/2	10	20	1934
Chase, Chevy	Film	1/8	10	8	1943
Chase, Ilka	Letters	4/8	4	8	1903
Chase, Lucia	Dance	3/6	3	24	1907
Chase, Sylvia	Television	2/5	2	23	1938
Chavez, Carlos	Music	4/6	6	13	1899
Chavez, Cesar	Politics	3/4	3	31	1927
Chayefsky, Paddy	Literature	1/2	1	29	1923
Checker, Chubby	Music	1/3	10	3	1941
Cheever, John	Literature	5/9	5	27	1912
Chekhov, Anton	Literature	1/8	1	17	1868
Chennault, Claire	Military	6/9	9	6	1890
Cher	Entertainment	2/5	5	20	1946
Chesterfield, Philip S., Lord	Literature	4/9	4	22	1694
Chesterton, G. K.	Literature	2/5	5	29	1847
Chevalier, Maurice	Film	3/9	9	12	1888
Chiang Kai-shek	Politics	1/4	10	31	1887
Child, Julia	Letters	6/8	8	15	1912
Childs, William	Literature	3/8	3	17	1903
Chippendale, Thomas	Design	5/6	6	5	1718
Chirico, Giorgio de	Visual Arts	1/7	7	10	1888
Chisholm, Shirley	Politics	2/3	2	30	1924
Chopin, Frédéric	Music	2/4	2	22	1810
Chopin, Kate	Literature	2/8	2	8	1851
Christian, Linda	Television	2/4	11	13	1923
Christie, Agatha	Literature	6/9	9	15	1891
Christie, Julie	Film	4/5	4	14	1941
Christo	Visual Arts	4/6	6	13	1935
Christy, June	Music	2/2	11	20	1925
Chrysler, Walter	Business	2/4	4	2	1875

NAME	FIELD	SET	MONTH	DAY	YEAR
Chung, Connie	Television	2/8	8	20	1946
Church, Frank	Politics	7/7	7	25	1924
Churchill, Clementine	Politics	1/4	4	1	1885
Churchill, Winston	Politics	2/3	11	30	1874
Ciardi, John	Literature	6/6	6	24	1916
Cicero, Marcus Tullius	Politics	1/1	1	1	B.C. 106
Cisneros, Henry	Politics	2/6	6	11	1947
Citroen, André G.	Business	2/5	2	5	1878
Clair, Rene	Film	2/2	11	11	1898
Clapton, Eric	Music	3/3	3	3	1945
Clark, Dane	Film	2/9	2	18	1915
Clark, Dick	Entertainment	2/3	11	30	1929
Clark, Petula	Music	2/6	11	15	1934
Clary, Robert	Dramatic Arts	1/3	3	1	1926
Clay, Lucius D.	Military	4/5	4	23	1897
Clayburgh, Jill	Film	3/4	4	30	1944
Cleaver, Eldridge	Politics	4/8	8	31	1935
Clemente, Roberto	Sports	8/9	8	18	1934
Cleveland, Grover	President	3/9	3	18	1837
Cliburn, Van	Music	3/7	7	12	1934
Clift, Montgomery	Film	1/8	10	17	1920
Clooney, Rosemary	Music	5/5	5	23	1928
Close, Glenn	Film	1/3	3	19	1947
Cobb, Lee J.	Film	3/9	12	9	1911
Cobb, Ty	Sports	3/9	12	18	1886
Coburn, Charles	Film	1/6	6	19	1877
Coburn, James	Film	4/8	8	31	1928
Coca, Imogene	Television	2/9	11	18	1908
Cocker, Joe	Music	2/5	5	2	1944
Coco, James	Film	3/3	3	21	1930
Cocteau, Jean	Literature	5/7	7	5	1889
Cody, William F. (Buffalo Bill)	Entertainment	2/8	2	26	1846
Cohan, George M.	Music	3/7	7	3	1878
Colbert, Claudette	Film	4/9	9	13	1905
Cole, Nat King	Music	3/8	3	17	1919
Cole, Natalie	Music	2/6	2	6	1950
Coleman, Dabney	Television	1/3	1	3	1932
Coleman, Gary	Television	2/8	2	8	1968
Coleman, Ornette	Music	1/3	3	19	1930
Coleridge, Samuel Taylor	Literature	1/3	10	21	1772

NAME	FIELD	SET	MONTH	DAY	YEAR
Colette	Literature	1/1	1	28	1873
Collins, Dorothy	Music	2/9	11	18	1926
Collins, Joan	Television	5/5	5	23	1933
Collins, Judy	Music	1/5	5	1	1939
Collins, Martha Layne	Politics	3/7	12	7	1936
Collins, Marva	Politics	4/8	8	31	1936
Collins, Wilkie	Literature	1/8	1	8	1824
Colman, Ronald	Film	2/9	2	9	1891
Coltrane, John	Music	5/9	9	23	1926
Columbus, Christopher	Exploration	1/3	10	30	1451
Comaneci, Nadia	Sports	2/3	11	12	1961
Comden, Betty	Dramatic Arts	3/5	5	3	1919
Como, Perry	Music	5/9	5	18	1912
Conn, Billy	Sports	1/8	10	8	1917
Connally, John	Politics	2/9	2	27	1917
Connery, Sean	Film	7/8	8	25	1930
Conniff, Ray	Music	2/6	11	6	1916
Connors, Chuck	Film	1/4	4	10	1921
Connors, Jimmy	Sports	2/9	9	2	1952
Conrad, Charles (Pete)	Exploration	2/6	6	2	1930
Conrad, Joseph	Literature	3/3	12	3	1857
Conrad, Robert	Television	1/3	3	1	1935
Conrad, William	Television	9/9	9	27	1920
Conreid, Hans	Film	4/6	4	15	1917
Constable, John	Visual Arts	2/6	6	11	1776
Conte, Richard	Film	3/6	3	24	1914
Conti, Tom	Film	2/4	11	22	1941
Coogan, Jackie	Film	1/8	10	26	1914
Cook, Barbara	Music	1/7	10	25	1927
Cook, James	Exploration	1/1	10	28	1728
Cook, Peter	Entertainment	2/8	11	17	1937
Cooke, Alistair	Television	2/2	11	20	1908
Coolidge, Calvin	President	4/7	7	4	1872
Coolidge, Rita	Music	1/5	5	1	1945
Cooper, Alice	Music	2/4	2	4	1948
Cooper, Gary	Film	5/7	5	7	1901
Cooper, Jackie	Film	6/9	9	15	1921
Cooper, James Fenimore	Literature	6/9	9	15	1789
Cooper, Leroy Gordon, Jr.	Exploration	3/6	3	6	1927
Cooper, Michael	Sports	4/6	4	15	1956

NAME	FIELD	SET	MONTH	DAY	YEAR
Coote, Robert	Dramatic Arts	2/4	2	4	1909
Copernicus, Nicolaus	Sciences	1/2	2	19	1473
Copland, Aaron	Music	2/5	2	14	1900
Coppola, Francis Ford	Film	4/7	4	7	1939
Cordero, Angel	Sports	5/8	5	8	1942
Corey, Irwin (Professor)	Entertainment	2/7	7	29	1912
Corey, Wendell	Film	2/3	3	20	1914
Corneille, Pierre	Literature	6/6	6	6	1606
Cornell, Katharine	Dramatic Arts	2/7	2	16	1893
Cornwallis, Charles	Military	3/4	12	31	1738
Corot, Jean Baptiste	Visual Arts	7/7	7	16	1796
Correll, Charles	Television	1/2	2	1	1890
Cosby, Bill	Television	3/7	7	12	1937
Cosell, Howard	Television	3/7	3	25	1920
Costello, Dolores	Film	8/9	9	17	1904
Costello, Elvis	Music	7/8	8	25	1954
Costello, Lou	Film	3/6	3	6	1906
Cotten, Joseph	Film	5/6	5	15	1905
Courbet, Gustave	Visual Arts	1/6	6	10	1819
Courrèges, André	Design	3/9	3	9	1923
Courtenay, Tom	Film	2/7	2	25	1937
Cousins, Norman	Letters	6/6	6	24	1915
Cousteau, Jacques	Exploration	2/6	6	11	1910
Coward, Noel	Dramatic Arts	3/7	12	16	1899
Cowper, William	Literature	2/8	11	26	1731
Cox, Wally	Entertainment	3/6	12	6	1924
Crabbe, Buster	Film	2/7	2	7	1907
Crain, Jeanne	Film	5/7	5	25	1925
Crane, Hart	Literature	3/7	7	21	1899
Crane, Stephen	Literature	1/2	11	1	1871
Crane, Walter	Visual Arts	6/8	8	15	1845
Cranston, Alan	Politics	1/6	6	19	1914
Crawford, Broderick	Film	3/9	12	9	1911
Crawford, Joan	Film	3/5	3	23	1904
Crenna, Richard	Television	2/3	11	30	1927
Crichton, Michael	Literature	1/5	10	23	1942
Crick, Francis	Sciences	6/8	6	8	1916
Crist, Judith	Letters	4/5	5	22	1922
Croce, Jim	Music	1/1	10	1	1942
Crockett, Davy	Exploration	8/8	8	17	1786

NAME	FIELD	SET	MONTH	DAY	YEAR
Cromwell, Oliver	Politics	5/5	5	5	1599
Cronkite, Walter	Television	2/4	11	4	1916
Cronyn, Hume	Dramatic Arts	7/9	7	18	1921
Crosby, Bing	Music	2/5	5	2	1901
Crosby, Bob	Music	5/8	8	23	1913
Crosby, David	Music	5/8	8	14	1914
Crosby, Gary	Television	6/9	6	27	1933
Cross, Christopher	Music	3/5	5	3	1951
Crothers, Scatman	Film	5/5	5	23	1910
Crowley, Aleister	Philosophy	1/3	10	12	1875
Cruikshank, George	Visual Arts	9/9	9	27	1792
Crystal, Billy	Entertainment	3/5	3	14	1947
Cugat, Xavier	Music	1/1	10	1	1900
Cukor, George	Film	7/7	7	7	1899
Cullen, Bill	Television	2/9	2	18	1920
Culp, Robert	Television	7/8	8	16	1930
cummings, e. e.	Literature	1/5	10	14	1894
Cummings, Robert	Film	6/9	6	9	1908
Cummins, Peggy	Film	3/9	12	18	1925
Cunningham, Imogen	Visual Arts	3/4	4	12	1883
Cuomo, Mario	Politics	6/6	6	15	1932
Curie, Marie	Sciences	2/7	11	7	1867
Curtis, Jamie Lee	Film	2/4	11	22	1958
Curtis, Tony	Film	3/6	6	3	1925
Cusack, Cyril	Dramatic Arts	2/8	11	26	1910
Cushing, Peter	Dramatic Arts	5/8	5	26	1913
Custer, George	Military	3/5	12	5	1839
Czar Ivan the Terrible	Royal	4/9	9	4	1530
Czar Peter the Great	Royal	6/9	6	9	1672
D'Amboise, Jacques	Dance	1/7	7	28	1934
D'Israeli, Isaac	Politics	2/5	5	11	1766
Da Vinci, Leonardo	Visual Arts	4/6	4	15	1452
Daguerre, Louis	Sciences	2/9	11	18	1789
Dahl, Arlene	Film	2/8	8	11	1924
Dailey, Dan	Film	3/5	12	14	1917
Dale, Jim	Dramatic Arts	6/8	8	15	1936
Daley, Cass	Entertainment	7/8	7	17	1915
Daley, Richard F.	Politics	5/6	5	15	1902
Dalí, Salvador	Visual Arts	2/5	5	11	1904
Daltry, Roger	Music	1/3	3	1	1945

NAME	FIELD	SET	MONTH	DAY	YEAR
Daly, James	Television	1/5	10	23	1918
Damita, Lili	Film	1/7	7	19	1901
Damone, Vic	Music	3/6	6	12	1928
Dana, Vic	Music	8/8	8	26	1942
Dandridge, Dorothy	Film	2/9	11	9	1922
Dangerfield, Rodney	Entertainment	2/4	11	22	1921
Daniels, Bebe	Film	1/5	1	14	1901
Danilova, Alexandra	Dance	2/2	11	20	1907
Dankworth, John	Music	2/9	9	20	1927
Danner, Blythe	Dramatic Arts	2/3	2	3	1943
Dano, Royal	Dramatic Arts	2/7	11	16	1927
Dantine, Helmut	Film	1/7	10	7	1917
Danton, Ray	Dramatic Arts	1/9	9	19	1931
Darin, Bobby	Music	5/5	5	14	1936
Darío, Rubén	Literature	1/9	1	18	1867
Darling, Joan	Dramatic Arts	5/9	9	23	1925
Darnell, Linda	Film	1/7	10	16	1921
Darren, James	Film	6/8	6	8	1936
Darrieux, Danielle	Film	1/5	5	1	1917
Darrow, Clarence	Law	4/9	4	18	1857
Darwell, Jane	Film	1/6	10	15	1879
Darwin, Charles	Sciences	2/3	2	12	1809
Dassin, Jules	Film	3/9	12	18	1911
Daugherty, Duffy	Sports	8/9	9	8	1915
Daumier, Honoré	Visual Arts	2/8	2	26	1808
Dauphin, Claude	Film	1/8	8	19	1903
Davenport, Jim	Sports	8/8	8	17	1933
David, Jacques	Visual Arts	3/8	8	30	1748
Davies, Arthur B.	Visual Arts	8/9	9	26	1862
Davies, Marion	Film	1/3	1	3	1897
Davis, Al	Business	4/7	7	4	1929
Davis, Angela	Politics	1/8	1	26	1944
Davis, Bette	Film	4/5	4	5	1908
Davis, Billy, Jr.	Music	6/8	6	26	1940
Davis, Jefferson	Politics	3/6	6	3	1808
Davis, Jimmy	Politics	2/9	9	11	1902
Davis, Joan	Television	2/6	6	29	1907
Davis, Mac	Music	1/3	1	21	1942
Davis, Miles	Music	5/7	5	25	1926
Davis, Ossie	Film	3/9	12	18	1917

NAME	FIELD	SET	MONTH	DAY	YEAR
Davis, Patti	Letters	1/4	10	22	1952
Davis, Sammy, Jr.	Entertainment	3/8	12	8	1925
Davis, Tommy	Sports	3/3	3	21	1939
Davy, Humphry	Sciences	3/8	12	17	1778
Dawber, Pam	Television	1/9	10	18	1951
Day, Clarence	Literature	2/9	11	18	1874
Day, Dennis	Television	3/5	5	21	1917
Day, Doris	Film	3/4	4	3	1924
Day, Laraine	Film	1/4	10	13	1920
Dayan, Moshe	Military	2/5	5	2	1915
De Carlo, Yvonne	Film	1/9	9	1	1922
de Gaulle, Charles	Politics	2/4	11	22	1890
De Havilland, Olivia	Film	1/7	7	1	1916
De Kooning, Willem	Visual Arts	4/6	4	24	1904
De La Renta, Oscar	Design	4/7	7	22	1932
De La Tour, Georges	Visual Arts	1/3	3	19	1593
De Laurentiis, Dino	Film	8/8	8	8	1919
De Luise, Dom	Entertainment	1/8	8	1	1933
De Mille, Agnes	Dance	9/9	9	18	1905
De Mille, Cecil B.	Film	3/8	8	12	1881
De Niro, Robert	Film	8/8	8	17	1943
De Palma, Brian	Film	2/9	9	11	1940
De Sica, Vittorio	Film	7/7	7	7	1901
De Staël, Nicolas	Visual Arts	1/5	1	5	1914
Dean, Dizzy	Sports	1/7	1	16	1911
Dean, James	Film	2/8	2	8	1931
Dean, Jimmy	Music	1/8	8	10	1928
Dearie, Blossom	Music	2/4	4	29	1926
DeBerg, Steve	Sports	1/1	1	19	1954
Debs, Eugene V.	Politics	2/5	11	5	1855
Debussy, Claude	Music	4/8	8	22	1862
DeCamp, Rosemary	Television	2/5	11	14	1910
Decamps, Alexandre	Visual Arts	3/3	3	3	1803
Decatur, Stephen	Politics	1/5	1	5	1779
Dee, Frances	Film	2/8	11	26	1907
Dee, Ruby	Film	1/9	10	27	1924
Dee, Sandra	Film	4/5	4	23	1942
DeFore, Don	Television	7/8	8	25	1917
Degas, Edgar	Visual Arts	1/7	7	19	1834
DeHaven, Gloria	Film	5/7	7	23	1924

NAME	FIELD	SET	MONTH	DAY	YEAR
Dekker, Albert	Film	2/3	12	20	1905
Del Rio, Dolores	Film	3/8	8	3	1905
Delacroix, Ferdinand	Visual Arts	4/8	4	26	1798
Delaunay, Robert	Visual Arts	3/4	4	12	1885
Delibes, Léo	Music	2/3	2	21	1836
Delius, Frederick	Music	1/2	1	29	1862
Delon, Alain	Film	2/8	11	8	1935
Demarest, William	Film	2/9	2	27	1892
Dempsey, Jack	Sports	6/6	6	24	1895
Dempsey, Tom	Sports	1/3	1	12	1947
Demuth, Charles	Visual Arts	2/8	11	8	1883
Deneuve, Catherine	Film	1/4	10	22	1940
Denis, Maurice	Visual Arts	2/7	11	25	1870
Dennis, Sandy	Dramatic Arts	4/9	4	27	1937
Denver, John	Music	3/4	12	31	1943
Depardieu, Gerard	Film	3/9	12	27	1948
Derain, André	Visual Arts	1/6	6	10	1880
Derek, Bo	Film	2/2	11	20	1956
Derek, John	Film	3/8	8	12	1926
Dern, Bruce	Film	4/6	6	4	1936
Descartes, René	Philosophy	3/4	3	31	1596
Desmond, Johnny	Music	2/5	11	14	1925
Deukmejian, George	Politics	6/6	6	6	1928
Devane, William	Television	5/9	9	5	1937
Devine, Andy	Television	1/7	10	7	1905
Devries, William C.	Sciences	1/3	12	19	1943
Dewhurst, Colleen	Dramatic Arts	3/6	6	3	1926
Dey, Susan	Television	1/2	12	10	1952
Di Sant'Angelo, Giorgio	Design	5/5	5	5	1939
Diaghilev, Serge	Dance	1/3	3	19	1872
Diamond, Neil	Music	1/6	1	24	1941
Dickens, Charles	Literature	2/7	2	7	1812
Dickerson, Eric	Sports	2/8	8	2	1960
Dickey, Bill	Sports	6/6	6	6	1907
Dickey, James	Literature	2/2	2	2	1923
Dickinson, Angie	Television	3/9	9	30	1932
Dickinson, Emily	Literature	1/3	12	10	1830
Diddley, Bo	Music	3/3	12	30	1928
Diderot, Denis	Literature	1/5	10	5	1713
Didion, Joan	Literature	3/5	12	5	1934

NAME	FIELD	SET	MONTH	DAY	YEAR
Diebenkorn, Richard	Visual Arts	4/4	4	22	1922
Diefenbaker, John	Politics	9/9	9	18	1895
Dietrich, Marlene	Film	3/9	12	27	1901
Diller, Barry	Film	2/2	2	2	1942
Diller, Phyllis	Entertainment	7/8	7	17	1917
Dillinger, John	Crime	4/6	6	22	1903
Dillman, Bradford	Film	4/5	4	14	1930
Dillon, Matt	Film	2/9	2	18	1964
DiMaggio, Joe	Sports	2/7	11	25	1914
Dine, Jim	Visual Arts	6/7	6	16	1935
Dinesen, Isak	Literature	4/8	4	17	1883
Dior, Christian	Design	1/3	1	21	1905
Dirac, Paul	Sciences	8/8	8	8	1902
Dirksen, Everett	Politics	1/4	1	4	1896
Disney, Walt	Film	3/5	12	5	1901
Disraeli, Benjamin	Politics	3/3	12	21	1804
Ditka, Mike	Sports	1/9	10	18	1939
Dix, Dorothea	Letters	4/4	4	4	1804
Dix, Dorothy	Literature	2/9	11	18	1870
Dix, Otto	Visual Arts	2/3	12	2	1859
Dix, Richard	Film	7/9	7	18	1894
Dixon, Alan J.	Politics	7/7	7	7	1927
Doctorow, E. L.	Literature	1/6	1	6	1931
Dodge, Mary Mapes	Literature	1/8	1	26	1831
Dohnányi, Ernst von	Music	7/9	7	27	1877
Dolby, Ray	Sciences	1/9	1	18	1933
Dole, Elizabeth	Politics	2/7	7	29	1936
Dole, Robert J.	Politics	4/7	7	22	1923
Domingo, Plácido	Music	1/3	1	21	1941
Domino, Antoine (Fats)	Music	2/8	2	26	1928
Donahue, Phil	Television	3/3	12	21	1935
Donat, Robert	Film	3/9	3	18	1905
Donen, Stanley	Film	4/4	4	13	1924
Dongen, Kees von	Visual Arts	1/8	1	26	1877
Donlevy, Brian	Film	2/9	2	9	1899
Donovan	Music	1/5	5	1	1943
Doolittle, Hilda (H.D.)	Literature	1/9	9	10	1886
Doolittle, James H.	Military	3/5	12	14	1896
Doppler, Christian J.	Sciences	2/2	11	29	1803
Dorati, Antal	Music	4/9	4	9	1906

NAME	FIELD	SET	MONTH	DAY	YEAR
Doré, Gustave	Visual Arts	1/6	1	6	1832
Dors, Diana	Film	1/5	10	23	1931
Dorsett, Tony	Sports	4/7	4	7	1954
Dorsey, Jimmy	Music	2/2	2	29	1904
Dorsey, Tommy	Music	1/2	11	19	1905
Dos Passos, John	Literature	1/5	1	14	1896
Dostoevsky, Fyodor	Literature	2/2	11	11	1821
Doubleday, Abner	Publishing	6/8	6	26	1819
Douglas, Helen Gahagen	Politics	2/7	11	25	1900
Douglas, Kirk	Film	3/9	12	9	1916
Douglas, Melvyn	Film	4/5	4	5	1901
Douglas, Michael	Film	7/9	9	25	1944
Douglas, Mike	Television	2/8	8	11	1925
Douglas, Paul	Film	1/3	3	28	1892
Douglas, William O.	Law	1/7	10	16	1898
Dove, Billie	Film	5/5	5	14	1900
Down, Lesley-Anne	Film	3/8	3	17	1954
Downey, Morton	Music	2/5	11	14	1901
Downs, Hugh	Television	2/5	2	14	1921
Downs, Johnny	Film	1/1	10	10	1913
Doyle, Arthur Conan	Literature	4/5	5	22	1859
Drakc, Alfred	Music	1/7	10	7	1914
Drake, Betsy	Film	2/9	9	11	1923
Drake, Tom	Film	5/8	8	5	1918
Dreier, Alex	Television	6/8	6	26	1916
Dreiser, Theodore	Literature	8/9	8	27	1871
Dressler, Marie	Film	2/9	11	9	1868
Drew, Ellen	Film	2/5	11	23	1915
Dreyfuss, Richard	Film	1/2	10	29	1947
Dru, Joanne	Film	1/4	1	31	1923
Drury, Allen	Literature	2/9	9	2	1918
Dryden, John	Literature	8/9	8	9	1631
Dryden, Kenny	Sports	8/8	8	8	1947
Drysdale, Don	Sports	5/7	7	23	1936
Du Bois, W. E. B.	Letters	2/5	2	23	1868
du Maurier, Daphne	Literature	4/5	5	13	1907
Du Pont, Pierre Samuel	Business	1/6	1	15	1870
Du Pont, Pierre Samuel IV	Politics	1/4	1	22	1936
Dubuffet, Jean	Visual Arts	3/7	7	3	1901
Duchamp, Marcel	Visual Arts	1/7	7	28	1887

NAME	FIELD	SET	MONTH	DAY	YEAR
Duchamp-Villon, Raymond	Visual Arts	2/5	11	5	1876
Duchin, Eddy	Music	1/4	4	1	1909
Duchin, Peter	Music	1/7	7	28	1937
Duff, Howard	Film	2/6	11	24	1917
Dufy, Raoul	Visual Arts	3/6	6	3	1877
Dukakis, Michael	Politics	2/3	11	3	1933
Duke of Windsor (Edward VIII)	Royal	5/6	6	5	1894
Dulles, Allen	Politics	4/7	4	7	1893
Dulles, John Foster	Politics	2/7	2	25	1888
Dumas, Alexandre	Literature	6/7	7	24	1802
Dumas, Alexandre (fils)	Literature	7/9	7	27	1824
Dunaway, Faye	Film	1/5	1	14	1941
Dunbar, Dixie	Film	1/1	1	19	1919
Duncan, Isadora	Dance	5/9	5	27	1878
Duncan, Sandy	Film	2/2	2	20	1946
Dunn, James	Film	2/2	11	2	1901
Dunne, Irene	Film	2/3	12	20	1901
Dunnock, Mildred	Dramatic Arts	1/7	1	25	1906
Durant, Ariel	Letters	1/5	5	10	1898
Durant, William J.	Letters	2/5	11	5	1885
Durante, Jimmy	Entertainment	1/2	2	10	1893
Duras, Marguerite	Literature	4/4	4	4	1914
Durbin, Deanna	Film	3/4	12	4	1921
Dürer, Albrecht	Visual Arts	3/5	5	21	1471
Durning, Charles	Film	1/2	2	28	1933
Durocher, Leo	Sports	7/9	7	27	1906
Durrell, Lawrence	Literature	2/9	2	27	1912
Duryea, Dan	Film	1/5	1	23	1907
Duvall, Robert	Film	1/5	1	5	1931
Duveneck, Frank	Visual Arts	1/9	10	9	1848
Dvorak, Ann	Film	2/8	8	11	1912
Dvořák, Antonín	Music	9/9	9	9	1841
Dylan, Bob	Music	5/6	5	24	1941
Eagels, Jeanne	Film	6/8	6	26	1890
Eakins, Thomas	Visual Arts	7/7	7	25	1844
Eames, Charles	Design	6/8	6	17	1907
Earhart, Amelia	Exploration	6/7	7	24	1897
Earp, Wyatt	Politics	1/3	3	19	1848
Eastman, George	Business	3/7	7	12	1854
Eastwood, Clint	Film	4/5	5	31	1930

NAME	FIELD	SET	MONTH	DAY	YEAR
Eban, Abba	Politics	2/2	2	2	1915
Eberly, Bob	Music	6/7	7	24	1915
Ebsen, Buddy	Film	2/4	4	2	1908
Eckstine, Billy	Music	7/8	7	17	1914
Eddy, Mary Baker	Religion	7/7	7	16	1821
Eddy, Nelson	Film	2/6	6	29	1901
Eden, Barbara	Television	5/8	8	23	1934
Edison, Thomas	Sciences	2/2	2	11	1847
Edwards, Vince	Television	7/7	7	7	1928
Egan, Richard	Television	2/5	11	14	1890
Eggar, Samantha	Film	3/5	3	5	1939
Ehrlich, Paul	Sciences	3/5	3	14	1854
Eiffel, Alexandre	Design	3/6	12	15	1882
Einstein, Albert	Sciences	3/5	3	14	1879
Eisenhower, Dwight	President	1/5	10	14	1890
Eisenhower, Julie Nixon	Politics	5/7	7	5	1948
Eisenhower, Mamie	Politics	2/5	11	14	1886
Eisenstein, Sergei	Film	1/5	1	23	1898
Ekberg, Anita	Film	2/9	9	29	1931
Ekland, Britt	Film	1/6	10	6	1942
Elam, Jack	Film	2/4	11	13	1916
Eldridge, Florence	Dramatic Arts	5/9	9	5	1901
Elgar, Edward	Music	2/6	6	2	1857
Eliot, George	Literature	2/4	11	22	1819
Eliot, T. S.	Literature	8/9	9	26	1888
Ellerbee, Linda	Television	6/8	8	15	1945
Ellington, Duke	Music	2/4	4	29	1899
Elliott, Denholm	Film	4/5	5	31	1922
Elliott, Sam	Television	8/9	8	9	1944
Ellis, Perry	Design	3/3	3	3	1940
Ellison, Ralph	Literature	1/3	3	1	1914
Emerson, Faye	Television	7/8	7	8	1917
Emerson, Ralph Waldo	Literature	5/7	5	25	1803
Emperor Charlemagne	Royal	4/6	4	6	742
Emperor Haile Selassie	Royal	5/7	7	23	1891
Emperor Hirohito	Royal	2/4	4	29	1901
Emperor Nero	Royal	3/4	12	13	37
Ensor, James	Visual Arts	4/4	4	13	1860
Entremont, Philippe	Music	6/7	6	7	1934
Epstein, Jacob	Visual Arts	8/9	8	9	1880

NAME	FIELD	SET	MONTH	DAY	YEAR
Erhard, Werner	Philosophy	5/9	9	5	1935
Erickson, Leif	Film	1/9	10	27	1911
Ernst, Max	Visual Arts	2/4	4	2	1891
Errol, Leon	Film	3/7	7	3	1881
Erté	Visual Arts	2/5	11	23	1892
Ervin, Sam	Politics	9/9	9	27	1896
Erving, Julius (Dr. J)	Sports	2/4	2	22	1950
Erwin, Stuart	Film	2/5	2	14	1902
Esposito, Phil	Sports	2/2	2	20	1942
Etting, Ruth	Music	2/5	11	23	1897
Evans, Linda	Television	2/9	11	18	1942
Evans, Maurice	Dramatic Arts	3/6	6	3	1901
Evans, Robert	Film	2/6	6	29	1930
Everly, Don	Music	1/2	2	1	1937
Everly, Phil	Music	1/1	1	19	1939
Fabergé, Peter Carl	Design	3/5	5	30	1846
Fabian (F. Anthony Forte)	Music	2/6	2	6	1943
Fabius, Laurent	Politics	2/8	8	20	1946
Factor, Max	Business	8/9	8	18	1904
Fadiman, Clifton	Letters	5/6	5	15	1904
Fahrenheit, Gabriel	Sciences	5/5	5	14	1686
Fairbanks, Douglas, Jr.	Film	3/9	12	9	1909
Fairbanks, Douglas, Sr.	Film	5/5	5	23	1883
Fairchild, Morgan	Television	2/3	2	3	1950
Faith, Percy	Music	4/7	4	7	1908
Falk, Peter	Television	7/9	9	16	1927
Falkenburg, Jinx	Entertainment	1/3	1	21	1919
Falla, Manuel de	Music	2/5	11	23	1876
Falwell, Jerry	Religion	2/8	8	11	1933
Fantin-Latour, Henri	Visual Arts	1/5	1	14	1836
Faraday, Michael	Sciences	4/9	9	22	1791
Farentino, James	Television	2/6	2	24	1938
Farley, James A.	Politics	3/5	5	30	1888
Farmer, Fanny	Letters	3/5	3	23	1857
Farmer, Frances	Film	1/9	9	19	1910
Farr, Felicia	Film	1/4	10	4	1932
Farrell, Charles	Film	8/9	8	9	1901
Farrell, Eileen	Music	2/4	2	13	1920
Farrell, Glenda	Film	3/6	6	30	1904
Farrow, Mia	Film	2/9	2	9	1949

NAME	FIELD	SET	MONTH	DAY	YEAR
Fasanella, Ralph	Visual Arts	2/9	9	2	1914
Fassbinder, Rainer Werner	Film	4/5	5	31	1946
Fast, Howard	Literature	2/2	11	11	1914
Faubus, Orval B.	Politics	1/7	1	7	1910
Faulkner, William	Literature	7/9	9	25	1897
Fawcett, Farrah	Television	2/2	2	2	1947
Faye, Alice	Film	5/5	5	5	1912
Feiffer, Jules	Visual Arts	1/8	1	26	1929
Feininger, Lyonel	Visual Arts	7/8	7	17	1871
Feinstein, Diane	Politics	4/6	6	22	1933
Feldman, Marty	Entertainment	7/8	7	8	1933
Feldshuh, Tovah	Dramatic Arts	3/9	12	27	1951
Feliciano, José	Music	1/9	9	10	1945
Fell, Norman	Television	3/6	3	24	1925
Fellini, Federico	Film	1/2	1	20	1920
Fender, Freddy	Music	4/6	6	4	1937
Ferber, Edna	Literature	6/8	8	15	1887
Ferguson, Maynard	Music	4/5	5	4	1928
Fermi, Enrico	Sciences	2/9	9	29	1901
Ferragamo, Vince	Sports	4/6	4	24	1954
Ferrari, Enzo	Design	2/2	2	20	1898
Ferraro, Geraldine	Politics	8/8	8	26	1935
Ferrer, Jose	Film	1/8	1	8	1912
Ferrer, Mel	Film	7/8	8	25	1917
Ferrigno, Lou	Television	2/9	11	9	1952
Feynman, Richard P.	Sciences	2/5	5	11	1918
Fiedler, Arthur	Music	3/8	12	17	1894
Field, Sally	Film	2/6	11	6	1946
Fielding, Henry	Literature	4/4	4	22	1707
Fields, Gracie	Entertainment	1/9	1	9	1898
Fields, Marshall	Business	8/9	8	18	1834
Fields, Totie	Entertainment	5/7	5	7	1931
Fields, W. C.	Film	1/1	1	19	1879
Fillmore, Abigail	Politics	3/4	3	13	1798
Fillmore, Millard	President	1/7	1	7	1800
Finch, Peter	Film	1/9	9	28	1916
Finney, Albert	Film	5/9	5	9	1936
Firkusny, Rudolf	Music	2/2	2	11	1912
Fischer-Dieskau, Dietrich	Music	1/5	5	28	1925
Fischl, Eric	Visual Arts	3/9	3	9	1948

NAME	FIELD	SET	MONTH	DAY	YEAR
Fisher, Carrie	Letters	1/3	10	21	1956
Fisher, Eddie	Music	1/8	8	10	1928
Fitzgerald, Barry	Film	1/3	3	10	1888
Fitzgerald, Ella	Music	4/7	4	25	1918
Fitzgerald, F. Scott	Literature	6/9	9	24	1896
Fitzgerald, Geraldine	Film	2/6	11	24	1912
Flack, Roberta	Music	1/2	2	10	1940
Flagg, Fannie	Entertainment	3/9	9	21	1944
Flagstad, Kirsten	Music	3/7	7	12	1895
Flanagan, Mike	Sports	3/7	12	16	1951
Flanner, Janet	Letters	3/4	3	13	1918
Flaubert, Gustave	Literature	3/3	12	12	1821
Fleetwood, Mick	Music	6/6	6	24	1942
Fleming, Alexander	Sciences	6/8	8	6	1881
Fleming, Ian	Literature	1/5	5	28	1908
Fleming, Peggy	Sports	7/9	7	27	1948
Fleming, Rhonda	Film	1/8	8	10	1923
Flynn, Errol	Film	2/6	6	20	1909
Flynt, Larry C.	Business	1/2	11	1	1942
Fo, Dario	Dramatic Arts	3/6	3	24	1926
Foch, Nina	Film	2/4	4	20	1924
Fonda, Henry	Film	5/7	5	16	1905
Fonda, Jane	Film	3/3	12	21	1937
Fonda, Peter	Film	2/5	2	23	1939
Fontaine, Joan	Film	1/4	10	22	1917
Fonteyn, Margot	Dance	5/9	5	18	1919
Foote, Horton	Literature	3/5	3	14	1916
Ford, Betty	Politics	4/8	4	8	1918
Ford, Edsel	Business	2/6	11	6	1893
Ford, Ford Madox	Literature	3/8	12	17	1873
Ford, Gerald	President	5/7	7	14	1913
Ford, Glenn	Film	1/5	5	1	1916
Ford, Harrison	Film	4/7	7	13	1942
Ford, Henry	Business	3/7	7	30	1863
Ford, Henry, II	Business	4/9	9	4	1917
Ford, John	Film	1/2	2	1	1895
Ford, Mary	Music	7/7	7	7	1924
Ford, Paul	Film	2/2	11	2	1901
Ford, Tennessee Ernie	Music	2/4	2	13	1919
Ford, Wallace	Film	2/3	2	12	1898

NAME	FIELD	SET	MONTH	DAY	YEAR
Ford, Wendal	Politics	8/9	9	8	1924
Forman, Milos	Film	2/9	2	18	1932
Forrestal, James	Politics	2/6	2	15	1892
Forster, E. M.	Literature	1/1	1	1	1879
Forsyth, Frederick	Literature	7/8	8	25	1938
Forsythe, John	Television	1/2	1	29	1918
Fosse, Bob	Dance	5/6	6	23	1927
Foster, Jodie	Film	1/2	11	19	1962
Foucault, Jean	Sciences	9/9	9	18	1819
Fournier, Pierre	Music	6/6	6	24	1906
Fowler, Mark S.	Politics	1/6	10	6	1941
Fowles, John	Literature	3/4	3	31	1926
Fox, James	Film	1/5	5	19	1939
Fox, Michael J.	Television	6/9	6	9	1961
Foxworth, Robert	Television	1/2	11	1	1941
Foxx, Redd	Entertainment	3/9	12	9	1922
Foyt, A. J.	Sports	1/7	1	16	1935
Fragonard, Jean Honoré	Visual Arts	4/5	4	5	1732
Frampton, Peter	Music	4/4	4	22	1950
France, Anatole	Literature	4/7	4	16	1844
Francescatti, Zino	Music	8/9	8	9	1905
Franciosa, Tony	Television	1/7	10	25	1928
Francis, Anne	Television	7/9	9	16	1932
Francis, Arlene	Television	1/2	10	20	1908
Francis, Connie	Music	3/3	12	12	1938
Francis, Kay	Film	1/4	1	13	1899
Francis, Sam	Visual Arts	7/7	7	25	1923
Franciscus, James	Television	1/4	1	31	1934
Franco, Francisco	Politics	3/4	12	4	1892
Frank, Anne	Letters	3/6	6	12	1929
Frankenheimer, John	Film	1/2	2	19	1930
Frankenthaler, Helen	Visual Arts	3/3	12	12	1928
Frankfurter, Felix	Law	2/6	11	15	1882
Franklin, Aretha	Music	3/7	3	25	1942
Franklin, Benjamin	Letters	1/8	1	17	1706
Fraser, James	Letters	1/1	1	1	1884
Frazier, Joe	Sports	1/8	1	17	1944
Freberg, Stan	Entertainment	7/8	8	7	1926
Freud, Sigmund	Psychology	5/6	5	6	1856
Friedan, Betty	Letters	2/4	2	4	1921

NAME	FIELD	SET	MONTH	DAY	YEAR
Friedkin, William	Film	2/8	8	29	1939
Frost, David	Television	4/7	4	7	1939
Frost, Robert	Literature	3/8	3	26	1874
Fry, Christopher	Literature	3/9	12	18	1907
Fulbright, J. William	Politics	4/9	4	9	1905
Fuller, Buckminster	Design	3/7	7	12	1895
Fuller, Margaret	Letters	5/5	5	23	1810
Fulton, Robert	Sciences	2/5	11	14	1765
Funicello, Annette	Television	1/4	10	22	1942
Funt, Allen	Television	7/9	9	16	1914
Füssli, J. H.	Visual Arts	2/7	2	7	1741
Gabin, Jean	Film	5/8	5	17	1904
Gable, Clark	Film	1/2	2	1	1901
Gabor, Eva	Entertainment	2/2	2	11	1921
Gabor, Jolie	Entertainment	2/9	9	29	1896
Gabor, Magda	Entertainment	1/7	7	10	1917
Gabor, Zsa Zsa	Entertainment	2/6	2	6	1919
Gagarin, Yuri	Exploration	3/9	3	9	1932
Gainsborough, Thomas	Visual Arts	5/5	5	14	1727
Galbraith, John Kenneth	Letters	1/6	10	15	1908
Galilei, Galileo	Sciences	2/7	2	25	1564
Gallo, Robert C.	Sciences	3/5	3	23	1937
Galsworthy, John	Literature	5/8	8	14	1867
Galway, James	Music	3/8	12	8	1939
Gamow, George	Sciences	3/4	3	4	1904
Gandhi, Indira	Politics	1/2	11	19	1917
Gandhi, Mahatma	Politics	1/2	10	2	1869
Gandhi, Rajiv	Politics	2/8	8	20	1944
Garbo, Greta	Film	9/9	9	18	1905
Garcia, Jerry	Music	1/8	8	1	1942
Gardenia, Vincent	Film	1/7	1	7	1922
Gardner, Ava	Film	3/6	12	24	1922
Gardner, Erle Stanley	Literature	7/8	7	17	1889
Gardner, John	Literature	3/7	7	21	1933
Garfield, James A.	President	1/2	11	19	1831
Garfield, John	Film	3/4	3	4	1913
Garfield, Lucretia	Politics	1/4	4	19	1832
Garfunkel, Art	Music	2/5	11	5	1941
Garibaldi, Giuseppe	Military	4/7	7	4	1807
Garland, Beverly	Television	1/8	10	17	1929

NAME	FIELD	SET	MONTH	DAY	YEAR
Garland, Judy	Music	1/6	6	10	1922
Garn, Jake	Politics	1/3	10	12	1932
Garner, Erroll	Music	6/6	6	15	1921
Garner, James	Television	4/7	4	7	1928
Garrett, Betty	Music	5/5	5	23	1919
Garson, Greer	Film	2/9	9	29	1908
Gaskell, Elizabeth	Literature	2/9	9	29	1810
Gastineau, Mark	Sports	2/2	11	20	1956
Gaudí, Antonio	Design	6/7	6	25	1852
Gauguin, Paul	Visual Arts	6/7	6	7	1848
Gavin, John	Politics	4/8	4	8	1928
Gay-Lussac, Joseph	Sciences	3/6	12	6	1778
Gayle, Crystal	Music	1/9	1	9	1951
Gaynor, Janet	Film	1/6	10	6	1906
Gaynor, Mitzi	Film	2/9	9	11	1930
Geer, Will	Film	3/9	3	9	1902
Geiger, Hans	Sciences	3/8	8	30	1882
Geldof, Bob	Music	1/5	10	5	1951
Genet, Jean	Literature	1/3	12	19	1910
Genovese, Vito	Crime	2/3	11	21	1897
Gentry, Bobbie	Music	7/9	7	27	1944
George, Dan (Chief)	Film	6/6	6	24	1899
George, Llewellyn	Philosophy	8/8	8	17	1876
George, Phyllis	Television	6/7	6	25	1949
Gere, Richard	Film	4/8	8	31	1949
Gershwin, George	Music	8/9	9	26	1898
Gershwin, Ira	Music	3/6	12	6	1896
Getty, Gordon P.	Business	2/3	12	20	1933
Getty, J. Paul	Business	3/6	12	15	1892
Geyer, Georgie Anne	Politics	2/4	4	2	1935
Giacometti, Alberto	Visual Arts	1/1	10	10	1901
Gibb, Barry	Music	1/9	9	1	1946
Gibb, Maurice	Music	3/4	12	22	1949
Gibb, Robin	Music	3/4	12	22	1949
Gibbon, Edward	Letters	4/9	4	27	1737
Gibran, Kahlil	Literature	3/6	12	6	1883
Gibson, Bob	Sports	2/9	11	9	1935
Gibson, Debbie	Music	4/8	8	31	1970
Gibson, Hoot	Film	6/8	8	6	1892
Gibson, William	Literature	2/4	11	13	1914

NAME	FIELD	SET	MONTH	DAY	YEAR
Gide, André	Literature	2/4	11	22	1869
Gielgud, John	Dramatic Arts	4/5	4	14	1904
Gilbert, W. S.	Literature	2/9	11	18	1836
Gilberto, Astrud	Music	3/3	3	30	1940
Gilford, Jack	Film	7/7	7	25	1913
Gilley, Mickey	Music	3/9	3	9	1936
Ginsberg, Allen	Literature	3/6	6	3	1926
Gish, Dorothy	Film	2/3	3	11	1898
Gish, Lillian	Film	1/5	10	14	1896
Givenchy, Hubert de	Design	2/3	2	21	1927
Givens, Robin	Television	2/9	11	27	1964
Glackens, William	Visual Arts	3/4	3	13	1870
Gladstone, William E.	Politics	2/3	12	29	1809
Glass, Philip	Music	1/4	1	31	1937
Glasser, Ira	Politics	4/9	4	18	1938
Glazunov, Alexander	Music	1/8	8	10	1865
Gleason, Jackie	Television	2/8	2	26	1916
Gleason, James	Film	5/5	5	23	1886
Glenn, John	Exploration	7/9	7	18	1921
Glinka, Mikhail Ivanovich	Music	1/6	6	1	1803
Glubb, John B.	Politics	4/7	4	16	1897
Gluck, Christoph	Music	2/7	7	2	1714
Gobel, George	Television	2/5	5	20	1920
Godard, Jean-Luc	Film	3/3	12	3	1930
Goddard, Paulette	Film	3/6	6	3	1911
Godden, Rumer	Literature	1/3	12	10	1907
Gödel, Kurt	Sciences	1/4	4	28	1906
Godunov, Alexander	Dance	1/2	11	28	1949
Goethe, Johann von	Literature	1/8	8	28	1749
Gogol, Nikolai	Literature	3/4	3	31	1809
Golan, Menachem	Film	4/5	5	31	1929
Goldberg, Arthur J.	Politics	8/8	8	8	1908
Goldberg, Whoopi	Entertainment	2/4	11	13	1949
Goldblum, Jeff	Film	1/4	10	22	1952
Golding, William	Literature	1/9	9	19	1911
Goldsmith, Oliver	Literature	1/2	11	10	1730
Goldwater, Barry	Politics	1/1	1	1	1909
Goldwyn, Samuel	Film	8/8	8	17	1882
Golgi, Camillo	Sciences	7/7	7	7	1844
Gonzalez, Pancho	Sports	5/9	5	9	1928

NAME	FIELD	SET	MONTH	DAY	YEAR
Goode, W. Wilson	Politics	1/8	8	19	1938
Goodman, Steve	Music	7/7	7	25	1948
Goodyear, Charles	Business	2/3	12	29	1800
Gorbachev, Mikhail	Politics	2/3	3	2	1931
Gorcey, Leo	Film	3/6	6	3	1915
Gordimer, Nadine	Literature	2/3	12	20	1923
Gordon, Dexter	Music	2/9	2	27	1923
Gordon, Gale	Film	2/2	2	2	1906
Gordon, Richard F., Jr.	Exploration	1/5	10	5	1929
Gordon, Ruth	Film	1/3	10	30	1896
Gordy, Berry, Jr.	Music	1/2	11	28	1929
Gore, Albert, Jr.	Politics	3/4	3	31	1948
Göring, Herman	Politics	1/3	10	3	1893
Gorky, Arshile	Visual Arts	1/7	10	25	1904
Gorky, Maxim	Literature	1/3	3	28	1868
Gorme, Eydie	Music	7/8	8	16	1932
Gorshin, Frank	Entertainment	4/5	4	5	1934
Gortner, Marjoe	Film	1/5	1	14	1945
Gosden, Freeman	Television	5/5	5	5	1896
Gossett, Louis, Jr.	Film	5/9	5	27	1936
Gottschalk, Louis	Music	8/8	8	26	1916
Gould, Elliott	Film	2/8	8	29	1938
Gould, Glenn	Music	7/9	9	25	1932
Gould, Morton	Music	1/3	12	10	1913
Goulet, Robert	Music	2/8	11	26	1933
Gounod, Charles	Music	6/8	6	17	1818
Gowdy, Curt	Television	4/7	7	31	1919
Goya, Francisco de	Visual Arts	3/3	3	30	1746
Graf, Steffi	Sports	5/6	6	14	1969
Graham, Bill	Entertainment	1/8	1	8	1931
Graham, Billy	Religion	2/7	11	7	1918
Graham, Bob	Politics	2/9	11	9	1936
Graham, Martha	Dance	2/5	5	11	1893
Grahame, Kenneth	Literature	3/8	3	8	1859
Gramm, William P.	Politics	7/8	7	8	1942
Grandma Moses	Visual Arts	7/9	9	7	1860
Grandy, Fred	Politics	2/6	6	29	1948
Granger, Farley	Film	1/7	7	1	1925
Granger, Stewart	Film	5/6	5	6	1913
Grant, Cary	Film	1/9	1	18	1904

NAME	FIELD	SET	MONTH	DAY	YEAR
Grant, Lee	Film	1/4	10	31	1929
Grant, Ulysses S.	President	4/9	4	27	1822
Granville, Bonita	Film	2/2	2	2	1923
Grass, Günter	Literature	1/7	10	16	1927
Graves, Peter	Television	3/9	3	18	1926
Graves, Robert	Literature	7/8	7	26	1895
Gray, Coleen	Film	1/5	10	23	1922
Gray, Thomas	Literature	3/8	12	26	1716
Grayson, Kathryn	Film	2/9	2	9	1922
Graziano, Rocky	Sports	6/7	6	7	1922
Greco, Buddy	Music	5/8	8	14	1926
Greco, José	Dance	3/5	12	23	1918
Green, Al	Music	4/4	4	13	1946
Green, Johnny	Music	1/1	10	10	1908
Greenaway, Kate	Literature	3/8	3	17	1846
Greenberg, Hank	Sports	1/1	1	1	1911
Greene, Graham	Literature	1/2	10	2	1904
Greene, Lorne	Television	2/3	2	12	1915
Greene, (Mean) Joe	Sports	6/9	9	24	1946
Greene, Richard	Film	7/8	8	25	1918
Greenspan, Alan	Business	3/6	3	6	1926
Greenstreet, Sydney	Film	3/9	12	27	1879
Greenwood, Charlotte	Dramatic Arts	6/7	6	25	1893
Greenwood, Joan	Film	3/4	3	4	1921
Gregory, Cynthia	Dance	7/8	7	8	1946
Gregory, Dick	Letters	1/3	10	12	1932
Gretzky, Wayne	Sports	1/8	1	26	1961
Grey, Joel	Music	2/4	4	11	1932
Grieg, Edvard	Music	6/6	6	15	1843
Griffin, Merv	Television	6/7	7	6	1925
Griffith, Andy	Television	1/6	6	1	1926
Griffith, D. W.	Film	1/4	1	22	1874
Griffith, Melanie	Film	8/9	8	9	1945
Grimes, Tammy	Entertainment	1/3	1	30	1934
Grimm, Jacob	Literature	1/4	1	4	1778
Grimm, Wilhelm	Literature	2/6	2	24	1786
Gris, Juan	Visual Arts	3/5	3	23	1887
Grissom, Virgil (Gus)	Exploration	3/4	4	3	1926
Gromyko, Andrei	Politics	6/7	7	6	1909
Gropius, Walter	Design	5/9	5	18	1883

NAME	FIELD	SET	MONTH	DAY	YEAR
Grosz, George	Visual Arts	7/8	7	26	1893
Guardi, Francesco	Visual Arts	1/4	10	4	1712
Guardino, Harry	Television	3/5	12	23	1925
Guccione, Robert	Business	3/8	12	17	1930
Guercino	Visual Arts	2/8	2	8	1591
Guevara, Ernesto (Che)	Politics	5/6	6	14	1928
Guggenheim, Peggy	Business	8/8	8	26	1898
Guggenheim, Simon	Business	3/3	12	30	1867
Guidi, Domenico	Visual Arts	6/6	6	6	1625
Guinness, Alec	Dramatic Arts	2/4	4	2	1914
Gunther, John	Literature	3/8	8	30	1901
Gurney, A. R., Jr.	Literature	1/2	11	1	1930
Guston, Philip	Visual Arts	6/9	6	27	1913
Gutenberg, Johannes	Sciences	2/5	2	23	1400
Guthrie, Arlo	Music	1/7	7	1	1947
Guthrie, Woody	Music	5/7	7	14	1912
Guttenberg, Steve	Film	6/8	8	24	1958
Gwynne, Fred	Film	1/7	7	10	1926
Hackett, Buddy	Entertainment	4/8	8	31	1924
Hackman, Gene	Film	1/3	1	30	1930
Haggard, Merle	Music	4/6	4	6	1937
Haig, Alexander, Jr.	Military	2/3	12	2	1924
Hale, Barbara	Television	4/9	4	18	1922
Hale, George	Sciences	2/6	6	29	1868
Hale, Nathan	Politics	6/6	6	6	1775
Haley, Alex	Literature	2/8	8	11	1921
Hall, Daryl	Music	1/2	10	11	1949
Hall, Jon	Film	2/5	2	23	1913
Hall, Juanita	Dramatic Arts	2/6	11	6	1901
Hall, Monty	Television	7/8	8	25	1923
Halston (Roy H. Frowick)	Design	4/5	4	23	1932
Hamill, Mark	Film	7/9	9	25	1951
Hamill, Pete	Letters	6/6	6	24	1935
Hamilton, Alexander	Politics	1/2	1	11	1757
Hamilton, Edith	Letters	3/8	8	12	1867
Hamilton, George	Film	3/8	8	12	1939
Hamlisch, Marvin	Music	2/6	6	2	1944
Hammarskjöld, Dag	Politics	2/7	7	29	1905
Hammer, Armand	Business	3/5	5	21	1898
Hammerstein, Oscar	Music	5/8	5	8	1847

NAME	FIELD	SET	MONTH	DAY	YEAR
Hammerstein, Oscar, II	Dramatic Arts	3/7	7	12	1895
Hammett, Dashiell	Literature	5/9	5	27	1894
Hampton, Lionel	Music	3/4	4	12	1913
Hamsun, Knut	Literature	4/8	8	4	1859
Hancock, Herbie	Music	3/4	4	12	1840
Hancock, John	Politics	1/5	1	23	1737
Handel, George Frederick	Music	2/5	2	23	1685
Handy, W. C.	Music	2/7	11	16	1873
Haney, Carol	Dance	3/6	12	24	1924
Hansberry, Lorraine	Literature	1/5	5	19	1930
Hanson, Howard	Music	1/1	10	28	1896
Harding, Warren G.	President	2/2	11	2	1865
Hardy, Oliver	Film	1/9	1	18	1892
Hardy, Thomas	Literature	2/6	6	2	1840
Haring, Keith	Visual Arts	4/5	5	4	1958
Harlow, Jean	Film	3/3	3	3	1911
Harper, Valerie	Television	4/8	8	22	1940
Harriman, Averell	Politics	2/6	11	15	1891
Harriman, E. Roland	Business	3/6	12	24	1895
Harris, Emmylou	Music	2/4	4	2	1947
Harris, Joel Chandler	Literature	3/9	12	9	1848
Harris, Julie	Dramatic Arts	2/3	12	2	1925
Harris, Phil	Film	6/6	6	24	1906
Harris, Richard	Film	1/1	10	1	1933
Harrison, Anna	Politics	7/7	7	25	1775
Harrison, Benjamin	President	2/8	8	20	1833
Harrison, Caroline	Politics	1/1	10	1	1832
Harrison, George	Music	2/7	2	25	1943
Harrison, Rex	Film	3/5	3	5	1908
Harrison, William Henry	President	2/9	2	9	1773
Harry, Deborah (Blondie)	Music	1/7	7	1	1945
Hart, Dolores	Film	1/2	10	20	1938
Hart, Gary	Politics	1/2	11	28	1937
Hart, Moss	Dramatic Arts	1/6	10	24	1904
Hart, William S.	Film	3/6	12	6	1870
Harte, Bret	Literature	7/8	8	25	1886
Hartford, Huntington	Business	4/9	4	18	1911
Hartley, Marsden	Visual Arts	1/4	1	4	1877
Hartman, David	Television	1/5	5	19	1935
Harvey, Laurence	Film	1/1	10	1	1928

NAME	FIELD	SET	MONTH	DAY	YEAR
Harvey, Lilian	Film	1/1	1	19	1906
Harvey, Paul	Letters	4/9	9	4	1918
Hassam, Childe	Visual Arts	1/8	10	17	1859
Hasso, Signe	Film	6/8	8	15	1915
Hatch, Orrin	Politics	3/4	3	22	1934
Hauer, Rutger	Film	1/5	1	23	1944
Haver, June	Film	1/6	6	10	1926
Havoc, June	Television	2/8	11	8	1916
Hawkins, Paula	Politics	1/6	1	24	1927
Hawn, Goldie	Film	2/3	11	21	1945
Haworth, Jill	Film	6/8	8	15	1945
Hawthorne, Nathaniel	Literature	4/7	7	4	1804
Hayakawa, S. I.	Politics	7/9	7	18	1906
Hayakawa, Sessue	Film	1/6	6	10	1890
Hayden, Sterling	Film	3/8	3	26	1916
Hayden, Tom	Politics	2/3	12	11	1939
Haydn, Franz Joseph	Music	3/4	3	31	1732
Hayes, Gabby	Film	5/7	5	7	1885
Hayes, Helen	Dramatic Arts	1/1	10	10	1900
Hayes, Isaac	Music	2/6	6	20	1942
Hayes, Peter Lind	Entertainment	6/7	6	25	1915
Hayes, Rutherford B.	President	1/4	10	4	1822
Hayes, Woody	Sports	2/5	2	14	1913
Hayward, Louis	Film	1/3	3	19	1909
Hayworth, Rita	Film	1/8	10	17	1918
Head, Edith	Design	1/1	10	28	1907
Hearns, Tom	Sports	1/9	10	18	1958
Hearst, Patty	Letters	2/2	2	20	1954
Hearst, William Randolph	Publishing	2/4	4	29	1863
Hearst, William Randolph, Jr.	Publishing	1/9	1	27	1908
Hecht, Anthony	Literature	1/7	1	16	1923
Hedren, Tippi	Film	1/1	1	19	1935
Heflin, Howell	Politics	1/6	6	19	1921
Hefner, Christie A.	Publishing	2/8	11	8	1952
Hefner, Hugh	Publishing	4/9	4	9	1926
Heifetz, Jascha	Music	2/2	2	2	1901
Heine, Heinrich	Literature	3/4	12	13	1797
Heisenberg, Werner	Sciences	3/5	12	5	1901
Held, Al	Visual Arts	1/3	10	12	1928
Heller, Joseph	Literature	1/5	5	1	1923

NAME	FIELD	SET	MONTH	DAY	YEAR
Hellman, Lillian	Literature	2/6	6	20	1905
Helms, Richard	Politics	3/3	3	30	1930
Helpmann, Robert	Dance	4/9	4	9	1909
Hemingway, Ernest	Literature	3/7	7	21	1899
Hemingway, Margaux	Film	1/2	2	19	1955
Hemmings, David	Film	2/9	11	18	1941
Henderson, Florence	Television	2/5	2	14	1934
Henderson, Skitch	Entertainment	1/9	1	27	1918
Hendrix, Jimi	Music	2/9	11	27	1942
Henie, Sonja	Sports	4/8	4	8	1910
Henning, Doug	Dramatic Arts	3/5	5	3	1947
Henreid, Paul	Film	1/1	1	10	1908
Henri, Robert	Visual Arts	6/6	6	24	1865
Henry, O. (William S. Porter)	Literature	2/9	9	11	1862
Henry, Patrick	Politics	2/5	5	29	1736
Henry the Navigator	Exploration	3/4	3	4	1394
Henson, Jim	Television	6/9	9	24	1936
Hepburn, Audrey	Film	4/5	5	4	1929
Hepburn, Katharine	Film	2/8	11	8	1909
Hepworth, Barbara	Visual Arts	1/1	1	10	1903
Herbert, George	Literature	3/4	4	3	1539
Herman, Pee-wee	Entertainment	8/9	8	27	1952
Herman, Woody	Music	5/7	5	16	1913
Herrick, Robert	Literature	6/8	8	24	1591
Herriot, James	Letters	3/9	3	9	1916
Hersey, John	Literature	6/8	6	17	1914
Hershey, Barbara	Film	2/5	2	5	1948
Hersholt, Jean	Film	3/7	7	12	1886
Hesse, Hermann	Literature	2/7	7	2	1877
Heston, Charlton	Film	1/4	10	4	1922
Heyerdahl, Thor	Exploration	1/6	10	6	1914
Hickok, James B. (Wild Bill)	Politics	5/9	5	27	1837
Hill, Arthur	Film	1/8	8	1	1922
Hill, Benny	Television	1/3	1	12	1925
Hill, George Roy	Film	2/3	3	20	1922
Hillary, Edmund	Exploration	2/7	7	20	1919
Hiller, Wendy	Dramatic Arts	6/8	8	15	1912
Hilton, Conrad	Business	3/7	3	25	1887
Hindemith, Paul	Music	2/7	11	16	1895
Hindenburg, Paul Ludwig von	Politics	1/2	10	2	1847

NAME	FIELD	SET	MONTH	DAY	YEAR
Hines, Gregory	Film	2/5	2	14	1946
Hines, Jerome	Music	2/8	11	8	1921
Hinkley, John W., Jr.	Crime	2/5	5	29	1955
Hirsch, Judd	Film	3/6	3	15	1935
Hirt, Al	Music	2/7	11	7	1922
Hiss, Alger	Letters	2/2	11	11	1904
Hitchcock, Alfred	Film	4/8	8	13	1899
Hitler, Adolf	Politics	2/4	4	20	1889
Ho Chi Minh	Politics	1/5	5	19	1890
Ho, Don	Music	4/8	8	13	1930
Hobart, Garret	Politics	3/6	6	3	1844
Hobby, Oveta Culp	Politics	1/1	1	19	1905
Hockney, David	Visual Arts	7/9	7	9	1937
Hodges, Gil	Sports	4/4	4	4	1924
Hodiak, John	Film	4/7	4	16	1914
Hoffa, James (Jimmy)	Politics	2/5	2	14	1913
Hoffer, Eric	Philosophy	7/7	7	25	1902
Hoffman, Abbie	Politics	2/3	11	30	1936
Hoffman, Dustin	Film	8/8	8	8	1937
Hoffman, Malvina	Visual Arts	6/6	6	6	1887
Hofmann, Hans	Visual Arts	3/3	3	21	1880
Hogan, Paul	Film	1/8	10	8	1939
Hogarth, William	Visual Arts	1/2	11	10	1697
Hogwood, Christopher	Music	1/9	9	1	1941
Hokusai, Katauhika	Visual Arts	1/3	10	21	1760
Holbrook, Hal	Dramatic Arts	2/8	2	17	1925
Holden, William	Film	4/8	4	17	1918
Holiday, Billie	Music	4/7	4	7	1915
Holliday, Judy	Film	3/6	6	21	1921
Holloway, Stanley	Dramatic Arts	1/1	10	1	1890
Holloway, Sterling	Film	1/4	1	4	1905
Holly, Buddy	Music	6/9	9	6	1936
Holm, Celeste	Film	2/4	4	29	1919
Holman, Libby	Music	5/5	5	23	1906
Holmes, Oliver Wendell, Jr.	Law	3/8	3	8	1841
Holmes, Oliver Wendell	Letters	2/8	8	29	1809
Holst, Gustav	Music	3/9	9	21	1874
Holt, Jack	Film	4/5	5	31	1888
Holt, Tim	Film	2/5	2	5	1918
Homer, Winslow	Visual Arts	2/6	2	24	1836

NAME	FIELD	SET	MONTH	DAY	YEAR
Hoover, Herbert	President	1/8	8	10	1874
Hoover, J. Edgar	Politics	1/1	1	1	1895
Hope, Bob	Entertainment	2/5	5	29	1903
Hopkins, Anthony	Dramatic Arts	3/4	12	31	1937
Hopkins, Gerard Manley	Literature	1/7	7	28	1824
Hopkins, Harry	Politics	8/8	8	17	1890
Hopkins, Miriam	Film	1/9	10	18	1902
Hopper, Dennis	Film	5/8	5	17	1936
Hopper, Edward	Visual Arts	4/7	7	22	1882
Hopper, Hedda	Letters	2/6	6	2	1890
Horace	Literature	3/8	12	8	B.C. 65
Horne, Lena	Music	3/6	6	30	1917
Horne, Marilyn	Music	1/7	1	16	1934
Horowitz, David	Politics	3/6	6	30	1937
Horowitz, Vladimir	Music	1/1	10	1	1904
Houseman, John	Dramatic Arts	4/9	9	22	1902
Houston, Whitney	Music	8/9	8	9	1963
Howard, Leslie	Film	4/6	4	24	1890
Howard, Ron	Film	1/3	3	1	1954
Howard, Trevor	Film	2/9	9	29	1916
Howes, Sally Ann	Dramatic Arts	2/7	7	20	1934
Hoyle, Fred	Sciences	6/6	6	24	1915
Hubble, Edwin	Sciences	2/2	11	20	1889
Hudson, Rock	Film	2/8	11	17	1925
Hughes, Howard	Business	3/6	12	24	1905
Hughes, Langston	Literature	1/2	2	1	1902
Hugo, Victor	Literature	2/8	2	26	1802
Hull, Bobby	Sports	1/3	1	3	1939
Humboldt, Friedrich	Exploration	5/9	9	14	1769
Humperdinck, Engelbert	Music	3/5	5	3	1936
Humphrey, Hubert	Politics	5/9	5	27	1911
Hunt, H. L.	Business	2/8	2	17	1889
Hunter, Ian	Film	4/6	6	13	1900
Hunter, Jeffrey	Film	2/5	11	23	1926
Hunter, Kim	Dramatic Arts	2/3	11	12	1922
Hunter, Ross	Film	5/6	5	6	1921
Hunter, Tab	Film	2/7	7	11	1931
Hurok, Sol	Entertainment	4/9	4	9	1884
Hurt, John	Film	1/4	1	22	1940
Hurt, William	Film	2/3	3	20	1950

NAME	FIELD	SET	MONTH	DAY	YEAR
Hussey, Olivia	Film	4/8	4	17	1951
Hussey, Ruth	Film	1/3	10	30	1914
Huston, John	Film	5/8	8	5	1906
Huston, Walter	Film	4/6	4	6	1884
Hutton, Barbara	Business	2/5	11	14	1912
Hutton, Betty	Film	2/8	2	26	1921
Hutton, Ina Rae	Music	3/4	3	13	1916
Hutton, Lauren	Film	2/8	11	17	1943
Huxley, Aldous	Literature	7/8	7	26	1894
Iacocca, Lee	Business	1/6	10	15	1924
Ian, Janis	Music	5/7	5	7	1950
Idol, Billy	Music	2/3	11	30	1955
Iglesias, Julio	Music	5/9	9	23	1943
Indiana, Robert	Visual Arts	4/9	9	13	1928
Inge, William	Dramatic Arts	6/6	6	6	1860
Ingram, Rex	Film	1/6	1	15	1892
Ingres, Jean-Auguste	Visual Arts	2/8	2	8	1780
Inouye, Daniel K.	Politics	7/9	9	7	1924
Ionesco, Eugène	Dramatic Arts	2/8	11	26	1912
Ireland, Jill	Film	4/6	4	24	1936
Irons, Jeremy	Film	1/9	9	19	1948
Irving, Amy	Film	1/9	9	10	1953
Irving, John	Literature	2/3	3	2	1942
Irving, Washington	Literature	3/4	4	3	1783
Isherwood, Christopher	Literature	8/8	8	26	1904
Ives, Burl	Music	5/6	6	14	1909
Ives, Charles	Music	1/2	10	20	1874
Jackson, Andrew	President	3/6	3	15	1767
Jackson, Anne	Dramatic Arts	3/9	9	3	1926
Jackson, Glenda	Film	5/9	5	9	1936
Jackson, Hurricane	Sports	8/9	8	9	1931
Jackson, Jesse	Politics	1/8	10	8	1941
Jackson, Kate	Television	1/2	10	29	1948
Jackson, Michael	Music	2/8	8	29	1958
Jackson, Rachel	Politics	6/6	6	15	1767
Jackson, Reggie	Sports	5/9	5	18	1946
Jacobi, Derek	Dramatic Arts	1/4	10	22	1938
Jaeckel, Richard	Film	1/1	10	10	1926
Jaffe, Sam	Film	3/8	3	8	1891
Jagger, Dean	Film	2/7	11	7	1903

NAME	FIELD	SET	MONTH	DAY	YEAR
Jagger, Mick	Music	7/8	7	26	1944
James, Dennis	Television	6/8	8	24	1917
James, Henry	Literature	4/6	4	15	1843
James, Jesse	Crime	5/9	9	5	1847
James, P. D.	Literature	3/8	8	3	1920
James, William	Literature	1/2	1	11	1842
Janácek, Leos	Music	3/7	7	3	1854
Jardine, Al	Music	3/9	9	3	1942
Jarreau, Al	Music	3/3	3	12	1940
Jarrett, Keith	Music	5/8	5	8	1945
Jarvis, Howard	Politics	4/9	9	22	1902
Javits, Jacob K.	Politics	5/9	5	18	1904
Jawlensky, Alexej Von	Visual Arts	3/4	3	13	1864
Jeffers, Robinson	Literature	1/1	1	10	1887
Jefferson, Martha Wayles	Politics	1/1	10	19	1748
Jefferson, Thomas	President	4/4	4	13	1743
Jenner, Bruce	Sports	1/1	10	28	1949
Jennings, Waylon	Music	6/6	6	15	1937
Jett, Joan	Music	4/9	9	22	1960
Jewett, Sarah Orne	Literature	3/9	9	3	1849
Joan of Arc	Politics	1/6	1	6	1412
Joel, Billy	Music	5/9	5	9	1949
John, Elton	Music	3/7	3	25	1947
Johns, Jasper	Visual Arts	5/6	5	15	1930
Johnson, Andrew	President	2/3	12	29	1808
Johnson, Ben	Film	4/6	6	13	1918
Johnson, Don	Television	3/6	12	15	1949
Johnson, Lady Bird	Letters	3/4	12	22	1912
Johnson, Lyndon B.	President	8/9	8	27	1908
Johnson, Philip C.	Design	7/8	7	8	1906
Johnson, Rafer	Sports	8/9	8	18	1935
Johnson, Samuel	Literature	9/9	9	18	1709
Johnson, Virginia	Dance	1/9	1	27	1950
Jolson, Al	Film	5/8	5	26	1886
Jones, Allan	Film	1/5	10	14	1907
Jones, Buck	Film	3/4	12	4	1889
Jones, Edward (Too Tall)	Sports	2/5	2	23	1951
Jones, Elvin	Music	9/9	9	9	1927
Jones, Grace	Music	1/5	5	19	1952
Jones, James	Literature	2/6	11	6	1921

NAME	FIELD	SET	MONTH	DAY	YEAR
Jones, James Earl	Film	1/8	1	17	1943
Jones, Jennifer	Film	2/3	3	2	1919
Jones, Spike	Music	3/5	12	14	1911
Jones, Tom	Music	6/7	6	7	1940
Jones, Tommy Lee	Film	6/9	9	15	1946
Jong, Erica	Literature	3/8	3	26	1942
Jonson, Ben	Literature	2/6	6	11	1572
Joplin, Janis	Music	1/1	1	19	1943
Joplin, Scott	Music	2/6	11	24	1868
Jory, Victor	Film	2/5	11	23	1902
Joyce, James	Literature	2/2	2	2	1882
Jung, Carl	Psychology	7/8	7	26	1875
Jurado, Katy	Film	1/7	1	16	1924
Kael, Pauline	Letters	1/6	6	19	1919
Kafka, Franz	Literature	3/7	7	3	1883
Kahn, Madeline	Film	2/9	9	29	1942
Kampelman, Max M.	Politics	2/7	2	7	1920
Kandinsky, Wassily	Visual Arts	3/4	12	4	1866
Kanin, Garson	Dramatic Arts	2/6	11	24	1912
Kant, Immanuel	Philosophy	4/4	4	22	1724
Kaplan, Gabe	Television	3/4	3	31	1945
Karajan, Herbert von	Music	4/5	4	5	1908
Karloff, Boris	Film	2/5	11	23	1887
Karns, Roscoe	Film	7/9	9	7	1893
Kasparov, Gary	Sports	4/4	4	13	1963
Katz, Alex	Visual Arts	6/7	7	24	1927
Kaufman, George S.	Dramatic Arts	2/5	2	14	1898
Kawabata, Yasunari	Literature	2/6	6	11	1899
Kaye, Danny	Film	1/9	1	18	1913
Kayser, Kaye	Entertainment	6/9	6	18	1905
Kazan, Elia	Dramatic Arts	7/9	9	7	1909
Kazan, Lainie	Music	5/7	5	16	1940
Kazantzakis, Nikos	Literature	2/3	12	2	1885
Keach, Stacy	Film	2/6	6	2	1941
Keaton, Buster	Film	1/4	10	4	1895
Keaton, Diane	Film	1/5	1	5	1946
Keaton, Michael	Film	9/9	9	9	1951
Keats, John	Literature	1/4	10	31	1795
Keel, Howard	Music	4/4	4	13	1917
Keeler, Ruby	Film	7/8	8	25	1909

NAME	FIELD	SET	MONTH	DAY	YEAR
Kefauver, Estes	Politics	7/8	7	26	1903
Keith, Brian	Film	2/5	11	14	1921
Keller, Helen	Letters	6/9	6	27	1880
Kellerman, Sally	Film	2/6	6	2	1938
Kelly, Ellsworth	Visual Arts	4/5	5	4	1923
Kelly, Emmett	Entertainment	3/9	12	9	1898
Kelly, Gene	Film	5/8	8	23	1912
Kelly, Grace	Film	2/3	11	12	1929
Kelly, Patsy	Film	1/3	1	12	1910
Kelvin, William T.	Sciences	6/8	6	26	1824
Kennedy, Edward (Ted)	Politics	2/4	2	22	1932
Kennedy, Ethel	Politics	2/4	4	11	1928
Kennedy, Joan Bennet	Politics	5/9	9	5	1936
Kennedy, John Fitzgerald	President	2/5	5	29	1917
Kennedy, John, Jr.	Business	2/7	11	25	1960
Kennedy, Joseph, Sr.	Politics	6/9	9	6	1888
Kennedy, Robert F.	Politics	2/2	11	20	1925
Kennedy, Rose	Politics	4/7	7	22	1890
Kent, Allegra	Dance	2/8	8	11	1937
Kent, Clark	Letters	2/2	2	29	1938
Kent, Corita	Visual Arts	2/2	11	20	1918
Kent, Rockwell	Visual Arts	3/6	6	21	1882
Kenton, Stan	Music	1/2	2	19	1912
Kenyatta, Jomo	Politics	1/1	10	28	1894
Kerkorian, Kirk	Business	6/6	6	6	1917
Kern, Jerome	Music	1/9	1	27	1885
Kerouac, Jack	Literature	3/3	3	12	1922
Kesey, Ken	Literature	8/9	9	17	1935
Khachaturian, Aram	Music	6/6	6	6	1903
Khashoggi, Adnan	Business	7/7	7	25	1935
Khrushchev, Nikita	Politics	4/8	4	17	1894
Kibbee, Guy	Film	3/6	3	6	1882
Kidder, Margot	Film	1/8	10	17	1948
Kierkegaard, Søren	Philosophy	5/5	5	5	1813
Kilgallen, Dorothy M.	Letters	3/7	7	3	1913
Kilmer, Joyce	Literature	3/6	12	6	1886
Kim, Dae Jung	Politics	1/6	1	6	1924
King, Alan	Entertainment	3/8	12	26	1927
King, B. B.	Music	7/9	9	16	1925
King, Billie Jean	Sports	2/4	11	22	1943

NAME	FIELD	SET	MONTH	DAY	YEAR
King, Carole	Music	2/9	2	9	1941
King Charles II	Royal	2/5	5	29	1630
King, Coretta Scott	Politics	4/9	4	27	1927
King Farouk	Royal	2/2	2	11	1920
King George V	Royal	3/6	6	3	1865
King, Henry	Film	6/6	6	24	1888
King Henry VIII	Royal	7/7	7	7	1491
King Hussein I	Royal	2/5	11	14	1889
King Hussein II	Royal	2/5	11	14	1935
King, Larry	Television	1/2	11	19	1933
King Louis XIV	Royal	5/9	9	5	1638
King Louis XVI	Royal	5/8	8	23	1754
King, Martin Luther, Jr.	Politics	1/6	1	15	1929
King, Micki	Sports	7/8	7	26	1944
King, Perry	Television	3/4	4	30	1948
King Richard I (the Lionhearted)	Royal	8/9	9	8	1157
King Saud	Royal	1/6	1	15	1902
Kingman, Dave	Sports	3/3	12	21	1948
Kingman, Dong	Visual Arts	3/4	3	31	1911
Kingsley, Ben	Film	3/4	12	31	1943
Kinnell, Galway	Literature	1/2	2	1	1927
Kinsey, Alfred	Sciences	5/6	6	23	1894
Kinski, Nastassja	Film	1/6	1	24	1960
Kipling, Rudyard	Literature	3/3	12	30	1865
Kirby, Durwood	Television	6/8	8	24	1912
Kirchner, Ernst Ludwig	Visual Arts	5/6	5	6	1880
Kirk, Rahsaan Roland	Music	7/8	8	7	1936
Kirkland, Gelsey	Dance	2/3	12	29	1952
Kirkpatrick, Jeane	Politics	1/2	11	19	1926
Kissinger, Henry	Politics	5/9	5	27	1923
Kitt, Eartha	Music	1/8	1	26	1928
Klee, Paul	Visual Arts	3/9	12	18	1879
Klein, Calvin	Design	1/2	11	19	1942
Klemperer, Otto	Music	5/5	5	14	1885
Klimt, Gustav	Visual Arts	5/7	7	14	1862
Kline, Franz	Visual Arts	5/5	5	23	1910
Kline, Kevin	Film	1/6	10	24	1947
Klugman, Jack	Television	4/9	4	27	1922
Knievel, Evel	Sports	1/8	10	17	1938
Knight, Gladys	Music	1/5	5	28	1944

NAME	FIELD	SET	MONTH	DAY	YEAR
Knight, Ted	Television	3/7	12	7	1923
Knopf, Alfred A.	Publishing	3/9	9	12	1892
Koch, Edward I.	Politics	3/3	12	12	1924
Kodály, Zoltán	Music	3/7	12	16	1882
Koestler, Arthur	Literature	5/9	9	5	1905
Kokoschka, Oskar	Visual Arts	1/3	3	1	1886
Kollwitz, Kathë	Visual Arts	7/8	7	8	1867
Koppel, Ted	Television	2/8	2	8	1940
Korda, Alexander	Film	7/9	9	16	1893
Korda, Michael	Publishing	1/8	10	8	1933
Korman, Harvey	Television	2/6	2	15	1927
Korngold, Erich Wolfgang	Music	2/5	5	29	1897
Kosinski, Jerzy	Literature	5/6	6	14	1933
Kostelanetz, André	Music	3/4	12	22	1901
Kosygin, Aleksei	Politics	2/2	2	20	1904
Koufax, Sandy	Sports	3/3	12	30	1935
Kovacs, Ernie	Television	1/5	1	23	1919
Krafft-Ebing, Richard von	Psychology	5/8	8	14	1840
Kramer, Stanley	Film	2/9	9	29	1913
Krebs, Hans Adolf	Sciences	7/8	8	25	1900
Kreisler, Fritz	Music	2/2	2	2	1875
Kristofferson, Kris	Film	4/6	6	22	1936
Krupa, Gene	Music	1/6	1	15	1909
Kuhn, Bowie	Sports	1/1	10	28	1926
Kuniyoshi, Yasuo	Visual Arts	1/9	9	1	1893
Kurosawa, Akira	Film	3/5	3	23	1910
Ky, Nguyen Cao	Politics	8/9	9	8	1930
L'Engle, Madeleine	Literature	2/2	11	29	1918
La Fontaine, Jean de	Literature	7/8	7	8	1621
LaBelle, Patti	Music	1/4	10	4	1944
Ladd, Alan	Film	3/9	9	3	1913
Ladd, Cheryl	Television	3/7	7	12	1951
Lafayette, Marquis de	Military	6/9	9	6	1757
Lagerfeld, Karl	Design	1/9	9	10	1938
Lagerlöf, Selma	Literature	2/2	11	20	1858
LaGuardia, Fiorello	Politics	2/3	12	11	1880
Laine, Cleo	Music	1/1	10	28	1927
Laing, R. D.	Psychology	1/7	10	7	1927
Lake, Arthur	Film	4/8	4	17	1905
Lake, Veronica	Film	2/5	11	14	1919

NAME	FIELD	SET	MONTH	DAY	YEAR
LaLanne, Jack	Sports	1/3	10	3	1914
Lalo, Édouard	Music	1/9	1	27	1823
Lamarr, Hedy	Film	2/9	9	11	1914
Lamb, Charles	Literature	1/2	2	10	1775
Lamm, Richard D.	Politics	3/8	8	3	1935
LaMotta, Jake	Sports	1/7	7	10	1921
Lamour, Dorothy	Film	1/3	12	10	1914
Lancaster, Burt	Film	2/2	11	2	1913
Lanchester, Elsa	Film	1/1	10	28	1902
Land, Edwin H.	Sciences	5/7	5	7	1909
Landers, Ann	Letters	4/7	7	4	1918
Landis, Carole	Film	1/1	1	1	1919
Landis, John	Film	3/8	8	3	1950
Landon, Alfred	Politics	9/9	9	9	1887
Landry, Tom	Sports	2/9	9	11	1924
Lane, Abbe	Entertainment	3/5	12	14	1933
Lane, Lola	Film	3/5	5	21	1906
Lane, Priscilla	Film	3/6	6	12	1917
Lane, Rosemary	Film	4/4	4	4	1913
Lang, Fritz	Film	3/5	12	5	1890
Langdon, Harry	Film	6/6	6	15	1884
Lange, Dorothea	Visual Arts	4/8	4	26	1895
Lange, Hope	Film	1/2	11	28	1931
Langella, Frank	Film	1/1	1	1	1946
Langford, Francis	Music	4/4	4	4	1914
Langtry, Lily	Entertainment	1/4	10	13	1853
Lansbury, Angela	Dramatic Arts	1/7	10	16	1925
Lansing, Robert	Television	5/6	6	5	1929
Lardner, Ring	Literature	3/6	3	6	1885
Larrieu-Smith, Francie	Sports	2/5	11	23	1952
Lasser, Louise	Television	2/4	4	11	1939
Lauder, Estée	Business	1/7	7	1	1908
Laughton, Charles	Film	1/7	7	1	1899
Lauper, Cyndi	Music	2/6	6	20	1953
Laurel, Stan	Film	6/7	6	16	1890
Lauren, Ralph	Design	1/5	10	14	1939
Laurie, Piper	Film	1/4	1	22	1932
Laver, Rod	Sports	8/9	8	9	1938
Lawford, Peter	Film	6/9	9	6	1923
Lawrence, Carol	Dramatic Arts	5/9	9	5	1934

NAME	FIELD	SET	MONTH	DAY	YEAR
Lawrence, D. H.	Literature	2/9	9	11	1885
Lawrence, Jacob	Visual Arts	7/9	9	7	1917
Lawrence, Steve	Music	7/8	7	8	1935
Lawrence, T. E. (of Arabia)	Letters	6/8	8	15	1888
Lawrence, Thomas	Visual Arts	4/4	4	13	1769
Le Carré, John	Literature	1/1	10	19	1931
Le Corbusier	Design	1/6	10	6	1887
Le Galienne, Eva	Dramatic Arts	1/2	1	11	1899
Leach, Bernard	Visual Arts	1/5	1	5	1887
Leachman, Cloris	Television	4/4	4	4	1926
Leahy, Frank	Business	8/9	8	27	1908
Leakey, Mary	Sciences	2/6	2	6	1913
Leakey, Richard E.	Sciences	1/3	12	19	1944
Lean, David	Film	3/7	3	25	1908
Lear, Edward	Literature	3/5	5	12	1812
Lear, Norman	Television	7/9	7	27	1922
Learned, Michael	Television	4/9	4	9	1939
Leary, Timothy	Letters	1/4	10	22	1920
Lederer, Francis	Film	2/6	11	6	1902
Lee, Brenda	Music	2/3	12	11	1944
Lee, Bruce	Film	2/9	11	27	1940
Lee, Christopher	Film	5/9	5	27	1922
Lee, Harper	Literature	1/4	4	28	1926
Lee, Michele	Television	6/6	6	24	1942
Lee, Peggy	Music	5/8	5	26	1920
Lee, Robert E.	Military	1/1	1	19	1803
Léger, Fernand	Visual Arts	2/4	2	4	1881
Lehár, Franz	Music	3/4	4	30	1870
Lehman, John F., Jr.	Politics	5/9	9	14	1942
Leibman, Ron	Film	1/2	10	11	1937
Leigh, Janet	Film	6/7	7	6	1927
Leigh, Vivian	Film	2/5	11	5	1913
Leinsdorf, Erich	Music	2/4	2	4	1912
Lelouch, Claude	Film	1/3	10	30	1937
Lemmon, Jack	Film	2/8	2	8	1925
Lenin, Nikolai	Politics	4/4	4	22	1870
Lennon, Janet	Music	6/6	6	15	1946
Lennon, John	Music	1/9	10	9	1940
Lenya, Lotte	Dramatic Arts	1/1	10	19	1900
Leonard, Sheldon	Film	2/4	2	22	1907

NAME	FIELD	SET	MONTH	DAY	YEAR
Leonard, (Sugar) Ray	Sports	5/8	5	17	1956
Lerner, Alan Jay	Music	4/8	8	31	1918
LeRoy, Mervyn	Film	1/6	10	15	1900
Leslie, Joan	Film	1/8	1	26	1925
Lessing, Doris	Literature	1/4	10	22	1919
Lester, Richard	Film	1/1	1	19	1932
Letterman, David	Television	3/4	4	12	1947
Levant, Oscar	Entertainment	3/9	12	27	1906
Levertov, Denise	Literature	1/6	10	24	1923
Levine, Joseph E.	Film	9/9	9	9	1905
Lewes, George Henry	Literature	4/9	4	18	1817
Lewis, C. S.	Literature	2/2	11	29	1898
Lewis, Carl	Sports	1/7	7	1	1961
Lewis, Jerry	Entertainment	3/7	3	16	1926
Lewis, Jerry Lee	Music	2/9	9	29	1935
Lewis, Meriwether	Exploration	8/9	8	18	1774
Lewis, Shari	Television	1/8	1	17	1934
Lewis, Sinclair	Literature	2/7	2	7	1885
Lewis, Ted	Music	6/6	6	6	1891
Lewis, Wyndham	Literature	2/9	11	18	1882
Lewitt, Sol	Visual Arts	9/9	9	9	1928
Li, Choh Hao	Sciences	3/4	4	21	1913
Liberace	Music	5/7	5	16	1920
Lichtenstein, Roy	Visual Arts	1/9	10	27	1923
Liddy, G. Gordon	Politics	2/3	11	30	1930
Lie, Trygve H.	Politics	7/7	7	16	1896
Lightfoot, Gordon	Music	2/8	11	17	1938
Lillie, Beatrice	Music	2/5	5	29	1898
Lincoln, Abraham	President	2/3	2	12	1809
Lind, Jenny	Entertainment	1/6	10	6	1820
Lindbergh, Anne Morrow	Letters	4/6	6	22	1906
Lindbergh, Charles	Exploration	2/4	2	4	1902
Linden, Hal	Television	2/3	3	20	1931
Lindfors, Viveca	Film	2/3	12	29	1920
Lindsay, John V.	Politics	2/6	11	24	1921
Lindsay, Vachel	Literature	1/2	11	10	1879
Linkletter, Art	Television	7/8	7	17	1912
Linnaeus, Carolus	Sciences	5/5	5	23	1707
Lipchitz, Jacques	Visual Arts	4/8	8	22	1891
Liszt, Franz	Music	1/4	10	22	1811

NAME	FIELD	SET	MONTH	DAY	YEAR
Lithgow, John	Dramatic Arts	1/1	10	19	1945
Little, Rich	Entertainment	2/8	11	26	1938
Little Richard (Penniman)	Music	3/5	12	5	1932
Lloyd, Chris Evert	Sports	3/3	12	21	1954
Lloyd, Harold	Film	2/4	4	20	1889
Lloyd Webber, Andrew	Music	3/4	3	22	1948
Lo Bianco, Tony	Television	1/1	10	19	1936
Locke, Sondra	Film	1/5	5	28	1947
Lockhart, Gene	Film	7/9	7	18	1891
Lockhart, June	Television	6/7	6	25	1925
Lockwood, Margaret	Film	6/9	9	15	1916
Lodge, Henry Cabot, Jr.	Politics	5/7	7	5	1902
Loesser, Frank	Music	2/6	6	29	1910
Loewy, Raymond F.	Design	2/5	11	5	1893
Logan, Joshua	Dramatic Arts	1/5	10	5	1908
Loggia, Robert	Film	1/3	1	3	1930
Loggins, Kenny	Music	1/7	1	7	1948
Lollobrigida, Gina	Film	4/7	7	4	1928
Lombard, Carole	Film	1/6	10	6	1908
Lombardi, Vince	Sports	2/6	6	11	1913
Lombardo, Guy	Music	1/6	6	19	1902
Lon Nol	Politics	2/8	11	17	1913
London, Jack	Literature	1/3	3	12	1876
London, Julie	Music	8/9	9	26	1926
Long, Huey	Politics	3/8	8	30	1893
Long, Shelley	Television	5/8	8	23	1949
Longfellow, Henry W.	Literature	2/9	2	27	1807
Lopez, Nancy	Sports	1/6	1	6	1957
López Portillo, José	Politics	7/7	7	16	1920
Lopez, Trini	Music	5/6	5	15	1937
Lorca, Federico García	Literature	5/6	6	5	1898
Loren, Sophia	Film	2/9	9	20	1934
Lorentz, Hendrik	Sciences	7/9	7	18	1853
Lorre, Peter	Film	6/8	6	26	1904
Loudon, Dorothy	Dramatic Arts	8/9	9	17	1933
Louis, Joe	Sports	4/5	5	13	1914
Louise, Anita	Film	1/9	1	9	1915
Louise, Tina	Film	2/3	3	11	1934
Louvin, Charlie	Music	7/7	7	7	1927
Love, Bessie	Film	1/9	9	10	1893

NAME	FIELD	SET	MONTH	DAY	YEAR
Love, Mike	Music	3/6	3	15	1941
Lowe, Edmund	Film	3/3	3	3	1890
Lowell, Amy	Literature	2/9	2	9	1874
Lowell, James Russell	Literature	2/4	2	22	1819
Lowell, Robert	Literature	1/3	3	1	1917
Loy, Myrna	Film	2/8	8	2	1905
Lucas, George	Film	5/5	5	14	1944
Luce, Clare Boothe	Letters	1/4	4	10	1903
Luckinbill, Laurence	Television	2/3	11	21	1934
Lugosi, Bela	Film	1/2	10	20	1882
Lumet, Sidney	Film	6/7	6	25	1924
Lunceford, Jimmie	Music	6/6	6	6	1902
Lupino, Ida	Film	2/4	2	4	1918
Lupone, Patti	Dramatic Arts	3/4	4	21	1949
Lurie, Alison	Literature	3/9	9	3	1926
Lynde, Paul	Entertainment	4/6	6	13	1926
Lyng, Richard E.	Politics	2/6	6	29	1918
Lynley, Carol	Film	2/4	2	13	1942
Lynn, Janet	Sports	4/6	4	6	1953
Lynn, Loretta	Music	4/5	4	14	1936
Lyon, Ben	Film	2/6	2	6	1901
Lyon, Sue	Film	1/7	7	10	1946
Lysenko, Trofim	Sciences	2/9	9	29	1898
Maazel, Lorin	Music	3/6	3	6	1930
MacArthur, Douglas	Military	1/8	1	26	1880
MacArthur, James	Television	3/8	12	8	1937
Macaulay, Thomas	Literature	1/7	10	25	1800
Macchio, Ralph	Film	2/4	11	4	1961
MacDonald, Jeanette	Film	6/9	6	18	1901
MacDonald, John D.	Literature	6/7	7	24	1916
MacGraw, Ali	Film	1/4	4	1	1939
Mach, Ernst	Sciences	2/9	2	18	1838
Machiavelli, Niccolo	Philosophy	3/5	5	3	1469
Mack, Connie	Sports	2/4	2	22	1862
Macke, August	Visual Arts	1/3	1	3	1887
MacKenzie, Gisele	Music	1/1	1	10	1927
MacLaine, Shirley	Film	4/6	4	24	1934
MacLeish, Archibald	Literature	5/7	5	7	1892
Macmillan, Harold	Politics	1/2	2	10	1894
MacMurray, Fred	Film	3/8	8	30	1908

NAME	FIELD	SET	MONTH	DAY	YEAR
MacNeil, Robert	Television	1/1	1	19	1931
MacRae, Gordon	Music	3/3	3	12	1921
Macy, Bill	Dramatic Arts	5/9	5	18	1922
Madden, John	Television	1/4	4	10	1936
Maddox, Lester	Politics	3/9	9	30	1915
Madison, Dolly	Politics	2/5	5	2	1768
Madison, Guy	Television	1/1	1	19	1922
Madison, James	President	3/7	3	16	1751
Madonna	Music	7/8	8	16	1958
Magritte, René	Visual Arts	2/3	11	21	1898
Mahler, Gustav	Music	7/7	7	7	1860
Mailer, Norman	Literature	1/4	1	31	1923
Main, Marjorie	Film	2/6	2	24	1890
Majors, Lee	Television	4/5	4	23	1940
Makarova, Natalia	Dance	2/3	11	21	1940
Malamud, Bernard	Literature	4/8	4	26	1914
Malcolm X	Politics	1/5	5	19	1925
Malden, Karl	Film	3/4	3	22	1913
Mallarmé, Stéphane	Literature	3/9	3	18	1842
Malle, Louis	Film	1/3	10	30	1932
Malone, Dorothy	Film	1/3	1	30	1925
Malraux, André	Literature	2/2	11	2	1901
Maltin, Leonard	Television	3/9	12	18	1950
Mamet, David	Dramatic Arts	2/3	11	30	1947
Man Ray	Visual Arts	8/9	8	27	1890
Manchester, Melissa	Music	2/6	2	15	1951
Mancini, Henry	Music	4/7	4	16	1924
Mandrell, Barbara	Music	3/7	12	25	1948
Manet, Édouard	Visual Arts	1/5	1	23	1832
Mangione, Chuck	Music	2/2	11	29	1940
Manilow, Barry	Music	6/8	6	17	1946
Mann, Herbie	Music	4/7	4	16	1930
Mann, Thomas	Literature	6/6	6	6	1875
Mansfield, Katherine	Literature	1/5	10	14	1888
Manson, Charles	Crime	2/3	11	12	1934
Mantle, Mickey	Sports	1/2	10	20	1931
Manville, Tommy	Business	4/9	4	9	1894
Manzoni, Alessandro	Literature	3/7	3	7	1785
Mao Tse-tung	Politics	3/8	12	26	1893
Marc, Franz	Visual Arts	2/8	2	8	1880

NAME	FIELD	SET	MONTH	DAY	YEAR
Marceau, Marcel	Entertainment	3/4	3	22	1923
March, Fredric	Film	4/8	8	31	1897
March, Hal	Television	4/4	4	22	1920
Marcos, Ferdinand	Politics	2/9	9	11	1917
Margo	Film	1/5	5	10	1918
Margolin, Janet	Film	7/7	7	25	1943
Marin, Cheech	Film	4/7	7	13	1946
Marini, Marino	Visual Arts	2/9	2	27	1901
Maris, Roger	Sports	1/9	9	10	1934
Marisol	Visual Arts	4/5	5	22	1930
Markova, Alicia	Dance	1/3	12	1	1910
Marley, Bob	Music	2/5	2	5	1945
Marlowe, Christopher	Literature	2/6	2	6	1564
Márquez, Gabriel García	Literature	3/6	3	6	1928
Marriner, Neville	Music	4/6	4	15	1924
Marriott, J. Willard	Business	8/9	9	17	1900
Marsalis, Wynton	Music	1/9	10	18	1961
Marsh, Jean	Television	1/7	7	1	1934
Marsh, Reginald	Visual Arts	3/5	3	14	1898
Marshall, Catherine	Literature	9/9	9	27	1914
Marshall, E. G.	Television	6/9	6	18	1910
Marshall, Herbert	Film	5/5	5	23	1890
Marshall, Penny	Television	1/6	10	15	1945
Martin, Billy	Sports	5/7	5	16	1928
Martin, Dean	Music	6/8	6	17	1917
Martin, Dick	Television	1/3	1	30	1928
Martin, Judith	Literature	4/9	9	13	1938
Martin, Mary	Dramatic Arts	1/3	12	1	1913
Martin, Pamela Sue	Television	1/5	1	5	1954
Martin, Quinn	Television	4/5	5	22	1922
Martin, Strother	Dramatic Arts	3/8	3	26	1919
Martin, Tony	Music	3/7	12	25	1913
Martino, Al	Music	1/7	10	7	1927
Martins, Peter	Dance	1/9	10	27	1946
Marvin, Lee	Film	1/2	2	19	1924
Marx, Chico	Film	2/4	2	22	1891
Marx, Groucho	Film	1/2	10	2	1890
Marx, Harpo	Film	2/5	11	23	1892
Marx, Karl	Philosophy	5/5	5	5	1818
Marx, Zeppo	Film	2/7	2	25	1901

NAME	FIELD	SET	MONTH	DAY	YEAR
Mary Stuart (Queen of Scots)	Royal	3/7	12	16	1542
Masaccio	Visual Arts	3/3	12	21	1401
Masefield, John	Literature	1/6	6	1	1878
Mason, James	Film	5/6	5	15	1909
Mason, Marsha	Film	3/4	4	3	1942
Mason, Pamela	Television	1/3	3	10	1922
Massenet, Jules	Music	3/5	5	12	1842
Massine, Léonide	Dance	8/9	8	9	1896
Masters, Edgar Lee	Literature	5/8	8	23	1869
Mastroianni, Marcello	Film	1/9	9	28	1923
Mata Hari	Politics	7/8	8	7	1876
Matheson, Tim	Film	3/4	12	31	1947
Mathis, Johnny	Music	3/9	9	30	1935
Matisse, Henri	Visual Arts	3/4	12	31	1869
Matthau, Walter	Film	1/1	10	1	1920
Mattingly, Don	Sports	3/4	4	21	1961
Mature, Victor	Film	1/2	1	29	1916
Maugham, Somerset	Literature	1/9	1	27	1874
Maupassant, Guy de	Literature	5/8	8	5	1850
Max, Peter	Visual Arts	1/1	10	19	1939
Maxwell, Elsa	Letters	5/6	5	24	1883
May, Elaine	Dramatic Arts	3/4	4	21	1932
Mayakovsky, Vladimir	Literature	2/7	7	29	1893
Mayfield, Curtis	Music	3/6	6	3	1942
Mayo, Virginia	Film	2/3	11	30	1920
Mays, Willie	Sports	5/6	5	6	1931
Mazurki, Mike	Film	3/7	12	25	1909
Mazursky, Paul	Film	4/7	4	25	1930
McBride, Patricia	Dance	5/8	8	23	1942
McCallum, David	Television	1/9	9	19	1933
McCambridge, Mercedes	Film	3/8	3	17	1918
McCarthy, Kevin	Television	2/6	2	15	1914
McCarthy, Mary	Literature	3/6	6	21	1912
McCartney, Paul	Music	6/9	6	18	1942
McClure, Doug	Television	2/5	5	11	1938
McClure, James A.	Politics	3/9	12	27	1924
McCluskey, Roger	Politics	6/8	8	24	1930
McCovey, Willie	Sports	1/1	1	10	1938
McCoy, Tim	Film	1/4	4	10	1891
McCrae, Carmen	Music	4/8	4	8	1922

NAME	FIELD	SET	MONTH	DAY	YEAR
McCrea, Joel	Film	2/5	11	5	1905
McCullers, Carson	Literature	1/2	2	19	1917
McDowall, Roddy	Film	8/9	9	17	1928
McDowell, Malcolm	Film	1/6	6	19	1943
McEnroe, John	Sports	2/7	2	16	1959
McFarland, Spanky	Film	1/2	10	2	1928
McGavin, Darren	Television	5/7	5	7	1922
McGoohan, Patrick	Television	1/3	3	19	1928
McGuire, Dorothy	Film	5/6	6	14	1919
McKenna, Siobhan	Dramatic Arts	5/6	5	24	1922
McKinley, William	President	1/2	1	29	1843
McKuen, Rod	Literature	2/4	4	29	1933
McLaglen, Victor	Film	1/3	12	10	1886
McLean, Don	Music	1/2	10	2	1945
McLuhan, Marshall	Letters	3/7	7	21	1911
McMahon, Ed	Television	3/6	3	6	1923
McMahon, Jim	Sports	3/8	8	21	1959
McNair, Barbara	Television	3/4	3	4	1939
McNichol, Kristy	Television	9/9	9	9	1962
McPhee, John	Letters	3/8	3	8	1931
McQueen, Butterfly	Film	1/7	1	7	1911
Meadows, Jayne	Television	9/9	9	27	1923
Meany, George	Politics	7/8	8	16	1894
Meeker, Ralph	Film	2/3	11	21	1920
Meese, Edwin	Politics	3/3	12	3	1931
Mehta, Zubin	Music	2/4	4	29	1936
Meir, Golda	Politics	3/5	5	3	1898
Melanie (Melanie Safka)	Music	1/3	1	3	1947
Mellencamp, John Cougar	Music	1/7	10	7	1951
Mellon, Andrew	Business	3/6	3	24	1855
Mellon, Paul	Visual Arts	2/6	6	11	1907
Melville, Herman	Literature	1/8	8	1	1819
Mencken, H. L.	Letters	3/9	9	12	1880
Mendel, Gregor	Sciences	4/7	7	22	1822
Mendelssohn, Felix	Music	2/3	2	3	1809
Mendes, Sergio	Music	2/2	2	11	1941
Menjou, Adolphe	Film	2/9	2	18	1890
Menotti, Gian-Carlo	Music	7/7	7	7	1911
Menuhin, Yehudi	Music	4/4	4	22	1916
Menzies, Robert	Politics	2/3	12	20	1894

NAME	FIELD	SET	MONTH	DAY	YEAR
Mercer, Bobby	Music	2/5	5	2	1946
Mercer, Mabel	Music	2/3	2	3	1900
Mercouri, Melina	Film	1/9	10	18	1925
Meredith, Burgess	Film	2/7	11	16	1908
Meredith, George	Literature	2/3	2	12	1828
Merman, Ethel	Entertainment	1/7	1	16	1909
Merrick, David	Dramatic Arts	2/9	11	27	1912
Merrill, Dina	Film	3/9	12	9	1925
Merrill, Gary	Film	2/8	8	2	1915
Merton, Thomas	Literature	1/4	1	31	1915
Mesmer, Frank Anton	Sciences	5/5	5	23	1734
Michael, George	Music	6/7	6	25	1963
Michelangelo	Visual Arts	3/6	3	6	1475
Michener, James A.	Literature	2/3	2	3	1907
Mickey Mouse	Entertainment	2/9	11	18	1928
Midler, Bette	Film	1/3	12	1	1945
Mies van der Rohe, Ludwig	Design	3/9	3	27	1886
Mifune, Toshiro	Film	1/4	4	1	1920
Miles, Sarah	Film	3/4	12	31	1941
Miles, Sylvia	Film	9/9	9	9	1932
Miles, Vera	Film	5/8	8	23	1930
Milhaud, Darius	Music	4/9	9	4	1892
Millais, John	Visual Arts	6/8	6	8	1829
Milland, Ray	Film	1/3	1	3	1905
Millay, Edna St. Vincent	Literature	2/4	2	22	1892
Miller, Ann	Film	3/4	4	12	1932
Miller, Arthur	Dramatic Arts	1/8	10	17	1915
Miller, Glenn	Music	1/3	3	1	1904
Miller, Henry	Literature	3/8	12	26	1891
Miller, Jonathan	Dramatic Arts	3/7	7	21	1934
Miller, Mitch	Music	4/7	7	4	1911
Miller, Roger	Music	1/2	1	2	1936
Millet, Jean François	Visual Arts	1/4	10	4	1814
Mills, Donald	Music	2/4	4	29	1915
Mills, Donna	Television	2/3	12	11	1947
Mills, Hayley	Film	4/9	4	18	1946
Mills, Herbert	Music	3/4	4	12	1912
Mills, John	Film	2/4	2	22	1908
Mills, Wilbur	Politics	5/6	5	24	1909
Milne, A. A.	Literature	1/9	1	18	1882

NAME	FIELD	SET	MONTH	DAY	YEAR
Milstein, Nathan	Music	3/4	12	31	1904
Milton, John	Literature	3/9	12	9	1608
Mimieux, Yvette	Film	1/8	1	8	1942
Mineo, Sal	Film	1/1	1	10	1939
Mingus, Charles	Music	4/4	4	22	1922
Minnelli, Liza	Entertainment	3/3	3	12	1946
Minnelli, Vincente	Film	1/2	2	28	1913
Miranda, Carmen	Film	2/9	2	9	1914
Miró, Joan	Visual Arts	2/4	4	20	1893
Mishima, Yukio	Literature	1/5	1	14	1925
Mitchell, Cameron	Film	2/4	11	4	1918
Mitchell, George John	Politics	2/8	8	20	1933
Mitchell, Joan	Visual Arts	2/3	2	12	1926
Mitchell, John	Politics	5/9	9	5	1913
Mitchell, Joni	Music	2/7	11	7	1943
Mitchell, Margaret	Literature	2/8	11	8	1900
Mitchell, Martha	Politics	2/9	9	2	1918
Mitchell, Thomas	Dramatic Arts	2/7	7	11	1892
Mitchum, James	Film	5/8	5	8	1941
Mitchum, Robert	Film	6/8	8	6	1917
Mitgang, Herbert	Letters	1/2	1	20	1920
Mix, Tom	Film	1/6	1	6	1880
Modigliani, Amedeo	Visual Arts	3/7	7	12	1884
Moffo, Anna	Music	6/8	6	26	1935
Moholy-Nagy, László	Visual Arts	2/7	7	20	1895
Molière (Jean Baptiste Poquelin)	Literature	1/6	1	15	1622
Molotov, Vyacheslav	Politics	3/9	3	9	1890
Momaday, N. Scott	Literature	2/9	2	27	1934
Mondale, Joan	Politics	8/8	8	8	1930
Mondale, Walter	Politics	1/5	1	5	1928
Mondrian, Piet	Visual Arts	3/7	3	7	1872
Monet, Claude	Visual Arts	2/5	11	14	1840
Monk, Thelonious	Music	1/1	10	10	1918
Monroe, Earl	Sports	2/3	11	21	1944
Monroe, James	President	1/4	4	28	1758
Monroe, Marilyn	Film	1/6	6	1	1926
Monroe, Vaughn	Music	1/7	10	7	1911
Monsarrat, Nicholas	Literature	3/4	3	22	1910
Montagu, Ashley	Literature	1/6	6	28	1905
Montaigne, Michel de	Literature	1/2	2	28	1533

NAME	FIELD	SET	MONTH	DAY	YEAR
Montalban, Ricardo	Film	2/7	11	25	1930
Montana, Joe	Sports	2/6	6	11	1956
Montand, Yves	Film	1/4	10	13	1921
Montesquieu, Charles de	Literature	1/9	1	18	1689
Monteverdi, Claudio	Music	5/6	5	15	1567
Montez, Maria	Film	6/6	6	6	1918
Montgomery, Elizabeth	Television	4/6	4	15	1933
Montgomery, George	Film	2/8	8	29	1916
Montgomery, Robert	Film	3/5	5	21	1904
Montgomery, Wes	Music	3/6	3	6	1925
Montoya, Carlos	Music	3/4	12	13	1903
Moody, Ron	Dramatic Arts	1/8	1	8	1924
Moog, Robert A.	Sciences	5/5	5	23	1934
Moore, Clayton (Lone Ranger)	Film	5/9	9	14	1914
Moore, Colleen	Film	1/8	8	19	1900
Moore, Constance	Film	1/9	1	18	1922
Moore, Demi	Film	2/2	11	11	1962
Moore, Dudley	Film	1/4	4	19	1935
Moore, Garry	Television	1/4	1	31	1915
Moore, Henry	Visual Arts	3/7	7	30	1898
Moore, Marianne	Literature	2/6	11	15	1887
Moore, Mary Tyler	Television	2/3	12	29	1937
Moore, Melba	Music	1/2	10	29	1945
Moore, Roger	Film	1/5	10	14	1927
Moore, Terry	Film	1/1	1	1	1932
Moreau, Jeanne	Film	1/5	1	23	1928
Moreno, Rita	Dramatic Arts	2/3	12	11	1931
Morgan, Frank	Film	1/6	6	1	1890
Morgan, Henry	Television	3/4	3	31	1915
Morgan, J. Pierpont	Business	4/8	4	17	1837
Morgan, Jaye P.	Music	3/3	12	3	1931
Morgan, John Pierpont, Jr.	Business	7/9	9	7	1867
Morgenthau, Henry, Jr.	Politics	2/5	5	11	1891
Morgenthau, Robert M.	Politics	4/7	7	31	1919
Moriarty, Michael	Film	4/5	4	5	1941
Morisot, Berthe	Visual Arts	1/5	1	14	1841
Morley, Robert	Film	5/8	5	26	1908
Morris, Chester	Film	2/7	2	16	1901
Morris, James	Music	1/1	1	10	1947
Morrison, Jim	Music	3/8	12	8	1943

NAME	FIELD	SET	MONTH	DAY	YEAR
Morrison, Toni	Literature	2/9	2	18	1931
Morrison, Van	Music	4/8	8	31	1945
Morrow, Vic	Film	2/5	2	14	1932
Morton, Ferdinand (Jelly Roll)	Music	2/9	9	20	1885
Moses, Edward	Sports	4/8	8	31	1958
Moss, Sterling	Television	8/9	9	17	1929
Mother Teresa	Religion	8/9	8	27	1910
Motherwell, Robert	Visual Arts	1/6	1	24	1915
Mowat, Farley	Letters	3/5	5	12	1921
Mowbray, Alan	Film	8/9	8	18	1893
Moyers, Bill	Television	5/6	6	5	1934
Moynihan, Daniel Patrick	Politics	3/7	3	16	1927
Mozart, Wolfgang Amadeus	Music	1/9	1	27	1756
Mr. T	Television	3/5	5	21	1952
Mucha, Alphonse	Visual Arts	6/8	8	24	1860
Mudd, Roger	Television	2/9	2	9	1928
Muldaur, Maria	Music	3/9	9	12	1942
Mull, Martin	Entertainment	8/9	8	18	1943
Mulligan, Gerry	Music	4/6	6	4	1927
Munch, Charles	Music	8/9	9	26	1891
Munch, Edvard	Visual Arts	3/3	12	12	1863
Mundt, Karl	Politics	3/6	6	3	1900
Muni, Paul	Film	4/9	9	22	1895
Munsel, Patrice	Music	5/5	5	14	1925
Munson, Thurman	Sports	6/7	6	7	1947
Murdoch, Iris	Literature	6/7	7	15	1919
Murdoch, Rupert	Publishing	2/5	5	11	1931
Murillo, Bartolomé	Visual Arts	1/1	1	1	1617
Murnau, F. W.	Film	1/3	12	28	1888
Murphy, Eddie	Film	3/4	4	3	1961
Murphy, George	Politics	4/7	7	4	1902
Murray, Anne	Music	2/6	6	20	1945
Murray, Arthur	Dance	4/4	4	4	1895
Murray, Bill	Film	3/9	9	21	1950
Murray, Don	Film	4/7	7	31	1929
Murray, Ken	Entertainment	5/7	7	14	1903
Murrow, Edward R.	Television	4/7	4	25	1908
Musante, Tony	Television	3/6	6	30	1936
Musial, Stan	Sports	2/3	11	21	1920
Muskie, Edmund S.	Politics	1/3	3	28	1914

NAME	FIELD	SET	MONTH	DAY	YEAR
Mussolini, Benito	Politics	2/7	7	29	1883
Mussorgsky, Modest	Music	3/3	3	21	1839
Muybridge, Eadweard	Visual Arts	4/9	4	9	1830
Mydans, Carl M.	Literature	2/5	5	2	1907
Myerson, Bess	Politics	7/7	7	16	1924
Nabokov, Vladimir	Literature	4/5	4	23	1899
Nabors, Jim	Television	3/6	6	12	1933
Nader, Ralph	Politics	2/9	2	27	1934
Naipaul, V. S.	Literature	8/8	8	17	1932
Nakian, Ruben	Visual Arts	1/8	8	10	1897
Namath, Joe	Sports	4/5	5	31	1943
Nash, Graham	Music	1/5	1	5	1942
Nash, Ogden	Literature	1/8	8	19	1902
Nasser, Gamal	Politics	1/6	1	15	1918
Nast, Thomas	Visual Arts	9/9	9	27	1840
Nastase, Ilie	Sports	1/7	7	19	1946
Nation, Carry	Politics	2/7	11	25	1846
Natwick, Mildred	Film	1/6	6	19	1908
Navratilova, Martina	Sports	1/9	10	18	1956
Neal, Patricia	Film	1/2	1	20	1926
Neff, Hildegarde	Film	1/3	12	28	1925
Negri, Pola	Film	3/4	12	31	1894
Nehru, Jawaharlal	Politics	2/5	11	14	1889
Neiman, Leroy	Visual Arts	6/8	6	8	1926
Nelligan, Kate	Film	3/7	3	16	1951
Nelson, Barry	Film	4/7	4	16	1920
Nelson, Cindy	Sports	1/8	8	19	1955
Nelson, David	Television	1/6	10	24	1936
Nelson, Gene	Film	3/6	3	24	1920
Nelson, Harriet	Television	7/9	7	18	1911
Nelson, Judd	Film	1/2	11	28	1959
Nelson, Ozzie	Television	2/2	2	20	1907
Nelson, Rick	Music	5/8	5	8	1940
Nelson, Willie	Music	3/4	4	3	1933
Nero, Peter	Music	4/5	5	22	1934
Neruda, Pablo	Literature	3/7	7	12	1904
Nesbitt, Cathleen	Dramatic Arts	2/6	11	24	1889
Neuharth, Allen H.	Literature	3/4	3	22	1924
Neutra, Richard	Visual Arts	4/8	8	8	1892
Newhart, Bob	Television	5/9	9	5	1929

NAME	FIELD	SET	MONTH	DAY	YEAR
Newley, Anthony	Entertainment	6/9	9	24	1931
Newman, Barry	Film	2/7	11	7	1938
Newman, Paul	Film	1/8	1	26	1925
Newman, Phyllis	Dramatic Arts	1/3	3	19	1935
Newman, Randy	Music	1/2	11	28	1943
Newton, Isaac	Sciences	3/7	12	25	1642
Newton, Robert	Film	1/6	6	1	1905
Newton, Wayne	Music	3/4	4	3	1942
Newton-John, Olivia	Music	8/9	9	26	1948
Nichols, Mike	Dramatic Arts	2/6	11	6	1931
Nicholson, Jack	Film	4/4	4	22	1937
Nicklaus, Jack	Sports	1/3	1	21	1940
Nicks, Stevie	Music	5/8	5	26	1948
Nielsen, Leslie	Television	2/2	2	11	1926
Nietzsche, Friedrich	Philosophy	1/6	10	15	1844
Nijinsky, Vaslav	Dance	1/3	12	28	1890
Nilsson, Birgit	Music	5/8	5	17	1923
Nimitz, Chester	Military	2/6	2	17	1915
Nimoy, Leonard	Television	3/8	3	26	1931
Nin, Anaïs	Literature	2/3	2	21	1887
Niven, David	Film	1/3	3	1	1910
Nixon, Richard	President	1/9	1	9	1913
Nobel, Alfred	Sciences	1/3	10	21	1833
Noguchi, Isamu	Design	2/8	11	17	1904
Nolan, Kathleen	Television	9/9	9	27	1933
Nolan, Lloyd	Film	2/8	8	11	1902
Nolde, Emil	Visual Arts	7/8	8	7	1867
Nolte, Nick	Film	2/8	2	8	1940
North, Oliver	Military	1/7	10	7	1943
North, Sheree	Television	1/8	1	17	1933
Norton, Ken	Sports	8/9	8	9	1945
Nostradamus, Michel de	Letters	3/5	12	23	1503
Novak, Kim	Film	2/9	2	18	1933
Novarro, Ramon	Film	2/6	2	6	1899
Novello, Ivor	Music	1/6	1	15	1893
Nunn, Sam	Politics	8/9	9	8	1938
Nureyev, Rudolf	Dance	3/8	3	17	1938
O'Brian, Hugh	Television	1/4	4	19	1930
O'Brien, Edmond	Film	1/9	9	10	1915
O'Brien, Margaret	Film	1/6	1	15	1937

NAME	FIELD	SET	MONTH	DAY	YEAR
O'Brien, Pat	Film	2/2	11	11	1899
O'Casey, Sean	Literature	3/3	3	30	1880
O'Connell, Helen	Music	5/5	5	23	1920
O'Connor, Carroll	Television	2/8	8	2	1924
O'Connor, Donald	Film	1/8	8	28	1925
O'Connor, Flannery	Literature	3/7	3	25	1925
O'Hara, John	Literature	1/4	1	31	1905
O'Hara, Maureen	Film	8/8	8	17	1921
O'Herlihy, Dan	Television	1/5	5	1	1919
O'Keeffe, Georgia	Visual Arts	2/6	11	15	1887
O'Neal, Patrick	Television	8/9	9	26	1927
O'Neal, Ryan	Film	2/4	4	20	1941
O'Neal, Tatum	Film	2/5	11	5	1963
O'Neill, Eugene	Dramatic Arts	1/7	10	16	1888
O'Neill, Jennifer	Film	2/2	2	20	1949
O'Neill, Thomas P. (Tip)	Politics	3/9	12	9	1912
O'Neill, William A.	Politics	2/8	8	11	1930
O'Sullivan, Maureen	Film	5/8	5	17	1911
O'Toole, Peter	Film	2/8	8	2	1932
Oakie, Jack	Film	2/3	11	12	1903
Oakley, Annie	Entertainment	4/8	8	13	1859
Oates, Joyce Carol	Literature	6/7	6	16	1938
Oates, Warren	Film	5/7	7	5	1928
Oberon, Merle	Film	1/2	2	19	1911
Odets, Clifford	Dramatic Arts	7/9	7	18	1906
Odetta	Music	3/4	12	31	1930
Offenbach, Jacques	Music	2/6	6	20	1819
Ohm, Georg Simon	Sciences	3/7	3	16	1787
Oland, Warner	Film	1/3	10	3	1880
Oldenburg, Claes	Visual Arts	1/1	1	28	1929
Olivier, Laurence	Dramatic Arts	4/5	5	22	1907
Olmsted, Frederick	Design	4/8	4	26	1822
Onassis, Aristotle	Business	1/6	1	15	1906
Onassis, Christina	Business	2/3	12	11	1950
Onassis, Jacqueline Kennedy	Publishing	1/7	7	28	1929
Ono, Yoko	Music	2/9	2	18	1933
Opel, John R.	Business	1/5	1	5	1925
Ophüls, Max	Film	5/6	5	6	1902
Oppenheimer, Robert J.	Sciences	4/4	4	22	1904
Orff, Carl	Music	1/7	7	10	1895

NAME	FIELD	SET	MONTH	DAY	YEAR
Orlando, Tony	Music	3/4	4	3	1944
Ormandy, Eugene	Music	2/9	11	18	1899
Orozco, José Clemente	Visual Arts	2/5	11	23	1883
Orr, Bobby	Sports	2/3	3	20	1948
Orwell, George	Literature	6/7	6	25	1903
Osborne, Ozzy	Music	3/3	12	3	1948
Osmond, Donny	Music	3/9	3	9	1957
Osmond, Marie	Music	1/4	10	13	1959
Oswald, Lee Harvey	Crime	1/9	10	18	1939
Ovid	Literature	2/3	3	2	B.C. 43
Owens, Buck	Music	3/8	8	12	1929
Owens, Jesse	Sports	3/9	9	12	1913
Ozawa, Seiji	Music	1/9	9	1	1935
Pacino, Al	Film	4/7	4	25	1940
Paderewski, Ignace	Music	2/8	11	8	1860
Paganini, Niccolò	Music	1/9	10	27	1782
Page, Geraldine	Dramatic Arts	2/4	11	22	1924
Page, Patti	Music	2/8	11	8	1927
Paige, Janis	Dramatic Arts	7/9	9	16	1922
Paige, Satchel	Sports	7/7	7	7	1906
Paisley, Ian	Politics	4/6	4	6	1926
Palance, Jack	Film	2/9	2	18	1920
Palmer, Betsy	Film	1/2	11	2	1929
Palmer, Lilli	Dramatic Arts	5/6	5	24	1914
Pandit, Nehru	Politics	8/9	8	18	1900
Papas, Irene	Film	3/9	9	3	1929
Papp, Joseph	Dramatic Arts	4/6	6	22	1921
Park, Chong Hoon	Politics	1/1	1	19	1919
Park, Chung Hee	Politics	3/9	9	30	1917
Parker, Bonnie	Crime	1/1	10	1	1910
Parker, Charlie	Music	2/8	8	29	1920
Parker, Dorothy	Literature	4/8	8	22	1893
Parker, Eleanor	Film	6/8	6	26	1922
Parker, Fess	Television	7/8	8	16	1925
Parker, Jean	Film	2/8	8	11	1912
Parkman, Francis	Literature	7/9	9	16	1823
Parks, Bert	Television	3/3	12	30	1914
Parr, Jack	Television	1/5	5	1	1918
Parrish, Maxfield	Visual Arts	7/7	7	25	1870
Parsons, Estelle	Film	2/2	11	20	1927

NAME	FIELD	SET	MONTH	DAY	YEAR
Parsons, Louella	Letters	6/8	8	6	1881
Partch, Harry	Music	6/6	6	24	1901
Parton, Dolly	Music	1/1	1	19	1946
Pascal, Blaise	Sciences	1/6	6	19	1623
Pasha, Enver	Politics	2/5	11	23	1881
Pasternak, Boris	Literature	1/2	2	10	1890
Pasteur, Louis	Sciences	3/9	12	27	1822
Pastora, Eden	Military	1/4	1	22	1937
Pater, Walter	Letters	4/8	8	4	1839
Paton, Alan	Literature	1/2	1	11	1903
Patterson, Floyd	Sports	1/4	1	4	1935
Patton, George	Military	2/2	11	11	1885
Pauling, Linus	Sciences	1/2	2	28	1901
Pavarotti, Luciano	Music	1/3	10	12	1935
Pavlov, Ivan	Sciences	5/9	9	14	1849
Pavlova, Anna	Dance	1/3	1	3	1885
Paxton, Tom	Music	1/4	10	31	1937
Paycheck, Johnny	Music	4/5	5	31	1941
Payne, John	Film	5/5	5	23	1912
Payton, Barbara	Film	2/7	11	16	1927
Payton, Walter	Sports	7/7	7	25	1954
Peale, Charles Wilson	Visual Arts	4/6	4	15	1741
Peale, Raphael	Visual Arts	2/8	2	17	1774
Peale, Rembrandt	Visual Arts	2/4	2	22	1778
Peary, Robert Edwin	Exploration	5/6	5	6	1856
Peck, Gregory	Film	4/5	4	5	1916
Peerce, Jan	Music	3/6	6	3	1904
Péguy, Charles	Literature	1/7	1	7	1873
Pei, I. M.	Design	4/8	4	26	1917
Pelé	Sports	1/5	10	23	1940
Pendergrass, Teddy	Music	3/8	3	26	1950
Penn, Arthur H.	Film	9/9	9	27	1922
Penn, Irving	Visual Arts	6/7	6	16	1917
Penn, Sean	Film	8/8	8	17	1960
Penn, William	Politics	1/5	10	14	1644
Penney, J. C.	Business	7/9	9	16	1875
Peppard, George	Film	1/1	10	1	1928
Pepper, Claude	Politics	8/9	9	8	1900
Pepys, Samuel	Letters	2/5	2	23	1633
Percy, Charles H.	Politics	9/9	9	27	1919

NAME	FIELD	SET	MONTH	DAY	YEAR
Percy, Walker	Literature	1/5	5	28	1916
Pereira, William L.	Design	4/7	4	25	1909
Peréz, Alan Garcia	Politics	5/5	5	23	1949
Perkins, Anthony	Film	4/4	4	4	1932
Perlman, Itzhak	Music	4/8	8	31	1945
Perón, Eva	Politics	2/4	2	4	1931
Perón, Juan	Politics	1/8	10	8	1895
Perrine, Valerie	Film	3/9	9	3	1943
Perry, Lincoln (Stepin Fetchit)	Film	3/5	5	30	1892
Pershing, John J. (Blackjack)	Military	4/9	9	13	1860
Persichetti, Vincent	Music	6/6	6	6	1915
Persoff, Nehemiah	Film	5/8	8	14	1920
Pertschuk, Michael	Politics	1/3	1	12	1933
Peters, Bernadette	Entertainment	1/2	2	28	1948
Peters, Jean	Film	1/6	10	15	1926
Peters, Roberta	Music	4/5	5	4	1930
Peterson, Oscar	Music	6/8	8	15	1925
Petrarch (Francesco Petrarca)	Literature	2/7	7	20	1304
Petrillo, James	Politics	3/7	3	16	1892
Phillips, Mackenzie	Television	1/2	11	10	1959
Phillips, Michelle	Music	4/6	4	6	1944
Phillips, Oail (Bum)	Sports	2/9	9	29	1923
Phoenix, River	Film	5/8	8	23	1970
Piaf, Edith	Music	1/3	12	19	1915
Piatigorsky, Gregor	Music	4/8	4	17	1903
Picabia, Francis	Visual Arts	1/4	1	22	1879
Picasso, Pablo	Visual Arts	1/7	10	25	1881
Picasso, Paloma	Design	1/4	4	19	1949
Pickens, Slim	Film	2/6	6	29	1919
Pickett, Wilson	Music	3/9	3	18	1941
Pickford, Mary	Film	4/8	4	8	1893
Pidgeon, Walter	Film	5/9	9	23	1897
Pierce, Franklin	President	2/5	11	23	1804
Pincay, Laffit	Sports	2/3	12	29	1946
Piniella, Lou	Sports	1/8	8	28	1943
Pinter, Harold	Literature	1/1	10	10	1930
Pinza, Ezio	Music	5/9	5	18	1895
Piranesi, Giambattista	Visual Arts	1/4	10	4	1720
Pissaro, Camille	Visual Arts	1/7	7	10	1830
Planck, Max	Sciences	4/5	4	23	1858

NAME	FIELD	SET	MONTH	DAY	YEAR
Plant, Robert	Music	2/8	8	20	1948
Plath, Sylvia	Literature	1/9	10	27	1932
Pleasance, Donald	Film	1/5	10	5	1919
Pleshette, Suzanne	Television	1/4	1	31	1937
Plisetskaya, Maya	Dance	2/2	11	20	1925
Plowright, Joan	Dramatic Arts	1/2	10	28	1929
Plummer, Christopher	Film	3/4	12	13	1929
Poe, Edgar Allan	Literature	1/1	1	19	1809
Poitier, Sydney	Film	2/2	2	20	1924
Polanski, Roman	Film	8/9	8	18	1933
Polk, James K.	President	2/2	11	2	1795
Pollack, Sidney	Film	1/7	7	1	1934
Pollock, Jackson	Visual Arts	1/1	1	28	1912
Ponti, Carlo	Film	2/3	12	11	1913
Pope, Alexander	Literature	3/5	5	21	1688
Pope John Paul I	Religion	1/8	10	17	1912
Pope John Paul II	Religion	5/9	5	18	1920
Pope John XXIII	Religion	2/7	11	25	1881
Pope Paul VI	Religion	8/9	9	26	1897
Pope Pius X	Religion	2/6	6	2	1835
Pope Pius XI	Religion	4/5	5	31	1857
Pope Pius XII	Religion	2/3	3	2	1876
Porsche, Ferdinand	Design	3/9	9	3	1875
Porter, Cole	Music	6/9	6	9	1893
Porter, Katherine Anne	Literature	5/6	5	15	1890
Post, Emily	Letters	1/3	10	3	1873
Poston, Tom	Television	1/8	10	17	1921
Potok, Chaim	Literature	2/8	2	17	1929
Potter, Beatrice	Literature	1/7	7	28	1886
Potter, Beatrix	Visual Arts	6/7	7	6	1866
Potvin, Dennis	Sports	1/2	10	29	1953
Poulenc, Francis	Music	1/7	1	7	1899
Pound, Ezra	Literature	1/3	10	30	1885
Powell, Bud	Music	9/9	9	27	1924
Powell, Dick	Film	2/5	11	14	1904
Powell, Eleanor	Film	2/3	11	21	1910
Powell, Jane	Film	1/4	4	1	1929
Power, Tyrone	Film	5/5	5	5	1913
Powers, Francis Gary	Military	8/8	8	17	1929
Powers, Stefanie	Television	2/2	11	2	1942

NAME	FIELD	SET	MONTH	DAY	YEAR
Preminger, Otto	Film	3/5	12	5	1906
Prentiss, Paula	Film	3/4	3	4	1939
Presley, Elvis	Music	1/8	1	8	1935
Presley, Priscilla	Television	5/6	5	24	1945
Preston, Billy	Music	9/9	9	9	1946
Preston, Robert	Film	6/8	6	8	1918
Previn, André	Music	4/6	4	6	1929
Previn, Dory	Music	1/4	10	22	1929
Price, Dennis	Film	5/6	6	23	1915
Price, Leontyne	Music	1/2	2	10	1927
Price, Margaret	Music	4/4	4	13	1934
Price, Vincent	Film	5/9	5	27	1911
Pride, Charley	Music	3/9	3	18	1939
Priest, Ivy Baker	Politics	7/9	9	7	1905
Prima, Louie	Music	3/7	12	7	1912
Prince Albert	Royal	8/8	8	26	1819
Prince Aly Khan	Royal	4/4	6	13	1911
Prince Charles	Royal	2/5	11	14	1948
Prince Philip	Royal	1/6	6	10	1921
Prince Rainier III	Royal	4/5	5	31	1923
Prince (Rogers Nelson)	Music	6/7	6	7	1958
Princess Anne	Royal	6/8	8	15	1950
Princess Caroline	Royal	1/5	1	23	1957
Princess Diana	Royal	1/7	7	1	1961
Princess Lee Radziwill	Royal	3/3	3	3	1933
Princess Margaret	Royal	3/8	8	21	1930
Principal, Victoria	Television	1/3	1	30	1950
Pritikin, Nathan	Sciences	2/8	8	29	1915
Prokofiev, Sergei	Music	4/5	4	23	1891
Proust, Marcel	Literature	1/7	7	10	1871
Prowse, Juliet	Dance	7/9	9	25	1936
Pryor, Richard	Entertainment	1/3	12	1	1940
Pucci, Emilio	Design	2/2	11	20	1914
Puccini, Giacomo	Music	3/4	12	22	1858
Purl, Linda	Television	2/9	9	2	1955
Pushkin, Alexander	Literature	6/6	6	6	1799
Pyle, Denver	Television	2/5	5	11	1920
Pynchon, Thomas	Literature	5/8	5	8	1937
Quaid, Dennis	Film	4/9	4	9	1954
Quaid, Randy	Film	1/1	10	1	1950

NAME	FIELD	SET	MONTH	DAY	YEAR
Quant, Mary	Design	2/2	2	11	1934
Quarry, Jerry	Sports	5/6	5	15	1945
Quatro, Suzi	Music	3/6	6	3	1950
Quayle, Anthony	Dramatic Arts	7/9	9	7	1913
Queen Elizabeth I	Royal	8/9	9	17	1533
Queen Elizabeth II	Royal	3/4	4	21	1926
Queen Isabella I	Royal	1/5	5	1	1451
Queen Victoria	Royal	5/6	5	24	1819
Quinlan, Kathleen	Film	1/2	11	19	1954
Quinn, Anthony	Film	3/4	4	21	1915
Rabbit, Eddie	Music	2/9	11	27	1941
Rachmaninoff, Sergei	Music	4/5	4	23	1873
Racine, Jean Baptiste	Literature	3/4	12	22	1639
Rackham, Arthur	Visual Arts	1/9	9	19	1867
Radcliffe, Ann	Literature	7/9	7	9	1764
Radner, Gilda	Film	1/6	6	28	1946
Raeburn, Henry	Visual Arts	3/4	3	4	1756
Raffin, Deborah	Television	3/4	3	13	1953
Raft, George	Film	9/9	9	27	1895
Ragen, David	Letters	8/8	8	26	1925
Rainer, Luise	Film	1/3	1	12	1912
Raines, Ella	Film	6/8	8	6	1921
Rainey, Gertrude (Ma)	Music	4/8	4	26	1886
Raitt, Bonnie	Music	2/8	11	8	1949
Raitt, John	Dramatic Arts	1/1	1	19	1917
Ralston, Vera	Film	3/7	7	12	1919
Rambo, Dack	Television	2/4	11	13	1941
Rampal, Jean-Pierre	Music	1/7	1	7	1922
Rampling, Charlotte	Film	2/5	2	5	1946
Rand, Ayn	Literature	2/2	2	2	1905
Rand, Sally	Entertainment	3/4	4	12	1903
Randall, Tony	Television	2/8	2	26	1920
Rankin, Jeannette	Politics	2/6	6	11	1881
Ransom, John Crowe	Literature	3/4	4	30	1888
Raphael	Visual Arts	4/6	4	6	1483
Rathbone, Basil	Film	4/6	6	13	1892
Rather, Dan	Television	1/4	10	31	1931
Ratoff, Gregory	Film	2/4	4	20	1893
Rattigan, Terence M.	Literature	1/6	6	10	1911
Rauschenberg, Robert	Visual Arts	1/4	10	22	1925

NAME	FIELD	SET	MONTH	DAY	YEAR
Ravel, Maurice	Music	3/7	3	7	1875
Rawlings, Marjorie Kinnan	Literature	8/8	8	8	1896
Rawls, Lou	Music	1/3	12	1	1936
Ray, Aldo	Film	7/9	9	25	1926
Ray, James Earl	Crime	1/3	3	10	1928
Ray, Johnnie	Music	1/1	1	10	1927
Ray, Satyajit	Film	2/5	5	2	1922
Rayburn, Gene	Television	3/4	12	22	1917
Rayburn, Sam	Politics	1/6	1	6	1882
Raye, Martha	Entertainment	8/9	8	27	1916
Raymond, Gene	Film	4/8	8	13	1908
Reagan, Nancy	Politics	6/7	7	6	1921
Reagan, Ronald	President	2/6	2	6	1911
Reasoner, Harry	Television	4/8	4	17	1923
Rebozo, C. G. (Bebe)	Business	2/8	11	17	1912
Redding, Otis	Music	9/9	9	9	1941
Reddy, Helen	Music	1/7	10	25	1941
Redford, Robert	Film	8/9	8	18	1937
Redgrave, Lynn	Film	3/8	3	8	1943
Redgrave, Michael	Dramatic Arts	2/3	3	20	1908
Redgrave, Vanessa	Film	1/3	1	30	1937
Redon, Odilon	Visual Arts	4/4	4	22	1840
Reed, Donna	Television	1/9	1	27	1921
Reed, John Shepard	Business	2/7	2	7	1939
Reed, Lou	Music	2/3	3	2	1942
Reed, Oliver	Film	2/4	2	13	1938
Reed, Rex	Letters	1/2	10	2	1938
Reed, Robert	Television	1/1	10	19	1932
Reed, Walter	Sciences	4/9	9	13	1851
Reed, Willis	Sports	6/7	6	25	1942
Reems, Harry	Film	8/9	8	27	1947
Reese, Della	Music	6/7	7	6	1931
Reese, Harold (Pee Wee)	Sports	5/7	7	23	1919
Reeve, Christopher	Film	7/9	9	25	1952
Reeves, Dan	Sports	1/1	1	19	1944
Reeves, Steve	Film	1/3	1	21	1926
Regan, Donald T.	Politics	3/3	12	21	1918
Rehnquist, William H.	Law	1/1	10	1	1924
Reich, Steve	Music	1/3	10	3	1936
Reid, Kate	Dramatic Arts	2/4	11	4	1930

NAME	FIELD	SET	MONTH	DAY	YEAR
Reid, Wallace	Film	4/6	4	15	1890
Reiner, Carl	Television	2/3	3	20	1922
Reiner, Fritz	Music	1/3	12	19	1888
Reiner, Rob	Film	3/6	3	6	1945
Reinhardt, Max	Dramatic Arts	9/9	9	9	1873
Remarque, Erich Maria	Literature	4/6	6	22	1898
Rembrandt van Rijn	Visual Arts	6/7	7	15	1605
Remick, Lee	Film	3/5	12	14	1935
Remington, Frederic	Visual Arts	1/4	10	4	1861
Renault, Mary	Literature	4/9	9	4	1905
Renoir, Jean	Film	6/9	9	15	1894
Renoir, Pierre-Auguste	Visual Arts	2/7	2	25	1841
Resnais, Alain	Film	3/6	6	3	1922
Respighi, Ottorino	Music	7/9	7	9	1879
Retton, Mary Lou	Sports	1/6	1	24	1968
Reuther, Walter	Politics	1/9	9	1	1907
Revere, Paul	Politics	1/3	1	12	1735
Reverend Ike	Religion	1/6	6	1	1935
Revson, Charles	Business	1/2	10	11	1906
Rey, Alejandro	Film	2/8	2	8	1930
Reynolds, Burt	Film	2/2	2	11	1936
Reynolds, Debbie	Film	1/4	4	1	1932
Reynolds, Frank	Television	2/2	11	29	1923
Reynolds, Joshua	Visual Arts	7/7	7	16	1723
Reynolds, Marjorie	Television	3/8	8	12	1921
Rheingold, Howard	Letters	7/7	7	7	1947
Rhodes, Cecil	Politics	5/7	7	5	1853
Ribicoff, Abraham A.	Politics	4/9	4	9	1910
Rich, Buddy	Music	3/6	6	3	1917
Rich, Charlie	Music	3/5	12	14	1932
Rich, Irene	Film	1/4	10	13	1897
Richards, Keith	Music	3/9	12	18	1943
Richardson, Dorothy	Literature	5/8	5	17	1873
Richardson, Ralph	Dramatic Arts	1/3	12	19	1902
Richardson, Tony	Film	5/6	6	5	1928
Richie, Lionel	Music	2/6	6	20	1950
Richter, Charles F.	Sciences	4/8	4	26	1900
Richter, Conrad	Literature	1/4	10	13	1890
Richter, Hans	Music	4/4	4	4	1843
Richter, Sviatoslav	Music	2/3	3	20	1914

NAME	FIELD	SET	MONTH	DAY	YEAR
Rickenbacker, Eddie	Politics	1/8	10	8	1890
Rickey, Branch W.	Business	2/3	12	20	1881
Rickles, Don	Entertainment	5/8	5	8	1926
Rickover, Hyman	Military	1/9	1	27	1900
Riddle, Nelson	Music	1/6	6	1	1921
Ride, Sally K.	Exploration	5/8	5	26	1951
Ridgway, Matthew B.	Military	3/3	3	3	1895
Riegle, Donald W., Jr.	Politics	2/4	2	4	1938
Rigg, Diana	Television	2/7	7	20	1938
Riggins, John	Sports	4/8	8	4	1949
Riley, Terry	Music	6/6	6	24	1935
Rilke, Rainer Maria	Literature	3/4	12	4	1875
Rimbaud, Arthur	Literature	1/2	10	20	1854
Rimsky-Korsakov, Nikolai	Music	3/9	3	18	1844
Ritchard, Cyril	Dramatic Arts	1/3	12	1	1898
Ritter, John	Television	8/9	9	17	1948
Ritter, Tex	Film	1/3	1	12	1906
Ritter, Thelma	Film	2/5	2	14	1905
Rivera, Chita	Dramatic Arts	8/8	8	17	1923
Rivera, Diego	Visual Arts	3/8	12	8	1886
Rivera, Geraldo M.	Television	3/7	7	3	1943
Rivers, Joan	Television	1/3	10	12	1935
Rivers, Johnny	Music	2/7	11	7	1942
Rivers, Larry	Visual Arts	8/8	8	17	1923
Rizzo, Frank L.	Politics	1/5	10	23	1920
Rizzuto, Phil	Television	6/9	9	24	1917
Roach, Hal	Film	1/5	1	14	1892
Roach, Max	Music	1/1	1	10	1925
Robards, Jason, Jr.	Dramatic Arts	7/8	7	26	1922
Robb, Lynda Bird	Politics	1/3	3	19	1943
Robbins, Harold	Literature	3/5	5	21	1916
Robbins, Jerome	Dance	1/2	10	11	1918
Robbins, Marty	Music	8/9	9	26	1925
Roberts, Oral	Religion	1/6	1	24	1918
Robertson, Cliff	Film	9/9	9	9	1925
Robertson, Dale	Television	5/7	7	14	1923
Robeson, Paul	Film	4/9	4	9	1898
Robespierre, Maximilien	Politics	5/6	5	6	1758
Robinson, Bill (Bojangles)	Dance	5/7	5	25	1878
Robinson, Bill (Smokey)	Music	1/2	2	19	1940

NAME	FIELD	SET	MONTH	DAY	YEAR
Robinson, Edward G.	Film	3/3	12	12	1893
Robinson, John (Jackie)	Sports	1/4	1	31	1919
Robinson, Sugar Ray	Sports	3/5	5	3	1920
Robson, Flora	Dramatic Arts	1/3	3	28	1902
Robustelli, Andy	Sports	3/6	12	6	1930
Rockefeller, David	Business	3/6	6	12	1915
Rockefeller, John Davison	Business	7/8	7	8	1839
Rockefeller, John Davison III	Business	3/3	3	21	1906
Rockefeller, John Davison IV	Politics	6/9	6	18	1937
Rockefeller, John Davison, Jr.	Business	1/2	1	29	1874
Rockefeller, Laurance S.	Business	5/8	5	26	1910
Rockefeller, Nelson A.	Politics	7/8	7	8	1908
Rockefeller, William	Business	4/5	5	31	1841
Rockefeller, Winthrop	Politics	1/5	5	1	1912
Rockne, Knute	Sports	3/4	3	4	1888
Rockwell, Norman	Visual Arts	2/3	2	3	1894
Rodgers, Jimmie F.	Music	9/9	9	18	1933
Rodgers, Richard	Music	1/6	6	28	1902
Rodin, Auguste	Visual Arts	2/3	11	12	1840
Roentgen, Wilhelm Konrad	Sciences	3/9	3	27	1845
Rogers, Buddy	Film	4/8	8	13	1904
Rogers, Ginger	Film	7/7	7	16	1911
Rogers, Kenny	Music	3/8	8	21	1938
Rogers, Roy	Entertainment	2/5	11	5	1912
Rogers, Wayne	Television	4/7	4	7	1933
Rogers, Will	Entertainment	2/4	11	4	1879
Rogers, Will, Jr.	Film	1/2	10	20	1911
Rohmer, Eric	Film	3/3	3	21	1920
Roland, Gilbert	Film	2/3	12	11	1905
Rolle, Esther	Dramatic Arts	2/8	11	8	1933
Romberg, Sigmund	Music	2/7	7	29	1887
Romero Barcelo, Carlos A.	Politics	4/9	9	4	1932
Romero, Cesar	Film	2/6	2	15	1907
Rommel, Erwin	Military	2/6	11	15	1891
Romney, George	Visual Arts	3/6	12	15	1734
Romney, George W.	Politics	7/8	7	8	1907
Romulo, Carlos P.	Politics	1/5	1	14	1901
Ronstadt, Linda	Music	6/7	7	15	1946
Rooney, Andrew A.	Letters	1/5	1	14	1919
Rooney, Mickey	Film	5/9	9	23	1920

NAME	FIELD	SET	MONTH	DAY	YEAR
Roosevelt, Anna Eleanor	Politics	3/5	5	3	1906
Roosevelt, Edith Kermit	Politics	6/8	8	6	1861
Roosevelt, Eleanor	Politics	1/2	10	11	1884
Roosevelt, F. D., Jr.	Politics	8/8	8	17	1914
Roosevelt, Franklin D.	President	1/3	1	30	1882
Roosevelt, James	Politics	3/5	12	23	1907
Roosevelt, Theodore	President	1/9	10	27	1858
Rose, Billy	Dramatic Arts	6/9	9	6	1899
Rose, David	Music	6/6	6	24	1910
Rose, Pete	Sports	4/5	4	14	1942
Roseboro, John	Sports	4/5	5	13	1933
Rosenberg, Ethel	Politics	1/9	9	28	1915
Rosenbloom, Slapsie Maxie	Film	6/9	9	6	1904
Ross, Betsy	Politics	1/1	1	1	1752
Ross, Diana	Music	3/8	3	26	1944
Ross, Katharine	Film	1/2	1	29	1943
Ross, Lanny	Entertainment	1/1	1	19	1906
Ross, Lillian	Letters	6/8	6	8	1927
Rossellini, Roberto	Film	5/8	5	8	1906
Rossetti, Christina	Literature	3/5	12	5	1830
Rossetti, Dante Gabriel	Visual Arts	3/5	5	12	1828
Rossini, Gioacchino	Music	2/2	2	29	1792
Rostropovich, Mstislav	Music	3/3	3	12	1927
Rote, Kyle	Sports	1/9	10	27	1928
Roth, David Lee	Music	1/1	10	10	1955
Roth, Lillian	Entertainment	3/4	12	13	1910
Roth, Philip	Literature	1/3	3	19	1933
Rothko, Mark	Visual Arts	7/9	9	25	1903
Rouault, Georges	Visual Arts	5/9	5	27	1871
Roundtree, Richard	Film	7/9	9	7	1942
Rousseau, Henri	Visual Arts	3/5	5	21	1844
Rousseau, Jean Jacques	Literature	1/6	6	28	1712
Rousseau, Théodore	Visual Arts	4/6	4	15	1812
Rowan, Dan	Television	2/7	7	2	1922
Rowlands, Gena	Film	1/6	6	19	1936
Rozelle, Pete	Television	1/3	3	1	1926
Rubens, Peter Paul	Visual Arts	2/6	6	29	1577
Rubicam, Raymond	Business	6/7	6	16	1892
Rubin, William S.	Visual Arts	2/8	8	11	1927
Rubinstein, Arthur	Music	1/1	1	28	1889

NAME	FIELD	SET	MONTH	DAY	YEAR
Rudman, Warren B.	Politics	5/9	5	9	1930
Ruggles, Charles	Film	2/8	2	8	1886
Rukeyser, Louis	Television	1/3	1	30	1933
Rule, Janice	Dramatic Arts	6/8	8	15	1931
Runyon, Damon	Literature	1/4	10	4	1884
Rush, Barbara	Film	1/4	1	4	1930
Rush, Tom	Music	2/8	2	8	1941
Rushing, Jimmy	Music	8/8	8	26	1903
Ruskin, John	Letters	2/8	2	8	1819
Russell, Bertrand	Philosophy	5/9	5	18	1872
Russell, Jane	Film	3/6	6	21	1921
Russell, Kurt	Film	3/8	3	17	1951
Russell, Leon	Music	2/4	4	2	1941
Russell, Lillian	Entertainment	3/4	12	4	1861
Russell, Mark	Entertainment	5/8	8	23	1932
Russell, Rosalind	Film	4/6	6	4	1907
Ruth, George Herman (Babe)	Sports	2/6	2	6	1895
Rutherford, Ann	Film	2/2	11	2	1917
Rutherford, Margaret	Film	2/5	5	11	1892
Ryan, Nolan	Sports	1/4	1	31	1947
Ryan, Robert	Film	2/2	11	11	1909
Rydell, Bobby	Music	4/8	4	26	1942
Ryder, Albert P.	Visual Arts	1/3	3	19	1847
Rysbrack, Michael	Visual Arts	6/6	6	24	1693
Sabatini, Rafael	Literature	2/4	4	29	1875
Sabin, Albert	Sciences	8/8	8	26	1906
Sabu	Film	3/6	3	15	1924
Sackville-West, Vita	Literature	3/9	3	9	1892
Sadat, Anwar	Politics	3/7	12	25	1918
Sade, Marquis de	Literature	2/6	6	2	1740
Safer, Morley	Television	2/8	11	8	1931
Sagan, Carl	Sciences	2/9	11	9	1934
Sagan, Françoise	Literature	3/6	6	21	1935
Sager, Carol Bayer	Music	3/8	3	8	1947
Sahl, Mort	Entertainment	2/5	5	11	1927
Saint, Eva Marie	Film	4/7	7	4	1922
St. Cyr, Lili	Entertainment	3/6	6	3	1917
Saint Francis Xavier	Religion	4/8	4	17	1506
Saint James, Susan	Television	5/8	8	14	1946
St. John, Jill	Film	1/8	8	19	1940

NAME	FIELD	SET	MONTH	DAY	YEAR
Saint Laurent, Yves	Design	1/8	8	1	1936
Saint-Saëns, Camille	Music	1/9	10	9	1835
Sainte Marie, Buffy	Music	2/2	2	20	1941
Saki (H. H. Munro)	Literature	3/9	12	18	1870
Sales, Soupy	Television	1/8	1	8	1926
Salieri, Antonio	Music	8/9	8	18	1750
Salinger, J. D.	Literature	1/1	1	1	1919
Salinger, Pierre	Politics	5/6	6	14	1925
Salisbury, Harrison E.	Letters	2/5	11	14	1908
Salk, Jonas	Sciences	1/1	10	28	1914
Sand, George	Literature	1/7	7	1	1804
Sandburg, Carl	Literature	1/6	1	6	1878
Sanders, George	Film	3/7	7	3	1906
Sanders, Harland (Colonel)	Business	1/9	9	19	1890
Sands, Tommy	Music	8/9	8	27	1937
Santana, Carlos	Music	2/7	7	20	1940
Santayana, George	Letters	3/7	12	16	1863
Sarandon, Chris	Film	6/7	7	24	1942
Sarandon, Susan	Film	1/4	10	4	1946
Sarbanes, Paul	Politics	2/3	2	3	1933
Sardi, Vincent	Business	3/5	12	23	1888
Sarney, José	Politics	3/4	4	30	1930
Sarnoff, Dorothy	Letters	5/7	5	25	1917
Saroyan, William	Literature	4/8	8	31	1908
Sarrazin, Michael	Film	4/5	5	4	1940
Sarto, Andrea del	Visual Arts	7/7	7	16	1486
Sartre, Jean-Paul	Literature	3/6	6	21	1905
Sassoon, Vidal	Business	1/8	1	17	1928
Satie, Erik	Music	5/8	5	17	1866
Savalas, Telly	Television	1/3	1	21	1924
Saxon, John	Film	5/8	8	5	1935
Sayão, Bidu	Music	2/5	5	11	1902
Sayer, Leo	Music	3/5	5	21	1948
Sayers, Gale	Sports	3/5	5	30	1943
Scaggs, Boz	Music	6/8	6	8	1944
Scarlatti, Alessandro	Music	2/5	5	2	1659
Scarlatti, Domenico	Music	1/8	10	26	1685
Scheider, Roy	Film	1/2	11	10	1935
Schell, Maria	Film	1/6	1	15	1926
Schell, Maximilian	Film	3/8	12	8	1930

NAME	FIELD	SET	MONTH	DAY	YEAR
Schiller, Friedrich von	Literature	1/2	11	10	1759
Schirra, Walter (Wally)	Exploration	3/3	3	12	1923
Schlesinger, Arthur	Letters	1/6	10	15	1917
Schlesinger, James R.	Politics	2/6	2	15	1929
Schlesinger, John	Film	2/7	2	16	1926
Schlossberg, Caroline Kennedy	Law	2/9	11	27	1957
Schmeling, Max	Sports	1/9	9	28	1905
Schoenberg, Arnold	Music	4/9	9	13	1874
Schroder, Ricky	Film	4/4	4	13	1970
Schrödinger, Erwin	Sciences	3/8	8	12	1887
Schubert, Franz	Music	1/4	1	31	1797
Schuller, Robert	Television	7/9	9	16	1926
Schulz, Charles	Visual Arts	2/8	11	26	1922
Schumann, Robert	Music	6/8	6	8	1810
Schwarzenegger, Arnold	Film	3/7	7	30	1947
Schwarzkopf, Elisabeth	Music	3/9	12	9	1915
Schweitzer, Albert	Sciences	1/5	1	14	1875
Schwitters, Kurt	Visual Arts	2/6	6	20	1887
Scofield, Paul	Dramatic Arts	1/3	1	21	1922
Scorsese, Martin	Film	2/8	11	17	1942
Scott, Cyril	Music	9/9	9	27	1879
Scott, David	Exploration	6/6	6	6	1932
Scott, George C.	Film	1/9	10	18	1927
Scott, Jonathan	Visual Arts	1/3	10	30	1914
Scott, Lizabeth	Film	2/9	9	29	1922
Scott, Randolph	Film	1/5	1	23	1903
Scott, Walter	Literature	6/8	8	15	1771
Scotto, Renata	Music	2/6	2	24	1935
Scriabin, Alexander	Music	1/6	1	6	1872
Scribner, Charles, Jr.	Publishing	4/7	7	13	1933
Seale, Bobby	Politics	1/4	10	22	1936
Seaver, Tom	Sports	2/8	11	17	1944
Sebastian, John	Music	3/8	3	17	1944
Sedaka, Neil	Music	3/4	3	13	1939
Seeger, Pete	Music	3/5	5	3	1919
Segal, Erich	Literature	6/7	6	16	1937
Segal, George	Visual Arts	2/8	11	26	1924
Segal, George	Film	2/4	2	13	1934
Seger, Bob	Music	5/6	6	23	1947
Segovia, Andrés	Music	2/9	2	18	1894

NAME	FIELD	SET	MONTH	DAY	YEAR
Selleck, Tom	Television	1/2	1	29	1945
Sellers, Peter	Film	8/9	9	8	1925
Selznick, David O.	Film	1/5	5	10	1902
Sendak, Maurice	Visual Arts	6/9	6	18	1928
Sennett, Mack	Film	1/8	1	17	1884
Serisawa, Sueo	Visual Arts	1/4	4	10	1910
Serkin, Rudolf	Music	1/3	3	28	1903
Serling, Rod	Television	3/7	12	25	1924
Service, Robert	Literature	1/7	1	16	1874
Seurat, Georges	Visual Arts	2/3	12	2	1891
Severinsen, Doc	Television	7/7	7	7	1927
Sexton, Anne	Literature	2/9	11	9	1928
Seymour, Jane	Television	2/6	2	15	1951
Shahn, Ben	Visual Arts	3/9	9	12	1898
Shakespeare, William	Literature	4/5	4	23	1564
Shankar, Ravi	Music	4/7	4	7	1920
Shanker, Albert	Politics	5/9	9	14	1928
Sharif, Omar	Film	1/4	4	10	1932
Shatner, William	Television	3/4	3	22	1931
Shaw, Artie	Music	5/5	5	23	1910
Shaw, George Bernard	Literature	7/8	7	26	1856
Shaw, Robert	Film	8/9	8	9	1927
Shawn, Dick	Entertainment	1/3	12	1	1929
Shearer, Norma	Film	1/8	1	17	1926
Shearing, George	Music	4/8	8	13	1919
Sheeler, Charles	Visual Arts	7/7	7	16	1883
Sheen, Martin	Film	3/8	8	3	1940
Sheets, Millard	Visual Arts	6/6	6	24	1907
Shelley, Mary Wollstonecraft	Literature	3/8	8	30	1797
Shelley, Percy Bysshe	Literature	4/8	8	4	1792
Shepard, Sam	Dramatic Arts	2/5	11	5	1943
Sheperd, Cybill	Television	2/9	2	18	1950
Shepp, Archie	Music	5/9	5	27	1937
Sheridan, Ann	Film	2/3	2	21	1915
Sheridan, Richard Brinsley	Literature	1/3	10	30	1751
Sherman, William Tecumseh	Military	2/8	2	8	1820
Sherriff, R. C.	Literature	6/6	6	6	1896
Sherwood, Madeleine	Film	2/4	11	13	1922
Sherwood, Robert	Dramatic Arts	4/4	4	4	1896
Shields, Brooke	Film	4/5	5	31	1965

NAME	FIELD	SET	MONTH	DAY	YEAR
Shimkus, Joanna	Film	1/1	10	10	1944
Shire, Talia	Film	4/7	4	25	1946
Shirer, William L.	Literature	2/5	2	23	1904
Shockley, William	Sciences	2/4	2	13	1910
Shoemaker, Willie	Sports	1/8	8	19	1931
Shor, Toots	Business	5/6	5	6	1905
Shore, Dinah	Entertainment	1/3	3	1	1917
Short, Bobby	Music	6/9	9	15	1924
Shorter, Wayne	Music	7/8	8	25	1933
Shostakovich, Dimitri	Music	7/9	9	25	1906
Shriner, Herb	Dramatic Arts	2/5	5	29	1918
Shriver, Maria	Television	2/6	11	6	1955
Shriver, Pam	Sports	4/7	7	4	1962
Shue, Gene	Sports	3/9	12	18	1931
Shula, Don	Sports	1/4	1	4	1930
Shulman, Max	Literature	3/5	3	14	1919
Shultz, George	Politics	3/4	12	13	1920
Sibelius, Jean	Music	3/8	12	8	1865
Sidney, Sylvia	Film	8/8	8	8	1910
Siepi, Cesare	Music	1/2	2	10	1923
Signac, Paul	Visual Arts	2/2	11	11	1863
Signoret, Simone	Film	3/7	3	25	1921
Sills, Beverly	Music	5/7	5	25	1929
Silver, Horace	Music	2/9	9	2	1928
Silvers, Phil	Film	2/5	5	11	1911
Simenon, Georges	Literature	2/4	2	13	1903
Simmons, Jean	Film	1/4	1	31	1929
Simon, Carly	Music	6/7	6	25	1945
Simon, Neil	Dramatic Arts	4/7	7	4	1927
Simon, Norton	Business	2/5	2	5	1907
Simon, Paul	Music	1/4	10	13	1942
Simon, Paul	Politics	2/2	11	29	1928
Simone, Nina	Music	2/3	2	21	1933
Simpson, O. J.	Sports	7/9	7	9	1947
Simpson, Wallis	Royal	1/6	6	19	1896
Sinatra, Frank	Music	3/3	12	12	1915
Sinatra, Frank, Jr.	Entertainment	1/1	1	10	1944
Sinatra, Nancy	Music	6/8	6	8	1940
Sinclair, Upton	Literature	2/9	9	20	1878
Singer, Isaac Bashevis	Literature	5/7	7	14	1904

NAME	FIELD	SET	MONTH	DAY	YEAR
Singleton, Penny	Film	6/9	9	15	1908
Singleton, Zutty	Music	5/5	5	5	1909
Sitwell, Edith	Literature	7/9	9	7	1887
Skelton, Red	Entertainment	7/9	7	18	1913
Slick, Grace	Music	1/3	10	30	1939
Sloan, John	Visual Arts	2/8	8	2	1871
Sloane, Everet T.	Film	1/1	10	1	1909
Smetana, Bedrich	Music	2/3	3	2	1824
Smith, Alexis	Film	6/8	6	8	1921
Smith, Bessie	Music	4/6	4	15	1898
Smith, C. Aubrey	Film	3/7	7	21	1863
Smith, Howard K.	Television	3/5	5	12	1914
Smith, Jaclyn	Television	1/8	10	26	1947
Smith, Kate	Entertainment	1/5	5	1	1907
Smith, Keely	Music	3/9	3	9	1935
Smith, Lillian	Literature	3/3	12	12	1897
Smith, Maggie	Film	1/3	12	28	1934
Smith, Margaret Chase	Politics	3/5	12	14	1897
Smith, Roger	Television	3/9	12	18	1932
Smith, Stevie	Literature	2/9	9	20	1902
Smith, William French	Politics	8/8	8	26	1917
Smollett, Tobias	Literature	3/9	3	18	1721
Smothers, Dick	Television	2/2	11	20	1939
Smothers, Tom	Television	2/2	2	2	1937
Snead, Sam	Sports	5/9	5	27	1912
Snodgress, Carrie	Film	1/9	10	27	1946
Snow, C. P.	Literature	1/6	10	15	1905
Snow, Phoebe	Music	7/8	7	17	1947
Snyder, Tom	Television	3/5	5	12	1936
Soleri, Paolo	Design	3/6	6	21	1919
Solti, Georg	Music	1/3	10	21	1912
Solzhenitsyn, Aleksandr	Literature	2/3	12	11	1918
Somers, Suzanne	Television	1/7	10	16	1946
Sommer, Elke	Film	2/5	11	5	1941
Sondergaard, Gale	Film	2/6	2	15	1899
Sondheim, Stephen	Dramatic Arts	3/4	3	22	1930
Sontar, Judy Cook	Sports	1/6	6	28	1944
Sothern, Ann	Television	1/4	1	22	1909
Soul, David	Television	8/9	8	18	1943
Sousa, John Philip	Music	2/6	11	6	1854

NAME	FIELD	SET	MONTH	DAY	YEAR
Southey, Robert	Literature	3/8	8	12	1774
Soyer, Raphael	Visual Arts	3/7	12	25	1899
Soyinka, Wole	Literature	4/7	7	13	1934
Spacek, Sissy	Film	3/7	3	25	1949
Spark, Muriel	Literature	1/2	2	1	1918
Speck, Richard	Crime	3/6	12	6	1941
Speer, Albert	Letters	1/3	3	19	1905
Spelling, Aaron	Television	4/4	4	22	1925
Spencer, Scott	Literature	1/9	9	1	1945
Spender, Stephen	Literature	1/9	9	28	1909
Spielberg, Steven	Film	3/9	12	18	1947
Spillane, Mickey	Literature	3/9	3	9	1918
Spinks, Leon	Sports	2/7	7	11	1953
Spinoza, Baruch	Philosophy	2/6	11	24	1632
Spock, Benjamin	Sciences	2/5	5	2	1903
Springfield, Dusty	Music	4/7	4	16	1939
Springfield, Rick	Music	5/8	8	23	1949
Springsteen, Bruce	Music	5/9	9	23	1949
Stack, Robert	Television	1/4	1	13	1919
Stade, Frederica Von	Music	1/6	6	1	1945
Stafford, Jo	Music	2/3	11	12	1918
Stahl, Lesley	Television	3/7	12	16	1941
Stalin, Joseph	Politics	3/3	12	21	1879
Stallone, Sylvester	Film	6/7	7	6	1946
Stamp, Terence	Film	4/7	7	22	1939
Stang, Arnold	Television	1/9	9	28	1926
Stanley, Kim	Dramatic Arts	2/2	2	11	1925
Stanton, Elizabeth Cady	Letters	2/3	11	12	1815
Stanwyck, Barbara	Film	7/7	7	16	1907
Stapleton, Jean	Television	1/1	1	19	1923
Stapleton, Maureen	Film	3/6	6	21	1926
Starr, Belle	Crime	2/5	2	5	1848
Starr, Kay	Music	3/7	7	21	1922
Starr, Ringo	Music	7/7	7	7	1940
Stassen, Harold	Politics	4/4	4	13	1907
Staubach, Roger	Sports	2/5	2	5	1942
Steffens, Lincoln	Literature	4/6	4	6	1866
Steichen, Edward	Visual Arts	3/9	3	27	1879
Steig, William	Visual Arts	2/5	11	14	1907
Steiger, Rod	Film	4/5	4	14	1925

NAME	FIELD	SET	MONTH	DAY	YEAR
Stein, Gertrude	Literature	2/3	2	3	1874
Steinbeck, John	Literature	2/9	2	27	1902
Steinberg, David	Entertainment	8/9	8	9	1942
Steinberg, Jeffrey	Publishing	1/3	10	3	1946
Steinberg, Saul	Visual Arts	6/7	6	16	1914
Steinem, Gloria	Publishing	3/7	3	25	1934
Steinway, Henry	Music	2/6	2	15	1797
Stella, Joseph	Visual Arts	4/5	5	13	1880
Stendhal (Marie-Henri Beyle)	Literature	1/5	1	23	1783
Stengel, Casey	Sports	4/7	7	31	1891
Sterling, Jan	Film	3/4	4	3	1923
Stern, Isaac	Music	3/7	7	21	1920
Sterne, Laurence	Literature	2/6	11	24	1713
Stevens, Cat	Music	3/7	7	21	1948
Stevens, Connie	Film	8/8	8	8	1936
Stevens, George	Film	3/9	12	18	1904
Stevens, Inger	Film	1/9	10	18	1934
Stevens, Risë	Music	2/6	6	11	1913
Stevens, Stella	Film	1/1	10	1	1936
Stevens, Wallace	Literature	1/2	10	2	1879
Stevenson, Adlai	Politics	2/5	2	5	1900
Stevenson, Adlai Ewing, III	Politics	1/1	10	10	1813
Stevenson, Robert Louis	Literature	2/4	11	13	1850
Stewart, James	Film	2/5	5	20	1908
Stewart, Rod	Music	1/1	1	10	1945
Stieglitz, Alfred	Visual Arts	1/1	1	1	1864
Stills, Stephen	Music	1/3	1	3	1946
Stilwell, Joseph W.	Military	1/3	3	19	1883
Sting (Gordon Sumner)	Music	1/2	10	2	1951
Stockwell, Dean	Film	3/5	3	5	1936
Stokowski, Leopold	Music	4/9	4	18	1882
Stone, I. F.	Letters	3/6	12	24	1907
Stone, Irving	Literature	5/7	7	14	1903
Stone, Lewis	Film	2/6	11	15	1879
Stone, Sly	Music	3/6	3	15	1943
Storch, Larry	Television	1/8	1	8	1925
Storm, Gale	Television	4/5	4	5	1921
Stowe, Harriet Beecher	Literature	5/6	6	14	1811
Strachey, Lytton	Literature	1/3	3	1	1880
Stradivari, Antonio	Music	1/2	2	1	1644

NAME	FIELD	SET	MONTH	DAY	YEAR
Straight, Beatrice	Dramatic Arts	2/8	8	2	1918
Strasberg, Lee	Dramatic Arts	2/8	11	17	1901
Strasberg, Susan	Film	4/5	5	22	1938
Stratas, Teresa	Music	5/6	5	6	1938
Strauss, Johann	Music	3/5	3	14	1804
Strauss, Johann, Jr.	Music	1/7	10	25	1825
Strauss, Peter	Television	2/2	2	20	1947
Strauss, Richard	Music	2/6	6	11	1864
Stravinsky, Igor	Music	1/6	6	19	1882
Strawberry, Darryl	Sports	3/3	3	12	1962
Streep, Meryl	Film	4/6	6	22	1949
Streisand, Barbra	Music	4/6	4	24	1942
Strindberg, August	Literature	1/4	1	22	1849
Stritch, Elaine	Dramatic Arts	2/2	2	2	1928
Struthers, Sally	Television	1/7	7	28	1948
Stuart, Gilbert	Visual Arts	3/3	3	12	1755
Stuart, Jeb	Military	2/6	2	6	1833
Styron, William	Literature	2/6	6	11	1925
Suharto	Military	6/8	6	8	1921
Sullavan, Margaret	Film	5/7	5	16	1909
Sullivan, Arthur	Music	4/5	5	13	1842
Sullivan, Barry	Film	2/8	8	29	1912
Sullivan, Ed	Television	1/9	9	28	1902
Sullivan, Francis L.	Film	1/6	1	6	1906
Sullivan, John L.	Sports	1/6	10	15	1858
Sumac, Yma	Music	1/9	9	10	1927
Summer, Donna	Music	3/4	12	31	1948
Susann, Jacqueline	Literature	2/8	8	20	1921
Susskind, David	Television	1/3	12	19	1920
Sutherland, Donald	Film	7/8	7	17	1934
Sutherland, Joan	Music	2/7	11	7	1926
Suzman, Janet	Dramatic Arts	2/9	2	9	1939
Suzuki, Pat	Dramatic Arts	5/9	9	23	1931
Swayze, John Cameron	Television	4/4	4	4	1906
Swayze, Patrick	Film	8/9	8	18	1952
Sweet, Blanche	Film	6/9	6	18	1895
Swift, Jonathan	Literature	2/3	11	30	1667
Swigert, John	Exploration	3/8	8	30	1931
Swinburne, Algernon	Literature	4/5	4	5	1837
Swit, Loretta	Television	2/4	11	4	1937

NAME	FIELD	SET	MONTH	DAY	YEAR
Synge, John Millington	Literature	4/7	4	16	1871
Szell, George	Music	6/7	6	7	1897
Szent-Györgyi, Albert	Sciences	7/9	9	16	1893
Taft, Robert A.	Politics	8/9	9	8	1889
Taft, Robert, Jr.	Politics	2/7	2	25	1917
Taft, William Howard	President	6/9	9	15	1857
Tagore, Rabindranath	Literature	5/7	5	7	1861
Tailleferre, Germaine	Music	1/4	4	19	1892
Takamine, Jokichi	Sciences	2/3	11	3	1854
Talbot, Lyle	Film	2/8	2	8	1902
Tallchief, Maria	Dance	1/5	1	24	1925
Talmadge, Herman E.	Politics	8/9	8	9	1913
Tandy, Jessica	Dramatic Arts	6/7	6	7	1909
Tanguy, Yves	Visual Arts	1/5	1	5	1900
Tanner, Henry	Visual Arts	3/6	6	21	1859
Tarkenton, Fran	Sports	2/3	2	3	1940
Tarkington, Booth	Literature	2/7	7	29	1869
Tate, Allen	Literature	1/2	11	19	1899
Tate, Sharon	Film	1/6	1	24	1943
Tatum, Art	Music	1/4	10	13	1910
Taylor, Elizabeth	Film	2/9	2	27	1932
Taylor, James	Music	3/3	3	12	1948
Taylor, Maxwell	Military	8/8	8	26	1901
Taylor, Robert	Film	5/8	8	5	1911
Taylor, Rod	Film	1/2	1	11	1929
Taylor, Zachary	President	2/6	11	24	1784
Taylor-Young, Leigh	Television	1/7	1	25	1944
Tchaikovsky, Pyotr Ilyich	Music	5/7	5	7	1840
Te Kanawa, Kiri	Music	3/6	3	6	1944
Tebaldi, Renata	Music	1/2	2	1	1922
Teicher, Louis	Music	6/8	8	24	1924
Telemann, Georg Philipp	Music	3/5	3	14	1681
Temple, Shirley	Film	4/5	4	23	1928
Tennstedt, Klaus	Music	6/6	6	6	1926
Tennyson, Alfred, Lord	Literature	6/8	8	6	1809
Terkel, Studs	Letters	5/7	5	16	1912
Terry, Sonny	Music	1/6	10	24	1911
Terry-Thomas	Film	5/7	7	14	1911
Tesla, Nikola	Sciences	7/9	7	9	1856
Tex, Joe	Music	8/8	8	8	1933

NAME	FIELD	SET	MONTH	DAY	YEAR
Thackeray, William Makepeace	Literature	7/9	7	18	1811
Thalberg, Irving G.	Film	3/5	5	30	1899
Thant, U	Politics	1/4	1	22	1909
Tharp, Twyla	Dance	1/7	7	1	1941
Thatcher, Margaret	Politics	1/4	10	13	1925
Thaxter, Phyllis	Film	2/2	11	20	1921
Theismann, Joe	Sports	9/9	9	9	1949
Theroux, Paul	Letters	1/4	4	10	1941
Thiebaud, Wayne	Visual Arts	2/6	11	15	1920
Thomas, B. J.	Music	7/8	8	7	1942
Thomas, Danny	Television	1/6	1	6	1914
Thomas, Dylan	Literature	1/9	10	27	1914
Thomas, Heather	Television	8/9	9	8	1957
Thomas, Lowell	Television	4/6	4	6	1892
Thomas, Marlo	Television	2/3	11	21	1943
Thomas, Michael Tilson	Music	3/3	12	21	1944
Thomas, Richard	Television	4/6	6	13	1951
Thomson, Virgil	Music	2/7	11	25	1896
Thoreau, Henry David	Letters	3/7	7	12	1817
Thorpe, Jim	Sports	1/5	5	28	1888
Thulin, Ingrid	Film	1/9	1	27	1929
Thurber, James	Literature	3/8	12	8	1894
Tiegs, Cheryl	Business	9/9	9	27	1947
Tiepolo, Giovanni	Visual Arts	3/5	3	5	1696
Tierney, Gene	Film	1/2	11	28	1920
Tiffany	Music	1/2	10	2	1971
Tiffany, Charles	Visual Arts	2/6	2	15	1812
Tiffany, Louis Comfort	Design	2/9	2	18	1848
Tillis, Melvin	Music	8/8	8	8	1932
Tinker, Grant	Television	1/2	1	11	1926
Tiny Tim	Entertainment	3/4	4	12	1925
Tiomkin, Dimitri	Music	1/5	5	10	1899
Tito, Josip	Politics	5/7	5	25	1892
Tjader, Cal	Music	7/7	7	16	1925
Tobey, Mark	Visual Arts	2/3	12	11	1890
Tocqueville, Alexis de	Letters	2/7	7	29	1805
Todd, Richard	Film	2/6	6	11	1919
Todd, Richard	Sports	1/2	11	19	1953
Tokyo Rose	Politics	4/7	7	4	1916
Tolkien, J. R. R.	Literature	1/3	1	3	1892

NAME	FIELD	SET	MONTH	DAY	YEAR
Tolstoy, Leo	Literature	9/9	9	9	1828
Tomlin, Lily	Entertainment	1/9	9	1	1939
Tone, Franchot	Film	2/9	2	9	1905
Tooker, George	Visual Arts	5/8	8	5	1920
Toomey, Regis	Film	4/8	8	13	1902
Topol	Film	9/9	9	9	1935
Torme, Mel	Music	4/9	9	13	1923
Torn, Rip	Dramatic Arts	2/6	2	6	1931
Torricelli, Evangelista	Sciences	1/6	10	15	1608
Toscanini, Arturo	Music	3/7	3	25	1867
Toulouse-Lautrec, Henri de	Visual Arts	2/6	11	24	1864
Tower, John	Politics	2/9	9	29	1925
Townshend, Pete	Music	1/5	5	19	1945
Toynbee, Arnold	Letters	4/5	4	14	1889
Tracy, Spencer	Film	4/5	4	5	1900
Travolta, John	Film	2/9	2	18	1954
Trevino, Lee	Sports	1/3	12	1	1939
Trevor, Claire	Film	3/8	3	8	1908
Trible, Paul S., Jr.	Politics	2/3	12	29	1946
Trollope, Anthony	Literature	4/6	4	24	1815
Trudeau, Margaret	Politics	1/9	9	10	1948
Trudeau, Pierre Elliott	Politics	1/9	10	18	1919
Truffaut, François	Film	2/6	2	6	1932
Trujillo, Rafael	Politics	1/6	10	24	1891
Truman, Bess	Politics	2/4	2	13	1885
Truman, Harry S.	President	5/8	5	8	1884
Truman, Margaret	Letters	2/8	2	17	1924
Trumbull, John	Visual Arts	6/6	6	6	1756
Tuchman, Barbara	Letters	1/3	1	30	1912
Tucker, Forrest	Film	2/3	2	12	1919
Tucker, Richard	Music	1/8	8	28	1913
Tucker, Sophie	Music	1/4	1	13	1884
Tucker, Tanya	Music	1/1	10	10	1958
Tufts, Sonny	Film	7/7	7	16	1911
Tune, Tommy	Entertainment	1/2	2	28	1939
Turgenev, Ivan	Literature	2/9	11	9	1818
Turner, Ike	Music	2/5	11	5	1931
Turner, J. M. W.	Visual Arts	4/5	4	23	1914
Turner, Lana	Film	2/8	2	8	1920
Turner, Tina	Music	2/8	11	26	1938

NAME	FIELD	SET	MONTH	DAY	YEAR
Turpin, Ben	Film	8/9	9	17	1874
Tushingham, Rita	Film	3/5	3	14	1942
Tutu, Desmond	Politics	1/7	10	7	1931
Twachtman, John	Visual Arts	4/8	8	4	1853
Twain, Mark (Samuel Clemens)	Literature	2/3	11	30	1835
Twiggy	Film	1/9	9	19	1949
Tyler, Anne	Literature	1/7	10	25	1941
Tyler, John	President	2/3	3	29	1790
Tyson, Cicely	Film	1/3	12	19	1933
Tyson, Mike	Sports	3/6	6	30	1966
Udall, Morris	Politics	6/6	6	15	1922
Uggams, Leslie	Film	5/7	5	25	1943
Ulanova, Galina	Dance	1/1	1	10	1910
Ullmann, Liv	Film	3/7	12	16	1939
Undset, Sigrid	Literature	2/5	5	20	1882
Unitas, Johnny	Sports	5/7	5	7	1933
Unser, Al	Sports	2/5	5	29	1939
Updike, John	Literature	3/9	3	18	1932
Uris, Leon	Literature	3/8	8	3	1924
Ustinov, Peter	Film	4/7	4	16	1921
Vaccaro, Brenda	Film	2/9	11	18	1939
Vale, Jerry	Music	7/8	7	8	1931
Valenti, Jack	Film	5/9	9	5	1921
Valentine, Karen	Television	5/7	5	25	1947
Valentino, Rudolph	Film	5/6	5	6	1895
Valentino, V. G.	Design	2/5	5	11	1932
Valenzuela, Fernando	Sports	1/2	11	1	1960
Valéry, Paul	Literature	1/3	10	30	1871
Vallee, Rudy	Film	1/7	7	28	1901
Valli, Frankie	Music	3/5	5	3	1937
Van Allen, James A.	Sciences	7/9	9	7	1914
Van Buren, Abigail	Letters	4/7	7	4	1918
Van Buren, Hannah	Politics	3/8	3	8	1783
Van Buren, Martin	President	3/5	12	5	1782
Van Cleef, Lee	Film	1/9	1	9	1925
Van de Graaff, Robert	Sciences	2/3	12	20	1901
Van Doren, Mamie	Entertainment	2/6	2	6	1933
Van Dyke, Dick	Television	3/4	12	13	1925
Van Fleet, Jo	Film	3/3	12	30	1919
Van Gogh, Vincent	Visual Arts	3/3	3	30	1853

NAME	FIELD	SET	MONTH	DAY	YEAR
Van Patten, Dick	Television	3/9	12	9	1928
Van Peebles, Melvin	Film	3/9	9	21	1932
Vanderbilt, Gloria	Business	2/2	2	20	1924
Varèse, Edgard	Music	3/4	12	22	1885
Vasarely, Victor	Visual Arts	4/9	4	9	1908
Vasari, Giorgio	Visual Arts	3/7	7	30	1511
Vaughan, Sarah	Music	3/9	3	27	1924
Vaughan Williams, Ralph	Music	1/3	10	12	1872
Vaughn, Robert	Television	2/4	11	22	1932
Velázquez, Diego	Visual Arts	6/6	6	6	1599
Velez, Lupe	Film	7/9	7	18	1908
Venuta, Benay	Music	1/9	1	27	1916
Verdi, Giuseppe	Music	1/1	10	10	1813
Verdon, Gwen	Dance	1/4	1	13	1927
Vereen, Ben	Dance	1/1	10	10	1946
Verlaine, Paul	Literature	3/3	3	30	1844
Vermeer, Jan	Visual Arts	1/4	10	31	1632
Verne, Jules	Literature	2/8	2	8	1828
Verrett, Shirley	Music	4/5	5	31	1931
Vesco, Robert	Business	3/4	12	4	1935
Vespucci, Amerigo	Exploration	3/9	9	18	1452
Vidal, Gore	Literature	1/3	10	3	1925
Vidor, King	Film	2/8	2	8	1895
Villa, Francisco (Pancho)	Military	5/6	6	5	1878
Villa-Lobos, Heitor	Music	3/5	3	5	1887
Villella, Edward	Dance	1/1	10	1	1936
Villon, Jacques	Visual Arts	4/7	7	31	1875
Vincent, Jan-Michael	Film	6/7	7	15	1944
Vinton, Bobby	Music	4/7	4	16	1935
Viola, Frank	Sports	1/4	4	19	1960
Virgil	Literature	1/6	10	15	B.C. 70
Vivaldi, Antonio	Music	3/4	3	4	1678
Vlaminck, Maurice de	Visual Arts	4/4	4	4	1876
Voight, Jon	Film	2/3	12	29	1938
Volker, Paul A.	Business	5/9	9	5	1927
Voltaire (Françoise Arouet)	Literature	2/3	11	21	1694
Von Furstenburg, Diane	Design	3/4	12	31	1946
Von Stroheim, Erich	Film	4/9	9	22	1885
Von Sydow, Max	Film	1/4	4	10	1929
Von Zell, Harry	Television	2/7	7	11	1906

NAME	FIELD	SET	MONTH	DAY	YEAR
Vonnegut, Kurt	Literature	2/2	11	11	1922
Vuillard, Édouard	Visual Arts	2/2	11	11	1868
Wagner, Lindsay	Television	4/6	6	22	1949
Wagner, Richard	Music	4/5	5	22	1813
Wagner, Robert	Television	1/2	2	10	1930
Wain, Bea	Music	3/4	4	30	1917
Waite, Ralph	Television	4/6	6	22	1929
Waite, Terence	Politics	4/5	5	31	1939
Waits, Tom	Music	3/7	12	7	1949
Walken, Christopher	Film	3/4	3	31	1943
Walker, Clint	Film	3/5	5	30	1927
Walker, Jimmy	Politics	1/6	6	19	1881
Walker, Nancy	Dramatic Arts	1/5	5	10	1921
Walker, Robert	Film	1/4	10	13	1914
Walker, Robert, Jr.	Film	4/6	4	15	1940
Wallace, George C.	Politics	7/8	8	25	1919
Wallace, Henry	Politics	1/7	10	7	1888
Wallace, Irving	Literature	1/3	3	19	1916
Wallace, Lurleen	Politics	1/9	9	19	1926
Wallace, Mike	Television	5/9	5	9	1918
Wallach, Eli	Dramatic Arts	3/7	12	7	1915
Waller, Fats	Music	3/5	5	21	1904
Wallis, Hal	Film	5/9	9	14	1899
Wallop, Malcolm	Politics	2/9	2	27	1933
Walpole, Horace	Literature	6/9	9	24	1717
Walsh, William (Bill)	Sports	2/3	11	30	1931
Walston, Ray	Television	2/2	11	2	1914
Walter, Bruno	Music	6/9	9	15	1876
Walter, Jessica	Television	1/4	1	31	1944
Walters, Barbara	Television	7/9	9	25	1931
Walton, Bill	Sports	2/5	11	5	1952
Walton, Izaak	Letters	8/9	8	9	1593
Walton, William Turner	Music	2/3	3	29	1902
Wambaugh, Joseph	Literature	1/4	1	22	1937
Wanamaker, Sam	Dramatic Arts	5/6	6	14	1919
Wang, An	Business	2/7	2	7	1920
Wanger, Walter	Film	2/7	7	11	1894
Ward, Montgomery	Business	2/8	2	17	1843
Ward, Roger	Sports	1/1	1	10	1921
Ward, Simon	Dramatic Arts	1/1	10	19	1932

NAME	FIELD	SET	MONTH	DAY	YEAR
Warden, Jack	Television	9/9	9	18	1920
Warfield, William	Dramatic Arts	1/4	1	22	1920
Warhol, Andy	Visual Arts	6/8	8	6	1927
Waring, Fred	Music	6/9	6	9	1900
Warner, Harry	Film	3/3	12	12	1881
Warner, Jack	Film	2/8	8	2	1892
Warner, John W.	Politics	2/9	2	18	1927
Warren, Earl	Law	1/3	3	19	1891
Warren, Lesley Ann	Film	7/8	8	16	1946
Warren, Robert Penn	Literature	4/6	4	24	1905
Warrick, Ruth	Film	2/6	6	29	1915
Wartels, Nat	Publishing	1/1	1	19	1902
Warwick, Dionne	Music	3/3	12	12	1941
Washington, Dinah	Music	2/8	8	29	1924
Washington, George	President	2/6	2	24	1732
Washington, Grover, Jr.	Music	3/3	12	12	1943
Washington, Harold	Politics	4/6	4	15	1922
Washington, Martha	Politics	3/6	6	21	1731
Washington, Walter	Politics	4/6	4	15	1915
Waters, Muddy	Music	4/4	4	4	1915
Waterston, Sam	Film	2/6	11	15	1940
Watson, James D.	Sciences	4/6	4	6	1928
Watt, James	Sciences	1/1	1	19	1736
Watteau, Jean-Antoine	Visual Arts	1/1	10	10	1684
Watts, André	Music	2/6	6	20	1946
Watts, Charlie	Music	2/6	6	2	1941
Waugh, Evelyn	Literature	1/1	10	28	1903
Wayne, David	Film	1/3	1	30	1914
Wayne, John	Film	5/8	5	26	1907
Weaver, Dennis	Television	4/6	6	4	1924
Weaver, Earl Sidney	Sports	5/8	8	14	1930
Weaver, Fritz	Dramatic Arts	1/1	1	19	1926
Weaver, Sigourney	Film	1/8	10	8	1949
Webb, Jack	Television	2/4	4	2	1920
Webb, Jimmy	Music	6/8	8	15	1946
Webb, Mary	Literature	3/7	3	25	1881
Weber, Carl Maria von	Music	2/9	11	18	1786
Webern, Anton von	Music	3/3	12	3	1883
Weeks, Sinclair	Literature	6/6	6	15	1893
Weicker, Lowell P., Jr.	Politics	5/7	5	16	1931

NAME	FIELD	SET	MONTH	DAY	YEAR
Weill, Kurt	Music	2/3	3	2	1900
Weinberger, Caspar W.	Politics	8/9	8	18	1917
Weiskopf, Thomas	Sports	2/9	11	9	1942
Weissmuller, Johnny	Film	2/6	6	2	1903
Welch, Raquel	Film	5/9	9	5	1942
Weld, Tuesday	Film	8/9	8	27	1943
Welk, Lawrence	Music	2/3	3	11	1903
Welles, Orson	Film	5/6	5	6	1915
Wells, H. G.	Literature	3/9	9	21	1866
Wells, Kitty	Music	3/8	8	30	1919
Welty, Eudora	Literature	4/4	4	13	1909
Wesselmann, Tom	Visual Arts	2/5	2	23	1931
West, Dottie	Music	1/2	10	11	1952
West, Jerry	Sports	1/5	5	28	1938
West, Mae	Film	8/8	8	17	1892
West, Morris L.	Literature	4/8	4	26	1916
West, Nathanael	Literature	3/8	12	17	1902
West, Rebecca	Literature	3/7	12	25	1892
Weston, Brett	Visual Arts	3/7	12	16	1911
Weston, Edward	Visual Arts	3/6	3	24	1850
Wharton, Edith	Literature	1/6	1	24	1862
Whistler, James McNeill	Visual Arts	1/7	7	10	1834
White, Barry	Music	3/9	9	12	1944
White, Betty	Television	1/8	1	17	1924
White, Byron R.	Politics	6/8	6	8	1917
White, E. B.	Literature	2/7	7	11	1899
White, Mark W., Jr.	Politics	3/8	3	17	1940
White, Paul Dudley	Politics	6/6	6	6	1886
White, Stanford	Design	2/9	11	9	1853
White, Theodore H.	Letters	5/6	6	5	1915
White, Vanna	Television	2/9	2	18	1957
Whitelaw, Billie	Dramatic Arts	6/6	6	6	1932
Whiteman, Paul	Music	1/3	3	28	1890
Whiting, Margaret	Music	4/7	7	22	1924
Whitman, Walt	Literature	4/5	5	31	1819
Whitmore, James	Film	1/1	10	1	1921
Whitney, John Hay	Business	8/8	8	17	1904
Whittier, John Greenleaf	Literature	3/8	12	17	1807
Whitty, May	Film	1/6	6	19	1865
Whitworth, Kathy	Sports	9/9	9	27	1939

NAME	FIELD	SET	MONTH	DAY	YEAR
Widmark, Richard	Film	3/8	12	26	1914
Wilde, Cornell	Film	1/4	10	13	1915
Wilde, Oscar	Literature	1/7	10	16	1854
Wilder, Billy	Film	4/6	6	22	1906
Wilder, Gene	Film	2/6	6	11	1934
Wilder, Thornton	Dramatic Arts	4/8	4	17	1897
Wilding, Michael	Film	5/7	7	23	1912
William, Warren	Film	2/3	12	2	1894
Williams, Andy	Music	3/3	12	3	1928
Williams, Billy Dee	Film	4/6	6	4	1937
Williams, Cindy	Television	4/8	8	22	1947
Williams, Emlyn	Dramatic Arts	2/8	11	26	1905
Williams, Esther	Film	8/8	8	8	1923
Williams, Hank, Jr.	Music	5/8	5	26	1949
Williams, Joe	Music	3/3	12	12	1918
Williams, John	Music	2/8	2	8	1932
Williams, Paul	Music	1/9	9	19	1940
Williams, Robin	Entertainment	3/7	7	21	1952
Williams, Roger	Music	1/1	10	1	1926
Williams, Ted	Sports	3/8	8	30	1918
Williams, Tennessee	Dramatic Arts	3/8	3	26	1911
Williams, William Carlos	Literature	8/9	9	17	1883
Williamson, Nicol	Dramatic Arts	5/9	9	14	1938
Wills, Chill	Film	7/9	7	18	1903
Wills, Maury	Sports	1/2	10	2	1932
Wilson, Brian	Music	2/6	6	20	1942
Wilson, Carl	Music	3/3	12	21	1946
Wilson, Dennis	Music	3/4	12	4	1944
Wilson, Don	Television	1/9	9	1	1900
Wilson, Earl	Letters	3/5	5	3	1907
Wilson, Edith Boling	Politics	1/6	10	15	1872
Wilson, Edmund	Literature	5/8	5	8	1895
Wilson, Ellen Axson	Politics	5/6	5	15	1860
Wilson, Flip	Entertainment	3/8	12	8	1933
Wilson, Harold	Politics	2/3	3	11	1916
Wilson, Woodrow	President	1/3	12	28	1856
Winchell, Paul	Film	3/3	12	21	1922
Winchell, Walter	Letters	4/7	4	7	1897
Winfield, Dave	Sports	1/3	10	3	1951
Winfield, Paul	Film	4/5	5	22	1941

NAME	FIELD	SET	MONTH	DAY	YEAR
Wing, R. L.	Philosophy	1/7	7	19	1946
Winger, Debra	Film	5/7	5	16	1955
Winkler, Henry	Film	1/3	10	3	1945
Winter, Edgar	Music	1/3	12	28	1946
Winter, Johnny	Music	2/5	2	23	1944
Winterhalter, Hugo	Music	6/8	8	15	1910
Winters, Jonathan	Entertainment	2/2	11	11	1925
Winters, Shelley	Film	8/9	8	18	1922
Winwood, Steve	Music	3/5	5	12	1948
Wise, Robert	Film	1/9	9	10	1914
Withers, Jane	Television	3/4	4	12	1927
Wodehouse, P. G.	Literature	1/6	10	15	1881
Wolf, Hugo	Music	3/4	3	13	1860
Wolfe, Thomas	Literature	1/3	10	3	1900
Wolfe, Tom	Literature	2/3	3	2	1931
Wolfman Jack (Bob Smith)	Music	1/3	1	21	1938
Wonder, Stevie	Music	4/5	5	13	1950
Wong, Anna May	Film	1/3	1	3	1907
Wood, Grant	Visual Arts	2/4	2	13	1892
Wood, Natalie	Film	2/7	7	20	1938
Woodruff, Judy	Television	2/2	11	20	1946
Woodward, Bob	Letters	5/5	5	5	1943
Woodward, Joanne	Film	2/9	2	27	1930
Woodward, Robert	Literature	3/8	3	26	1943
Woodward, Robert Burns	Sciences	1/4	4	10	1917
Woolf, Virginia	Literature	1/7	1	25	1882
Woollcott, Alexander	Literature	1/1	1	19	1887
Woolley, Monty	Film	8/8	8	17	1888
Woolworth, F. W.	Business	4/4	4	13	1852
Wordsworth, Dorothy	Literature	3/7	12	25	1771
Wordsworth, William	Literature	4/7	4	7	1770
Worley, Jo Anne	Entertainment	6/9	9	6	1937
Worth, Irene	Dramatic Arts	5/6	6	23	1916
Wouk, Herman	Literature	5/9	5	27	1915
Wray, Fay	Film	1/9	9	10	1907
Wren, Christopher	Design	1/2	10	20	1632
Wright, Frank Lloyd	Design	6/8	6	8	1869
Wright, James C., Jr.	Politics	3/4	12	22	1922
Wright, Orville	Sciences	1/8	8	19	1871
Wright, Richard	Literature	4/9	9	4	1908

NAME	FIELD	SET	MONTH	DAY	YEAR
Wright, Teresa	Film	1/9	10	27	1918
Wright, Wilbur	Sciences	4/7	4	16	1867
Wrigley, Philip Knight	Business	3/5	12	5	1894
Wu, Yifang	Politics	1/8	1	26	1893
Wyatt, Jane	Television	1/8	8	10	1911
Wyeth, Andrew	Visual Arts	3/7	7	12	1917
Wyeth, Jamie	Visual Arts	6/7	7	6	1946
Wyeth, N. C.	Visual Arts	1/4	10	22	1882
Wyler, William	Film	1/7	7	1	1902
Wylie, Elinor	Literature	7/9	9	7	1885
Wyman, Bill	Music	1/6	10	24	1941
Wyman, Jane	Film	1/4	1	4	1914
Wynette, Tammy	Music	5/5	5	5	1942
Wynn, Ed	Film	2/9	11	9	1886
Wynn, Keenan	Film	7/9	7	27	1916
Wynter, Dana	Film	6/8	6	8	1932
Yarborough, Glenn	Music	1/3	1	12	1930
Yarrow, Peter	Music	4/5	5	31	1943
Yastrzemski, Carl	Sports	4/8	8	22	1939
Yeager, Steve	Sports	2/6	11	24	1948
Yeats, William Butler	Literature	4/6	6	13	1865
Yerby, Frank	Literature	5/9	9	5	1916
York, Dick	Television	4/9	9	4	1928
York, Michael	Film	3/9	3	27	1942
York, Susannah	Film	1/9	1	9	1941
Yorkin, Bud	Television	2/4	2	22	1926
Yorty, Sam	Politics	1/1	10	1	1909
Youmans, Vincent	Music	9/9	9	27	1898
Young, Andrew	Politics	3/3	3	12	1932
Young, Brigham	Religion	1/6	6	1	1801
Young, Chic	Visual Arts	1/9	1	9	1901
Young, Coleman	Politics	5/6	5	24	1918
Young, Faron	Music	2/7	2	25	1932
Young, Jessie Colin	Music	2/2	11	11	1944
Young, John Watts	Exploration	6/9	9	24	1930
Young, Lester	Music	8/9	8	27	1909
Young, Loretta	Film	1/6	1	6	1911
Young, Neil	Music	2/3	11	12	1945
Young, Robert	Television	2/4	2	22	1907
Young, Roland	Film	2/2	11	11	1887

NAME	FIELD	SET	MONTH	DAY	YEAR
Youngblood, Jack	Sports	1/7	1	16	1950
Younger, Cole	Crime	8/8	8	17	1844
Yourcenar, Marguerite	Literature	6/8	6	8	1903
Zanuck, Darryl F.	Film	5/9	9	5	1902
Zanuck, Richard	Film	3/4	12	13	1934
Zappa, Frank	Music	3/3	12	21	1940
Zappa, Moon Unit	Music	1/9	9	28	1967
Zeffirelli, Franco	Film	2/3	2	12	1923
Zetterling, Mai	Film	5/6	5	24	1925
Ziegfeld, Florenz	Entertainment	3/3	3	12	1869
Ziegler, Ron	Politics	3/5	5	12	1939
Zimbalist, Efrem	Music	4/9	4	9	1889
Zimbalist, Efrem, Jr.	Television	2/3	11	30	1923
Zimbalist, Stephanie	Television	1/6	10	6	1956
Zoeller, Fuzzy	Sports	2/2	11	11	1951
Zola, Émile	Literature	2/4	4	2	1840
Zorina, Vera	Dance	1/2	1	2	1917
Zorinsky, Edward	Politics	2/2	11	11	1928
Zukerman, Pinchas	Music	7/7	7	16	1948
Zukor, Adolph	Film	1/7	1	7	1873
Zumwalt, Elmo	Military	2/2	11	29	1920
Zurbarán, Francisco de	Visual Arts	2/7	11	7	1598

THE
NUMERIC
PERSONALITY
CHARTS

THE NUMERIC PERSONALITY CHART   Name: _____

Use the chart on these pages to note the set numbers of people who are important to you. As the chart fills up, you will begin to see numeric patterns emerging. By analyzing the numeric patterns in your personal universe, you will notice which set numbers, family numbers, or interval numbers you are attached to, and which are the most compatible or important in your life.

The large numbers running down the left side of the chart are family numbers. The five set numbers listed in each row to the right of the family number are the sets that share that family number. The single number listed under each set number is the set interval for that set. Below are areas for you to keep track of the frequency with which you are associated with particular interval numbers or odd-even combinations.

Interval numbers indicate a range of interests from very deep or focused (0) to very general or diverse (8). Family numbers reflect certain destiny paths and shared areas of concern. Set numbers represent specific personality characteristics.

Everyone has four odd and/or even numbers made up of the set, family, and interval numbers. A zero interval has the numeric value of one of its set numbers. Individuals with mostly odd numbers interact with life in an "active-originating-direct" way. Those with mostly even numbers use a more "reactive-adapting-subtle" style in their approach to the world around them. Those with half and half have a very balanced approach.

#	Set	Interval	Set	Interval
1	1/9	8	2/8	6
2	1/1	0	2/9	7
3	1/2	1	3/9	6
4	1/3	2	2/2	0
5	1/4	3	2/3	1
6	1/5	4	2/4	2
7	1/6	5	2/5	3
8	1/7	6	2/6	4
9	1/8	7	2/7	5

FREQUENCY: ____ ____ ____ ____ ____
ODD OR EVEN: 4 Odd 3 Odd Half and Half 3 Even 4 Even

Set: _____ Family: _____ Interval: _____ Odd: _____ Even: _____

3/7	4/6	5/5
4	2	0
3/8	4/7	5/6
5	3	1
4/8	5/7	6/6
4	2	0
4/9	5/8	6/7
5	3	1
5/9	6/8	7/7
4	2	0
3/3	6/9	7/8
0	3	1
3/4	7/9	8/8
1	2	0
3/5	4/4	8/9
2	0	1
3/6	4/5	9/9
3	1	0

FREQUENCY:								
INTERVAL NUMBER:	0	1	2	3	4	5	6	7	8

THE NUMERIC PERSONALITY CHART   Name: _____

Use the chart on these pages to note the set numbers of people who are important to you. As the chart fills up, you will begin to see numeric patterns emerging. By analyzing the numeric patterns in your personal universe, you will notice which set numbers, family numbers, or interval numbers you are attached to, and which are the most compatible or important in your life.

The large numbers running down the left side of the chart are family numbers. The five set numbers listed in each row to the right of the family number are the sets that share that family number. The single number listed under each set number is the set interval for that set. Below are areas for you to keep track of the frequency with which you are associated with particular interval numbers or odd-even combinations.

Interval numbers indicate a range of interests from very deep or focused (0) to very general or diverse (8). Family numbers reflect certain destiny paths and shared areas of concern. Set numbers represent specific personality characteristics.

Everyone has four odd and/ or even numbers made up of the set, family, and interval numbers. A zero interval has the numeric value of one of its set numbers. Individuals with mostly odd numbers interact with life in an "active-originating-direct" way. Those with mostly even numbers use a more "reactive-adapting-subtle" style in their approach to the world around them. Those with half and half have a very balanced approach.

#		
1	1/9 8	2/8 6
2	1/1 0	2/9 7
3	1/2 1	3/9 6
4	1/3 2	2/2 0
5	1/4 3	2/3 1
6	1/5 4	2/4 2
7	1/6 5	2/5 3
8	1/7 6	2/6 4
9	1/8 7	2/7 5

FREQUENCY: ____ ____   ____ ____ ____
ODD OR EVEN: 4 Odd   3 Odd   Half and Half   3 Even   4 Even

Set: _____ Family: _____ Interval: _____ Odd: _____ Even: _____

3/7	4/6	5/5
4	2	0
3/8	4/7	5/6
5	3	1
4/8	5/7	6/6
4	2	0
4/9	5/8	6/7
5	3	1
5/9	6/8	7/7
4	2	0
3/3	6/9	7/8
0	3	1
3/4	7/9	8/8
1	2	0
3/5	4/4	8/9
2	0	1
3/6	4/5	9/9
3	1	0

FREQUENCY:								
INTERVAL NUMBER:	0	1	2	3	4	5	6	7	8

THE NUMERIC PERSONALITY CHART   Name: _____

Use the chart on these pages to note the set numbers of people who are important to you. As the chart fills up, you will begin to see numeric patterns emerging. By analyzing the numeric patterns in your personal universe, you will notice which set numbers, family numbers, or interval numbers you are attached to, and which are the most compatible or important in your life.

The large numbers running down the left side of the chart are family numbers. The five set numbers listed in each row to the right of the family number are the sets that share that family number. The single number listed under each set number is the set interval for that set. Below are areas for you to keep track of the frequency with which you are associated with particular interval numbers or odd-even combinations.

Interval numbers indicate a range of interests from very deep or focused (0) to very general or diverse (8). Family numbers reflect certain destiny paths and shared areas of concern. Set numbers represent specific personality characteristics.

Everyone has four odd and/ or even numbers made up of the set, family, and interval numbers. A zero interval has the numeric value of one of its set numbers. Individuals with mostly odd numbers interact with life in an "active-originating-direct" way. Those with mostly even numbers use a more "reactive-adapting-subtle" style in their approach to the world around them. Those with half and half have a very balanced approach.

#				
1	1/9 8		2/8 6	
2	1/1 0		2/9 7	
3	1/2 1		3/9 6	
4	1/3 2		2/2 0	
5	1/4 3		2/3 1	
6	1/5 4		2/4 2	
7	1/6 5		2/5 3	
8	1/7 6		2/6 4	
9	1/8 7		2/7 5	

FREQUENCY: ____ ____   ____ ____ ____

ODD OR EVEN: 4 Odd   3 Odd   Half and Half   3 Even   4 Even

Set: _____ Family: _____ Interval: _____ Odd: _____ Even: _____

3/7 4	4/6 2	5/5 0
3/8 5	4/7 3	5/6 1
4/8 4	5/7 2	6/6 0
4/9 5	5/8 3	6/7 1
5/9 4	6/8 2	7/7 0
3/3 0	6/9 3	7/8 1
3/4 1	7/9 2	8/8 0
3/5 2	4/4 0	8/9 1
3/6 3	4/5 1	9/9 0

FREQUENCY:								
INTERVAL NUMBER: 0	1	2	3	4	5	6	7	8

THE NUMERIC PERSONALITY CHART   Name: _____

Use the chart on these pages to note the set numbers of people who are important to you. As the chart fills up, you will begin to see numeric patterns emerging. By analyzing the numeric patterns in your personal universe, you will notice which set numbers, family numbers, or interval numbers you are attached to, and which are the most compatible or important in your life.

The large numbers running down the left side of the chart are family numbers. The five set numbers listed in each row to the right of the family number are the sets that share that family number. The single number listed under each set number is the set interval for that set. Below are areas for you to keep track of the frequency with which you are associated with particular interval numbers or odd-even combinations.

Interval numbers indicate a range of interests from very deep or focused (0) to very general or diverse (8). Family numbers reflect certain destiny paths and shared areas of concern. Set numbers represent specific personality characteristics.

Everyone has four odd and/or even numbers made up of the set, family, and interval numbers. A zero interval has the numeric value of one of its set numbers. Individuals with mostly odd numbers interact with life in an "active-originating-direct" way. Those with mostly even numbers use a more "reactive-adapting-subtle" style in their approach to the world around them. Those with half and half have a very balanced approach.

1
| 1/9 | 2/8 |
| 8 | 6 |

2
| 1/1 | 2/9 |
| 0 | 7 |

3
| 1/2 | 3/9 |
| 1 | 6 |

4
| 1/3 | 2/2 |
| 2 | 0 |

5
| 1/4 | 2/3 |
| 3 | 1 |

6
| 1/5 | 2/4 |
| 4 | 2 |

7
| 1/6 | 2/5 |
| 5 | 3 |

8
| 1/7 | 2/6 |
| 6 | 4 |

9
| 1/8 | 2/7 |
| 7 | 5 |

FREQUENCY: ____   ____   ____   ____   ____
ODD OR EVEN: 4 Odd   3 Odd   Half and Half   3 Even   4 Even

Set: _____ Family: _____ Interval: _____ Odd: _____ Even: _____

3/7	4/6	5/5
4	2	0
3/8	4/7	5/6
5	3	1
4/8	5/7	6/6
4	2	0
4/9	5/8	6/7
5	3	1
5/9	6/8	7/7
4	2	0
3/3	6/9	7/8
0	3	1
3/4	7/9	8/8
1	2	0
3/5	4/4	8/9
2	0	1
3/6	4/5	9/9
3	1	0

FREQUENCY:

INTERVAL NUMBER:	0	1	2	3	4	5	6	7	8

THE NUMERIC PERSONALITY CHART   Name: _____

Use the chart on these pages to note the set numbers of people who are important to you. As the chart fills up, you will begin to see numeric patterns emerging. By analyzing the numeric patterns in your personal universe, you will notice which set numbers, family numbers, or interval numbers you are attached to, and which are the most compatible or important in your life.

The large numbers running down the left side of the chart are family numbers. The five set numbers listed in each row to the right of the family number are the sets that share that family number. The single number listed under each set number is the set interval for that set. Below are areas for you to keep track of the frequency with which you are associated with particular interval numbers or odd-even combinations.

Interval numbers indicate a range of interests from very deep or focused (0) to very general or diverse (8). Family numbers reflect certain destiny paths and shared areas of concern. Set numbers represent specific personality characteristics.

Everyone has four odd and/or even numbers made up of the set, family, and interval numbers. A zero interval has the numeric value of one of its set numbers. Individuals with mostly odd numbers interact with life in an "active-originating-direct" way. Those with mostly even numbers use a more "reactive-adapting-subtle" style in their approach to the world around them. Those with half and half have a very balanced approach.

1	1/9 8	2/8 6
2	1/1 0	2/9 7
3	1/2 1	3/9 6
4	1/3 2	2/2 0
5	1/4 3	2/3 1
6	1/5 4	2/4 2
7	1/6 5	2/5 3
8	1/7 6	2/6 4
9	1/8 7	2/7 5

FREQUENCY: ____ ____ ____ ____ ____

ODD OR EVEN: 4 Odd   3 Odd   Half and Half   3 Even   4 Even

Set: _____ Family: _____ Interval: _____ Odd: _____ Even: _____

3/7 4	4/6 2	5/5 0
3/8 5	4/7 3	5/6 1
4/8 4	5/7 2	6/6 0
4/9 5	5/8 3	6/7 1
5/9 4	6/8 2	7/7 0
3/3 0	6/9 3	7/8 1
3/4 1	7/9 2	8/8 0
3/5 2	4/4 0	8/9 1
3/6 3	4/5 1	9/9 0

FREQUENCY:

INTERVAL NUMBER:	0	1	2	3	4	5	6	7	8

ABOUT THE AUTHOR

Richard Elliot Poole is an internationally recognized artist. His paintings have been exhibited at the Los Angeles County Museum of Art, the Palace of the Legion of Honor in San Francisco, the San Francisco M. H. De Young Museum, and The Pasadena Art Museum. He has had numerous one-man shows throughout the world. Mr. Poole is an avid collector of Japanese prints and pre-Columbian art, along with musical recordings from many diverse cultures. His wide-ranging interests have resulted in one of the largest private collections of movie and documentary video recordings in the world. Richard Poole is listed in *Who's Who in American Art.*

About his art he has written: "I try to communicate my feelings and intangible impressions of my inner vision of the world around me. I wish to create a mood, energy, or impression of a specific event, place, or person. The act of painting is to me a meditative experience, which will convey whatever specific meaning the viewer wishes to feel from this. My hope is to share some common inner experiences with the viewer — form, movement, interrelationships, energy fields, nature, optical vibrations, symbolism, and man are the elements I'm trying to explore."

When the numbers came into his life, Richard Poole put aside his brushes, mastered the personal computer, and adapted his art to the exploration of the numeric personality system.